D1426715

# PRIVATOPIA

# PRIVATOPIA

Homeowner Associations and the Rise of
Residential Private Government

Evan McKenzie

Yale University Press
New Haven and London

Published with assistance from the Stern Memorial Fund.

Designed by Deborah Dutton.
Set in New Century Schoolbook text and Torino display type by
Keystone Typesetting, Inc., Orwigsburg, Pennsylvania.

Printed in the United States of America by
Vail-Ballou Press, Binghamton, New York.

McKenzie, Evan.
Privatopia : homeowner associations and the rise of residential
private government / Evan McKenzie.
p.   cm.
Includes bibliographical references and index.
ISBN 0–300–05876–4
1. Homeowners' associations—United States.   2. Homeowners'
associations—Law and legislation—United States.   I. Title.
HD7287.82.U6M39   1994
643'.1'06073—dc20          93–37340
CIP

A catalogue record for this book is available from the British Library.

The paper in this book meets the guidelines for permanence and
durability of the Committee on Production Guidelines for Book
Longevity of the Council on Library Resources.

10 9 8 7 6 5 4 3 2

For Cecilia and Hunter

# CONTENTS

Acknowledgments
xi

1
From Garden City
to Privatopia
1

2
Restrictive Covenants
and the Rise of
Common-Interest Housing
29

3

From Exclusivity to
Exclusion: Homeowner
Associations in the
Suburban Housing
Boom
56


4

The Expansion of
Privatopia: Land
Economics and the
Legacy of
Ebenezer Howard
79


5

The Community
Associations
Institute: The Care
and Feeding of
Residential Private
Governments
106


6

Homeowner
Associations as
Private Governments
122


7

CID Private
Governments and the
Law in California
150

8
Conclusion:
Reflections on
Privatopia and the
City
175


Notes
199


Index
231

# ACKNOWLEDGMENTS

I would like to thank those who helped me develop and refine the ideas presented in this book, and others who lent various kinds of support.

Attorney and writer Michael Lee Bowler was my coauthor on two articles that stimulated my interest in homeowner associations. Although circumstances prevented us from writing a book together as we intended,

I deeply appreciate his friendship and his contribution to my thinking on the subject.

Later, while completing my graduate studies at the University of Southern California, several professors encouraged me to pursue this unorthodox topic in my dissertation. I am grateful to Larry L. Berg, John R. Schmidhauser, Michael B. Preston, Mark E. Kann, and John A. Schutz for their challenging questions and their confidence in me.

At Yale University Press, editors Marian Ash and John S. Covell were unfailingly supportive, insightful, and patient.

I am especially grateful to Dennis R. Judd of the University of Missouri, who was helpful beyond measure as I revised the first draft of this manuscript. His detailed comments on organization, style, and tone were invaluable to me. His efforts far exceeded what any author has a right to expect and, for me, exemplified the way academic criticism would always function, if only we lived in a perfect world.

The following people were especially generous with their time and their wisdom: Siegrun Fox of Texas Tech University; writer Philip Langdon; Sanford Lakoff of the University of California at San Diego; Byron Hanke, whose work at the Federal Housing Administration and in the founding of the Community Associations Institute was so important; Thomas C. Brogan and Michael Adams at Albright College; Greg Wallace, a former student at Albright who helped me as a research assistant; Stephen Holloway, consultant to the California Assembly Committee on Housing and Urban Development; Robyn Boyer Stewart of Common Interest Advocates in Sacramento, California; Dean Woodson of the Florida Bureau of Condominiums; Gopal Ahluwalia and Michael F. Shibley of the National Association of Home Builders; Frank H. Spink, Jr., David E. Stahl, and Michael Singer of the Urban Land Institute; Doug Kleine, David Rhame, C. James Dowden, David Gibbons, Lincoln Cummings, and Clifford J. Treese, all currently or formerly associated with the Community Associations Institute; Stephen Cottrelle, Dorothy Sager, and Larry Holzman of the Maryland Condominium and Homeowner Association; and San Diego attorneys Gary J. Aguirre, James K. Eckmann, C. Bradley Hallen, and the firm Higgs, Fletcher & Mack.

I would like to thank Albright College and Dean Eugene Lubot, who, despite scarce resources, provided me with two summer grants that enabled me to travel for interviews and source materials.

My wife, Cecilia, remained supportive and encouraging while, over the course of six years, I spent more hours at the keyboard than either of us would have imagined possible and left for weeks at a time on research trips. Our son, Hunter, when he is old enough to read these words, may understand what was taking Daddy away from the more important activities that he had in mind for us, such as covering the furniture with small pieces of tape or racing madly around the back yard. Cecilia and Hunter, because you are so important to me, because you put up with so much, and because you represent part of a better future, this book is dedicated to you.

Although I could not have written this book without the help of these generous individuals, I readily acknowledge that all the errors, omissions, inaccuracies, and inadequacies contained in these pages are mine alone.

# PRIVATOPIA

1

# From Garden City to Privatopia

What is the teaching of history, but that great national
transformations, while ages in unnoticed preparation,
when once inaugurated, are accomplished with a rapidity
and resistless momentum proportioned to their
magnitude, not limited by it?
—Edward Bellamy, *Looking Backward: 2000–1887*

In 1898 a forty-eight-year-old English court stenographer named Ebenezer Howard borrowed from a friend a copy of Edward Bellamy's utopian
novel *Looking Backward*. "This I read," Howard said, "at a sitting, not at
all critically, and was fairly carried away by the eloquence and evidently
strong convictions of the author."[1] Howard became a convert to Bellamy's
belief that a perfect society was within humankind's immediate reach.

The novel is the narrative of Julian West, a Bostonian who in 1887 seeks relief from insomnia at the hands of a hypnotist, only to awaken in the year 2000. He discovers that society has undergone a peaceful but radical metamorphosis and now operates in a humane, rational way. Monopoly capitalism has given way to benevolent state ownership of industry, advanced science and technology have made life easier for all, and social and political conflicts have disappeared.[2]

West's experience turns out to be a dream, but Bellamy's faith in the possibility of a utopian future was genuine. As he wrote in his postscript to the novel, *"Looking Backward* was written in the belief that the Golden Age lies before us and not behind us, and is not far away. Our chilüren will surely see it, and we, too, who are already men and women, if we deserve it by our faith and by our works."[3]

Howard was profoundly inspired by the novel, especially by the idea of rapidly transforming a nation through rational planning. "This book pictured the whole American nation organised on cooperative princi- ples—this mighty change coming about with marvellous celerity." He saw the "splendid possibilities of a new civilisation based on service to the community and not on self-interest, at present the dominant motive. Then I determined to take such part as I could, however small it might be, in helping to bring a new civilisation into being."[4]

Howard, at once an idealist and a pragmatist, grew obsessed with putting Bellamy's ideas into practice immediately, but on the less am- bitious scale of a small city. As a Londoner, he saw around him the social consequences of the Industrial Revolution. Cities offered opportunities for culture and social interaction, but they were overcrowded, dirty, and cut off from the salutary effects of contact with nature. High housing costs ensured squalor for many and opulence for a few. Workers toiled for long hours at tedious jobs, yet they continued to stream in from the depopulated and impoverished countryside in search of factory work because wages were higher in the city. Howard's idea was to plan and build a new kind of town that would combine the best features of city and country—a "garden city."

Howard soon wrote his own book detailing the concept, *Tomorrow: A Peaceful Path to Real Reform*. When he was unable to find a publisher, his American friend George Dickman, managing director of Kodak Company, lent him fifty pounds, and with that subsidy the work was published.[5] It was reissued in 1902 under the title *Garden Cities of Tomorrow*.[6]

The book is a manual for the financing, building, and operation of a new kind of planned community, or what came to be known as a "new town." Howard lectured widely and soon had a following. His Garden City Association built two cities in England during his lifetime—Welwyn and Letchworth—and his following turned into a movement that heavily influenced the modern planning profession in many countries.[7]

Howard's admirers and critics alike concede the tremendous influence of his book. One of his early followers was Lewis Mumford, who wrote that *"Garden Cities of Tomorrow* has done more than any other single book to guide the modern town planning movement and to alter its objectives." One of his most vocal critics is Jane Jacobs, who noted that "virtually all modern city planning has been adapted from, and embroidered on, this silly substance." Whether silly or profound, there is no denying the enduring power of Howard's idea.[8]

## THE GARDEN CITY IDEA

Howard readily acknowledged that his garden city plan was to some extent a synthesis of several proposals by other writers who had addressed more limited issues, such as an organized migration of population for colonization, a nationalization of land ownership, and a model industrial town.[9] Howard's particular genius was the way he combined these and other elements into a plan capable of being realized in the present. Mumford has noted that "Howard's prime contribution was to outline the nature of a balanced community and to show what steps were necessary, in an ill-organized and disoriented society, to bring it into existence."[10]

The garden city idea as Howard conceived it had two elements meant to work in tandem: the comprehensive physical planning and political and economic organization of the model community. Both have been enormously influential.

### The Physical Plan

The garden city's physical plan was to be based on Howard's conceptual diagrams, but in practice, he said, it would be meticulously designed by a team of engineers, architects, surveyors, and other professionals to make the city self-sufficient. It was of "incalculable" importance, Howard said, "that the town is definitely planned, so that the whole question of municipal administration may be dealt with by one far-reaching scheme. . . . It is essential, as we have said, that there should be unity of design and purpose—that the town should be planned as a whole, and not left to grow up in a chaotic manner as has been the case with all English towns, and more or less so with the towns of all countries."[11]

Howard envisioned building from scratch on an undeveloped six-thousand-acre plot of land. At the center would be a city one thousand acres in area and about one-and-one-half miles in diameter that would house up to thirty thousand people.[12] The city is depicted as circular and crossed from center to circumference by six wide boulevards. At the center would be a five-and-one-half-acre Central Park surrounded by such public buildings as the town hall. Around this park would run a circular Crystal Palace, a glass arcade not unlike the modern shopping mall. Outside this arcade a series of circular streets lined with trees, houses, schools, and gardens would encircle the center. At the edge of the circular city would be the industries—the factories, warehouses, and coal and timber yards—all of which would face outward onto a circular railway encompassing the town and delivering goods to and from the city and its businesses.

Outside this perimeter would be a five-thousand-acre belt of agricultural land that would be home to an additional two thousand people engaged in farming. This greenbelt—which would be permanent—would provide food for the city, prevent its expansion beyond the planned optimum size, and isolate it from outside forces that could change it.[13]

Through this careful planning and the efficiency it would produce, Howard anticipated that the rent would be well within the reach of most citizens. Although the garden city's rent would be higher than typical rents in London, the Londoner was paying taxes for municipal services that would be included in rents paid in the garden city. Consequently, the price of living in a garden city would be "extremely moderate."[14]

## Political and Economic Organization

Howard's plan for the political and economic structure of his garden city included radical proposals for public land ownership, a novel form of government, and an economic system of publicly regulated monopolies.

The initial construction funds would be borrowed. All land occupied by the city and the agricultural belt would be owned by the municipality. The residents would pay rent to the city, and that money would be used to pay off the construction loan, build public works projects, and provide old-age pensions and medical care.[15] Subsidies for the poor would not be required, as pensions and voluntary charitable work would make such costs unnecessary. There would be little need for police protection because the new citizens "for the most part, will be of the law-abiding class," and the plan would "prevent the creation of those surroundings which make the intervention of the police so frequently necessary."[16]

The government Howard proposed was a democratically controlled corporate technocracy. Renters would elect the heads of various practical departments grouped under general headings: Public Control, with departments on finance, law, assessment, and inspection; Engineering, composed of departments representing the various elements of the physical plant; and Social Purposes, with such departments as education, music, and recreation. The chairmen and vice-chairmen of these departments would constitute the Central Council, which would be the governing body of the city.[17]

The city's constitution would more closely resemble the charter of a business corporation than the governing document of any existing nation or city: "The constitution is modelled upon that of a large and well-appointed business, which is divided into various departments, each department being expected to justify its own continued existence—its officers being selected, not so much for their knowledge of the business generally as for their special fitness for the work of their department."[18]

This principle reflected Howard's belief that politics, in the sense of various interests competing for favor in the distribution of government services and wealth, would be essentially eliminated in his planned city. In place of politics and ideology would be rational management of practical matters by experts, each elected to a particular department because of his or her expertise in the area and views on "clear and distinct issues." "The candidates would not be expected to specify their views upon a hundred and one questions of municipal policy upon which they had no definite opinions, and which would probably not give rise within their term of office to the necessity for recording their votes, but would simply state their views as to some special question or group of questions, a sound opinion upon which would be of urgent importance to the electors, because immediately connected with the welfare of the town."[19]

In essence, electoral choice would be profoundly but voluntarily restricted. Choice would consist of nothing more than voting for the best electrician, the smartest engineer, the best-trained librarian, and so forth, so that all these technicians might govern as a body. Howard simply assumes that voters would choose on the basis of expertise, thus preserving his democratic technocracy. He does not mention the possibility that they might cast their ballots on some other basis.

This governing group of technicians would possess more power over its renters than other local governments have over their citizens because the council would have all the powers of a landlord at common law: "In the council (or its nominees) are vested the rights and powers of the community as sole landlord of Garden City. . . . By stepping as a *quasi* public body into the rights of a private landlord, it becomes at once clothed with far larger powers for carrying out the will of the people than are possessed by other local bodies, and thus solves to a large extent the problem of local self-government"[20] (emphasis in original).

These greater powers would enable the garden city to operate a new kind of market that combines capitalist and socialist elements. Howard felt that "no line could be sharply drawn between municipal and individual enterprise," and he viewed markets as "semi-municipal enterprises." He therefore proposed that business be regulated by limiting the number of private retail traders and controlling the kind of trade to be conducted in each shop. A trader would ask for permission to rent a shop, and the council would then grant the trader a monopoly on that trade. But the monopoly could be broken and a competitor permitted to operate if the renters so decided by vote, based on the trader's methods, treatment of workers, and prices. This system, which Howard called "local option," would make the tradesmen "in a very real sense, municipal servants."[21]

Howard envisioned that the first garden city would colonize a second city like itself a few miles away, and those two a third, and so on. The cities would be connected by railways, and these clusters of "social cities" would be linked not only by their similar internal plans but by an overall regional plan. In this way the entire nation would eventually be transformed by Howard's garden city idea.[22] Howard felt that the utopian transformation of human society could come painlessly, through urban planning alone—without revolution, without authoritarian national government, and without conscious efforts to change the family, the educational system, the national political system, and other social institutions.

# THE RISE OF PRIVATOPIA

From the adoption in America of Blackstone's commentaries to the simultaneous pursuit of privatization in the 1980s, Britain and the United States have enjoyed a "two-way transatlantic traffic" in land planning and urban policy concepts.[23] The garden city was no exception. American ideas and experience were a part of Howard's inspiration, and later his garden city notion was transplanted from England to the United States.

Yet his ideas did not lead in the benign and cooperative direction he anticipated when they started to become popular in the United States in the 1920s. Howard's ideas came to be absorbed into an important stage in the intellectual heritage of a form of private housing known as common-interest developments (CIDS), a category that includes planned-unit developments of single-family houses (PUDS), condominiums, and cooperative apartments. Some aspects of Howard's utopian vision were retained, others excised, and new elements added as a new kind of residential construction evolved throughout the twentieth century.

Although the government of Great Britain took on a substantial role in building towns inspired by Howard's garden city, the same was not true in the United States.[24] Private developers and businessmen, rather than government, have long been the dominant forces in American urban planning. In *The Private City,* a history of Philadelphia, Sam Bass Warner argues that "from about the mid-nineteenth century onward, the successes and failures of American cities have depended upon the unplanned outcomes of the private market," a market whose nature had "determined the shape and quality of America's big cities." According to Warner's definition of privatism, the purpose of the citizen is to seek wealth while the job of the city is to be "a community of private money makers."[25]

Dennis Judd argues that "American urban growth has always been dictated primarily by private institutions and not by public policy," because public policy "follows rather than precedes the activities of the entrepreneurs who have changed the urban landscape." Consequently, "in American cities, politics has tended to be the handmaiden of the economic system."[26]

The dominant ideology of privatism worked against important aspects of Howard's plan. Perhaps the most significant of these was his approach to land tenure. Because private institutions and private property drive urban development, Howard's proposal for community ownership of all real property, with people renting their homes instead of owning them, has never found favor with America's private real estate developers. Instead, these entrepreneurs, aided by government, have consistently promoted private home ownership.[27]

Yet this same American privatism made fertile soil for Howard's idea of building entire communities. Economies of scale mean bigger profit, especially for private builders with the capital to construct and sell what amount to small cities. Since the 1920s large corporate builders have gradually risen to prominence in the housing construction business, making the single-family house a mass-produced consumer item, like the toaster or automobile.[28] These corporations began to build hundreds, then thousands, of houses at a time for short-term profit, not for long-term social transformation. So, although the corporations have planned and built on a grand scale, their communities have been premised on private home ownership and designed to safeguard property values. Howard's hope for "a new civilisation based on service to the community and not on self interest" has not been realized. Instead, American real estate development corporations, with government as a silent partner, have chosen to build a new kind of community that serves as a monument to privatism.

The complex interplay between Howard's ideas and the ambience of American privatism began long before Howard wrote his influential book. In 1871, at the age of twenty-one, he went to America with two friends to start a farm in Howard County, Nebraska. He proved to be a failure at farming, and within a few months he moved to Chicago and became a court reporter. In 1876 he returned to England, but his stay in America had affected him deeply. Through contact with Quakers and Christian Scientists, he acquired a humanist religious outlook emphasizing the power of the mind to translate ideas into reality. As one of Howard's biographers put it, "This tipping of the balance towards the ideal remained in Howard's mind all his life."[29] Although his idealism and bedrock optimism helped to make him an inspirational leader, it also colored his urban planning ideas, leaving him with "[a] tendency discernible in *Garden Cities of Tomorrow* to discount the existence of evil" and a relentless belief that humankind was capable of achieving perfection through the use of the mind.[30]

America influenced Howard in another sense as well: during his stay he witnessed cities being built from the ground up. As Lewis Mumford describes it, "No little stimulus came to him from his visit to America, where he had before him the constant spectacle of new communities being laid out every year on new land, and he was impressed by the possibility of a fresh start."[31]

Among the new communities that appeared in nineteenth-century America were a number of privately owned and operated luxury subdivisions for the rich that were at least as important in the lineage of CID housing as Howard's garden city. The developments were not cities but exclusive neighborhoods designed to be separate and shielded from their surroundings. To maintain the private parks, lakes, and other amenities of the subdivisions, developers created provisions for common ownership of the land by all residents and private taxation of the owners. To ensure that the land would not be put to other uses by subsequent owners, developers attached "restrictive covenants" to the deeds. Two of the earliest such developments were Gramercy Park in New York, which formed an association in 1831, and Louisburg Square in Boston, which did the same in 1844.[32]

These and other subdivisions pioneered what was to become one of the most significant trends in American urban history: the use by developers of common ownership plans and deed restrictions as private land-planning devices. Similar methods were used by nineteenth-century St. Louis subdividers who provided such services as street maintenance, snow removal, mowing, tree trimming, and street lighting to private neighborhoods through hundreds of "private street associations."[33] By 1928 scores of luxury subdivisions across the country were using deed restrictions—including racially restrictive covenants—as their legal architecture. To guarantee enforcement of the covenants, developers were organizing "homeowner associations" so that residents could sue those who violated the rules.

At the same time, the ideas of Ebenezer Howard began to influence many American planners and architects. Perhaps the most important group to reflect Howard's ideas and, in a sense, Americanize them, was the Regional Planning Association of America, a group of innovative thinkers that included Lewis Mumford. The RPAA, working with builder Alexander M. Bing, developed the planned community of Radburn, New Jersey, in 1928. The project was not completely executed, however, because of the Great Depression; but it inspired many imitators.[34] The "Radburn idea" became famous for keeping vehicle traffic separated from pedestrian walkways and for "reversing" the houses so that living areas faced a large interior greenbelt and the kitchen and service areas faced the street.[35] Radburn's most enduring contribution may be the form of private government, based on restrictive covenants administered through a homeowner association, originated for it by attorney and political scientist Charles Ascher.[36] Radburn's government, which was based on the Progressive city manager model, became the prototype for today's CID regimes.

The depression and World War II radically reduced new housing construction, but pent-up demand led to a postwar housing boom of unprecedented scale. Large developers began to build more complex developments, some of which had private governments. The developers also began efforts to standardize and institutionalize this form of housing in 1944 when the Urban Land Institute formed a Community Builders' Council headed by Jesse Clyde Nichols, builder of the Country Club District in Kansas City and one of the most influential proponents of CIDs and homeowner associations.[37]

Such developments were still primarily for the affluent, however. As late as 1962 there were fewer than five hundred homeowner associations in the United States, and the dominant form of middle-class housing was still the suburban "big-lot" subdivision.[38] But rising land prices and a population boom pressured developers to find ways to squeeze more people onto smaller parcels of land. With the endorsement of the Federal Housing Administration, which provided developers with detailed guidelines on how to create condominiums and PUDs that would receive federal mortgage insurance, the real estate industry began in the mid-1960s to promote common-interest housing for the middle class, offering open spaces owned in common in lieu of large private yards.

By the 1960s the real estate industry was increasingly dominated by large-scale corporate "community builders."[39] These builders made housing a mass-produced consumer commodity, and they found CIDs enormously profitable. The CIDs allowed them to build more units per acre while satisfying middle-class consumer preferences for such amenities as swimming pools, golf courses, parks, private beaches, recreation rooms, security gates and guards that would be prohibitively expensive for individual middle-class owners.

The CID movement received another boost from the "new town" boom, which began in the 1960s. Dozens of large, heavily planned and relatively self-contained communities were built, including Rancho Bernardo and Irvine, in California; Reston, Virginia; and Columbia, Maryland. Projected populations ranged as high as five hundred thousand.

The sponsors of these "instant cities," as Theodore Roszak called them, included such corporate giants as Gulf Oil, Humble Oil, Goodyear Tire and Rubber, Westinghouse, and General Electric.[40] Some developers received federal assistance, but that was withdrawn in the mid-1970s amid a rash of insolvencies.

Despite the mixed results of the new town movement, the preference for CID housing among large developers was by then strong. To reduce risk while continuing to reap substantial profits, the industry shifted to construction of smaller developments but applied the same principles it used with the bigger developments. Beginning in the mid-1970s, financially strapped local governments also found CID housing appealing because it had features of private infrastructure, allowing communities to grow and add property-tax payers at reduced public cost.

These private initiatives in housing policy, and their validation by government, brought about astonishing nationwide growth in CID construction. There were fewer than five hundred such homeowner associations in 1964. By 1970 there were 10,000 homeowner associations; by 1975 there were 20,000; by 1980, 55,000; by 1990, 130,000; and by 1992, there were 150,000 associations privately governing an estimated 32 million Americans. In 1990 there were 11.6 million CID housing units constituting more than 11 percent of American housing. Of these, 51 percent were planned-unit developments of single-family homes, 42 percent were condominiums, and 7 percent were housing cooperatives. By 2000 there is expected to be a total of 225,000 homeowner associations in the country.[41]

Such housing developments are concentrated in the sunbelt states, including Florida and California, but not because of regional consumer preferences. Rather, a great deal of new housing has been built in the sunbelt in the past few decades, and that new housing increasingly is CID housing. In fact, CIDs are spreading wherever residential construction is taking place. In a 1989 national survey, the Advisory Commission on Intergovernmental Relations (ACIR) found that CIDs were most common in California, Florida, and Texas. A second group of states in which CIDs were an important sector included New Jersey, New York, Virginia, Pennsylvania, Maryland, and Hawaii. ACIR found that 36 percent of CIDs were in the West, 33 percent in the South, 21 percent in the northeast, and 10 percent in the Midwest.[42]

CIDs have become so much the norm for new housing that, as the ACIR notes, "In many rapidly developing areas, such as those in California, nearly all new residential development is within the jurisdiction of residential community associations."[43] As CIDs spread, and as old housing is replaced by new CID housing, consumer choice is increasingly restricted. In short, growing numbers of Americans who wish to purchase new houses are going to be living in CIDs, and under the rule of private governments, regardless of their preferences.

## MORNING IN PRIVATOPIA

If Ebenezer Howard could awaken now, like Bellamy's protagonist Julian West, and look about him at the America in which his ideas have had so much impact, he might react with astonishment and disappointment. He would see more than thirty million Americans, or some 12 percent of the U.S. population, living in about 150,000 common-interest developments.[44] These developments are Americanized, third-generation descendants of Howard's utopian garden city idea. Our garden cities are a hybrid of Howard's utopian ideas and American privatism, and I use the term *privatopia* to capture the two concepts.

### Rancho Bernardo

If Ebenezer Howard happened to awaken twenty-five miles north of downtown San Diego, California, he would see a community of 33,250 known as Rancho Bernardo.[45] Started in 1961 by builder Harry L. Summers, Rancho Bernardo typifies the large CID and has served as a model for many smaller developments.[46] Summers began, like Howard, with 6,107 acres of undeveloped land, mainly rolling hills, on which he built a planned community that included housing, streets, recreation facilities, commercial areas, and light industry. It is easily distinguishable from the town of Poway to the east by the red tile roofs that top every building, the most notable of many tight architectural restrictions.

There are now about fourteen thousand dwellings in Rancho Bernardo, of which some eight thousand are single-family detached homes; the remainder is made up of single-family attached homes (generally called townhouses), condominiums, and apartments. When it is fully developed (by 1995, estimates say), Rancho Bernardo will house 41,200 people in about 17,900 dwellings. Rancho Bernardo is legally part of the city of San Diego, but it is to a large extent self-sufficient. A fifty-three-acre town center houses a large supermarket, many retail businesses, banks, and a retirement home. Two other parcels—one of fifty-five acres and the other of seven acres—accommodate a post office, library, fire station, movie theaters, financial institutions, auto service centers, hotels, and restaurants. There are several office buildings housing lawyers, physicians, and other professionals. Four smaller neighborhood commercial centers offer convenience goods and services. Two industrial parks occupying a total of 618 acres house such high-tech employers as UNISYS (Burroughs Corporation), National Cash Register, Hewlett Packard, Sony, Gould Electronics, and other, smaller, corporations.[47]

The development is divided into a variety of "neighborhoods"—which offer distinct architectural styles, housing prices, and lifestyles—that were created during the different phases of the project. For example, Seven Oaks is a retirement community. Oaks North is for people age forty-five and older. Westwood includes apartments and a large "family area" with playground. The Trails offers larger lots, more privacy, a bit more individuality, and prices in the high six figures.[48]

The plan includes complex and detailed architectural restrictions for each of the neighborhoods—restrictions that are rigidly enforced by the more than one dozen neighborhood homeowner associations run by elected directors. Even the most minute changes in the restrictions require the approval of the association. Richard Louv, who studied Rancho Bernardo for his book *America II,* describes the restrictions as follows:

> Even vegetable gardens are frowned upon—though some people do grow tiny ones out of their neighbors' view. Fences, hedges, or walls require approval, and may not be more than three feet tall. Signs, other than for-sale signs, are prohibited. Trees must be kept trimmed and may not grow above the level of the roof, which must be covered with red tiles. Residents are not allowed to park recreational vehicles or boats in their driveway; a special communal parking area is set aside for them. One village, designed for seniors, prohibits grandchildren from using the recreation center, and home visitation by grandchildren is strictly limited. The owners of patio homes (semidetached houses that share common grounds, except for patio areas) must gain their neighbors' approval before altering the patio, planting a rose-bush, or raising a canopy.[49]

Restrictions in some neighborhoods are so detailed as to regulate the color of curtains.[50] The rigidity with which these restrictions are interpreted and enforced is illustrated by a matter that had to be resolved by the California courts.[51] One phase of the development had a restriction providing that "no truck, camper, trailer, boat of any kind or other form of recreational vehicle shall be parked" in the project. One of the residents bought a new pickup truck with a camper shell to use for personal transportation. The association, through its management company, took him to court to enjoin him from parking the truck under his own carport and to recover $2,060 in fines for this "violation." After losing in the trial court, the management company appealed, only to see the appellate court side with the resident and hold the company's action unreasonable.

Yet this sort of action does not seem unreasonable to many Rancho Bernardo residents. They place a high value on the restrictions, feeling that the infringement on one's own freedom is a small price to pay for protection from the potential misdeeds of one's neighbors. Louv quotes one resident as saying, "Sure, they have some rules, like the one that regulates campers. But the community associations are here to protect our interests, not let the community deteriorate. That's not regulation; it's common sense. I don't know why anyone would look at it differently than I do, do you?"[52]

In addition to the neighborhood associations that enforce architectural restrictions, there are projectwide committees and corporate entities that perform other functions. Rancho Bernardo's political structure is so complex and sophisticated as to include regular reapportionment and redistricting.[53] At the top is the Rancho Bernardo Town Council, which has numerous specialty commissions within it to deal with such matters as senior services, civic-community relations, public services, and community appearance. The Rancho Bernardo Community Planning Board communicates directly with the San Diego Planning Commission to maintain control over the gradual build-out of the project.[54]

Through these groups Rancho Bernardo residents are better represented before the San Diego city government than virtually any other part of the city. The Bernardo Home Owners Corporation not only maintains an official liaison with the San Diego City Council, it also provides buses that transport hordes of residents to City Council meetings at which topics in which they have an interest are being addressed.[55]

The political clout of San Bernardo is increased through the concentration of wealthy and skilled professionals among its residents, many of whom are retired and have not only the skills but the time to act as community advocates. When the cable television company asked the City Council for a rate citywide increase, Rancho Bernardo's successful opposition to the increase was led by two residents: a former director of public utilities for Fort Wayne, Indiana, and a former utility rate specialist. Communication with the San Diego Police Department was handled on a monthly basis by a former detective for the Beverly Hills Police Department. The successful effort to get a new hospital for Rancho Bernardo was led by a physician who was a former hospital administrator. Talent, wealth, and position are found in extraordinary abundance among Rancho Bernardo residents.[56] Moreover, journalist Harold Keen notes, "the community's affluence is reflected in its sociological makeup and political leanings—predominantly white Anglo, conservative Republican, overwhelmingly pro-Reagan."[57]

## No More Pink Flamingos

Rancho Bernardo is larger than most CIDs, but it is not unique in exalting private rules and regulations for their own sake and in emphasizing property values over considerations of individual privacy and freedom.[58]

Some community associations have banned political signs, prohibited distribution of newspapers, and forbidden political gatherings in the common areas.[59]

In Ashland, Massachusetts, a Vietnam War veteran was told that he could not fly the American flag on Flag Day. The board backed down only after the resident called the press and the story appeared on the front page of a local newspaper.[60]

In Monroe, New Jersey, a homeowner association took a married couple to court because the wife, at age forty-five, was three years younger than the association's age minimum for residency. The association won in court, and the judge ordered the sixty-year-old husband to sell, rent the unit, or live without his wife.[61]

In Houston, Texas, a homeowner association took a woman to court for keeping a dog in violation of the rules of her CID. The association won, but she kept the dog anyway. The judge sent her to jail for contempt of court.[62]

In Fairbanks Ranch, an affluent CID in Southern California that lies behind six locked gates, there are forty-five private streets patrolled by private security officers who enforce a private speed limit. First-time speeders get a warning; the second offense brings a hearing and a reprimand; a third offense means a five-hundred-dollar fine, and the car and driver are banned from the private streets for a month.[63]

The Rancho Santa Fe Association was established in 1927 in San Diego County, California. It governs the sixty-two-hundred-acre development of lavish homes that includes twenty-five hundred voting members in eighteen hundred residences. It has sixty-five full-time employees and a $3 million annual budget. The association had enough political influence with the county government to forestall construction of a badly needed arterial road through the development, despite strong support for the route in the adjoining city of Encinitas.[64]

In Vista, California, a homeowner whose income dropped because of a lost job and a divorce fell behind in paying her monthly association dues. The association obtained a lien on her property for the $192.04 it was owed, plus legal fees and costs. She resumed paying the dues on time, but when she disputed the amount of fees, late charges, and costs (which brought the lien to $857.13), the association served her with a foreclosure summons. In desperation, the homeowner got an advance on a credit card and paid the full amount, but said, "To think that for a few dollars they can come in and take your house out from under you—I can't believe it."[65]

In Fort Lauderdale, Florida, condominium managers ordered a couple to stop entering and leaving their unit through their back door, claiming that they were wearing an unsightly path in the lawn by taking a short cut to the parking lot. The couple retained an attorney who filed a lawsuit seeking a court's permission for the couple to use their own back door.[66]

In Boca Raton, Florida, an association cited a homeowner and took her to court because her dog weighed more than thirty pounds, a violation of association rules. A court-ordered weighing ceremony was inconclusive, with the scales hovering between just under and just over the limit. After the story made national news, the association settled the suit on undisclosed terms.[67]

In Delaware County, Pennsylvania, a man put up a four-foot-high fence of black fabric in his back yard to keep his young son from falling off a four-hundred-foot cliff. His homeowner association took him to court, contending that he had violated a rule against fences, but a judge ruled in his favor.[68]

In Bucks County, Pennsylvania, a woman bought a twenty-two-room stone farmhouse in 1980. Six years later a development called Tyler Walk was completed next to her property, and a homeowner association was formed. In 1988 a resident of Tyler Walk reviewed the plans for the development and discovered that the woman's land was within the borders of Tyler Walk. The association began assessing her membership dues and contended that she had to live by the association's rules. She refused, and the association sued her. A judge ordered her to pay two thousand dollars in fees and late charges. When she still refused to pay, the association obtained a lien on her house and scheduled a sheriff's sale at which they attempted to sell two of her cars and a lawn mower. When there were no takers, the association had to pay towing fees for the cars. Despite the net loss, the association president said that the important thing was upholding a principle. "The law's the law," he said, and offered to forgo selling her property (but keeping the lien on her house) if the woman would agree to pay her dues in the future.[69]

Near Philadelphia is a development of $225,000 homes called Chartwell. Construction of the homes began in the late 1980s. A married couple bought one in 1989 and brought their sons' metal swing set with them when they moved in. One year later the association told them to take the swing set down, even though there were as yet no written rules regarding swing sets. When the rules finally appeared, they prescribed that all swing sets must be made of wood. Why? "It has to do with what the overall community should look like," said an attorney for the association. The couple then submitted a petition in support of his swing set that was signed by three-fourths of the homeowners, along with Environmental Protection Agency warnings about the dangers to children (in this case, aged two and four) posed by the poisonous chemicals used in pressure-treated wood—the type needed for swing sets. The association's response was to impose a daily fine of ten dollars until the set was removed and to refuse offers to compromise, which included painting the swing set in earth tones. The association also passed rules governing the placement of firewood, rabbit hutches, and trash cans on the curb. It even banned "offensive conduct," which it defined as "activity which in the judgment of the Board of Directors is noxious or offensive to other home lot owners." One homeowner asked, "Who are these little Hitlers making these rules?"[70]

In Santa Ana, California, the Townsquare Owners' Association posted notices throughout the complex accusing a resident of "parking in circular driveway kissing and doing bad things for over 1 hour." She was warned that she would be fined if another such incident happened. The woman denied the charge, retained legal counsel, and threatened a lawsuit for defamation, invasion of privacy, and infliction of emotional distress. The association issued an apology through its attorney, explaining it as a case of mistaken identity. The incident received national media attention and prompted the *Los Angeles Times* to publish an editorial asking, "How many individual freedoms are to be lost to proliferating homeowner association regulations" and saying that "condominium associations need to curb the tendency to regulate excessively."[71]

These examples illustrate the peculiar internal dynamics of these heirs to the garden city legacy. American CIDs are both like and unlike the garden city. The similarities include master planning of large-scale communities; isolation of the development from its surroundings and protection against change; capitalization on dislike of city life to attract residents; development of a government based on a corporate charter and attempts to replace politics with management; and creation of a government with greater powers than that of the city.

The differences, however, are profound. Designers of American CIDs dwell on the physical plan but slight the social and economic structure of the community, particularly Howard's quasi-socialist reforms; base land tenure on private ownership rather than rental from a public landlord; and do not create real, self-sufficient communities with a full economic base. American CIDs are not intended first and foremost as a vehicle for reforming society, as was the garden city. But the American CID may have greater potential for achieving Howard's goal of undermining the city than did the English new towns.

For these and other reasons, the American CID falls short of Howard's expectations regarding both the nature and the quality of relations between homeowners and their boards of directors—what could be called their micropolitics—and in their apparent impact on society, or macropolitics.

## The Micropolitics of Private Governments

Instead of having a benevolent public landlord, as Howard anticipated, CIDs feature a form of private government that takes an American preference for private home ownership and, too often, turns it into an ideology of hostile privatism. Preservation of property values is the highest social goal, to which other aspects of community life are subordinated. Rigid, intrusive, and often petty rule enforcement makes a caricature of Howard's benign managerial government, and the belief in rational planning is distorted into an emphasis on conformity for its own sake.

To many residents, association boards often seem to operate as though wearing blinders, rigidly enforcing technical rules against people's use of their own homes and ignoring the consequences of such intrusive behavior. Many CID residents casually accept the rationality of such management-mania, but others become angry and file lawsuits or refuse to obey and find themselves sued by the association. A California study found that 44 percent of board members had been harassed or threatened with lawsuit during the preceding year. The CID resident must choose between conformity and conflict.[72]

This predilection toward litigation is primarily the result of the particular kind of private government found in CIDs. To understand why this is so, one needs to understand some of the legal terms and concepts that distinguish today's CIDs from ordinary subdivisions.

Planned unit developments, or PUDs, are single-family detached homes built according to a master plan, generally in the suburbs. Condominiums, though at law really a form of ownership rather than a type of building, are usually multifamily housing—that is, buildings housing more than one family. Cooperative apartments, or co-ops, are generally converted apartment buildings in which owners have a share of stock in the entire building and the exclusive right to occupy a particular unit.[73]

These forms of housing have three distinct legal characteristics that set their residents apart from other Americans: common ownership of property, mandatory membership in the homeowner association, and the requirement of living under a private regime of restrictive covenants enforced by fellow residents.

First, residents own or exclusively occupy their own units, but they share ownership of the "common area" of the development used by all (hence the term "common interest"). The common area may include the entire building in the case of a condominium or co-op, with only the "air space" within the units being privately owned or controlled. In a PUD, the common area may include recreation centers, streets, front lawns, parks, and parking lots. Residents are assessed fees to pay for these facilities and for private services that range from police protection to local self-government—services that were once the province of cities. Because these amenities are privately supported, only residents are allowed to use them.

Second, because common property ownership requires organization of some sort, everyone who buys a home in a CID automatically becomes a member of a homeowner association, or HOA. These are nearly always nonprofit corporations. They are set up on paper by the developer of the project while the project is in the planning stage, not voluntarily organized by the residents after they move in. The only way to resign from the association is to sell one's home and move out.

Third, because the homeowner association itself needs organization if it is to function, all residents are governed by a corporate board of directors elected by the unit owners, renters being disenfranchised but still subject to the board's authority. The board runs the development, aided by a system of committees it administers and often by a professional property manager retained by the association. The operation of the development involves collecting assessments from all owners, handling the association's finances, maintaining the common property, filing and managing lawsuits on behalf of all owners, and enforcing against the owners and renters a set of private laws drawn up by the developer and known as "covenants, conditions and restrictions," or CC&Rs. Empowered by this quasi-constitution, the board is a private government.

Ebenezer Howard wanted his Central Council to have greater powers than a city, and he accomplished that goal by basing the council's powers in property ownership rather than in principles of government. Although he prescribed a landlord-tenant arrangement, he would probably recognize the same power dynamic at work in today's residential private governments. Through private property relations, the board of directors does, indeed, have greater power over its residents than does a city.

The CC&Rs enforced by the board are a complicated system of private covenants, known generically as "deed restrictions," built into the deeds to all the homes. This device, which dates to fourteenth-century England, permits a seller of land—such as the original developer and his successor, the board—to retain control over how the land is used after he sells it.[74] The sale is conditional on the buyer's agreement to abide by certain restrictions on the way he may use or dispose of the property. The promises "run with the land," meaning that all successive buyers are bound by the same covenants as the original purchaser.

Certain particular covenants, such as racial restrictions or covenants banning children, are invalid everywhere or in some states, and
many restrictive covenants were once viewed by English judges as undue
restraints on the free sale of property. But that view was not widely
followed in America, particularly in the early twentieth century, and
today restrictive covenants are an approved legal device.[75]

Today's real estate developers do not merely insert into the deeds a
covenant or two, as sellers did in earlier times, such as a promise not to
build a slaughterhouse or soap factory, or a promise not to build on a
parcel set aside as a park. Instead, they have lawyers draft a fat package
many pages long and full of elaborate restrictions that, taken as a whole,
dictate to a large extent the lifestyle of everybody in the project.

The rigidity that seems to characterize CID rule enforcement was
deliberately institutionalized by developers. It is maintained through
the rules and laws under which CID boards operate. Even if individual
board members wish to use prudent discretion in the enforcement of
restrictions, and make exceptions, it is often difficult for them to do so.
Individual association members can sue the board for failing to enforce
the rules. Moreover, attorneys and property managers who specialize in
servicing CIDs advocate strict rule enforcement in order to avoid setting
precedents that could be used to justify further exceptions, and, ultimately, undermine the entire regime. Even if many residents and board
members wish to change a rule, the task is made especially difficult
by developers' "super-majority" requirements, which mandate approval
from 75 percent of *all* owners, not just those voting.

This form of private government is strikingly different from that of
cities. In a variety of ways, these private governments are illiberal and
undemocratic. Most significantly boards of directors operate outside constitutional restrictions because the law views them as business entities
rather than governments. Moreover, courts accept the legal fiction that
all the residents have voluntarily agreed to be bound by the covenants by
virtue of having bought a unit in the development.

## Macropolitics: Secession of the Successful?

Rather than offering a solution to the problems of big cities, as
Howard intended, CIDs exacerbate them. The developments take over
many municipal functions for those who can pay the price, offering a

competing sector of pay-as-you-go utilities that the Advisory Commission on Intergovernmental Relations (ACIR) has called "the most significant privatization of local government responsibilities in recent times."[76] This privatization was undertaken without consideration of its implications and consequences, however, and it is different from other forms of privatization in a number of significant ways. Most important, it carries with it the possibility that those affluent enough to live in CIDs will become increasingly segregated from the rest of society.

The segregationist trend was actively promoted by the Federal Housing Administration, which in 1964 adopted an Urban Land Institute policy advocating that open spaces, recreation centers, and other common property in large, planned developments be owned by private homeowner associations.[77] The ULI argued that public ownership of such facilities should be discouraged because "the use of general tax funds for maintenance of facilities requires availability of such facilities to the general public." The "suitability" of this arrangement, ULI argued, "remains doubtful."[78]

In 1967 Stanley Scott argued that this policy amounted to the institutionalization of existing segregated housing patterns.[79] This impression was reinforced, he argued, by ULI's recommendation that homeowners and renters should not belong to the same organization because "normally renters and homeowners have different interests and do not mix well in an association."[80]

Scott's conclusions were prescient regarding the implications of the FHA/ULI policy:

> Our society has important goals other than the creation of high-quality, upper-class, single-family, amenity-filled neighborhoods whose property values are secure and whose home owners never fail to meet a mortgage installment—laudable as some of the latter objectives may be. In the next two or three decades residential patterns will be established or rearranged, and many other features of existing and future urban communities determined. The policies under which this is done will influence fundamentally the quality and nature of future urban life. Decisions made during this period will also influence the role, strength, effectiveness and perhaps even the survival of our institutions of *public* local self-government.[81] (Emphasis in original)

Instead of housing people from all walks of life, as Ebenezer Howard envisioned, CIDs compete with cities for the affluent, siphoning off their tax dollars, their expertise and participation, and their sense of identification with a community. Such developments have come to be invoked as part of a disturbing trend called the "secession of the successful" by liberal economist Robert Reich, who is Secretary of Labor under President Clinton. "In many cities and towns, the wealthy have in effect withdrawn their dollars from the support of public spaces and institutions shared by all and dedicated the savings to their own private services," Reich writes. "Condominiums and the omnipresent residential communities dun their members to undertake work that financially strapped local governments can no longer afford to do well—maintaining roads, mending sidewalks, pruning trees, repairing street lights, cleaning swimming pools, paying for lifeguards and, notably, hiring security guards to protect life and property. (The number of private security guards in the United States now exceeds the number of public police officers.)"[82]

Similar observations have been made by conservative social scientist Charles Murray, who views the growth of CIDs as a symbol of America becoming a "a caste society" with "utter social separation" of the rich from the rest of society. Murray envisions a day when this growing sector of rich Americans will come to view cities as the internal equivalent of Indian reservations—places of deprivation and dysfunction for which they have no responsibility.[83]

## CIDs AS UTOPIAN COMMUNITIES

Lamentable though they may be, such sentiments as those Murray anticipates are consistent with one aspect of the utopian tradition. Utopian thinkers are inspired to create their ideal worlds in large part because of their dissatisfaction with the world around them, and their solutions tend to be reactive and one-dimensional. As Frank E. Manuel and Fritzie P. Manuel note in their massive study of utopian thought, "The great utopians have all borne witness to their anger at the world, their disgust with society, their acute suffering as their sensibilities are assailed from all sides. They withdraw from this world into a far simpler form of existence which they fantasy. The escape from everyday conflicts and disappointments has a childlike quality. And their way back from utopia, their return to the real world they had abandoned, is often characterized by devotion to a fixed idea with which they become obsessed. They clutch frantically at this overvalued idea that at once explains all evil and offers the universal remedy, and they build an impregnable fortress around it."[84]

This description fits Ebenezer Howard reasonably well, with his revulsion at the perceived evils of cities and his vision of solving them all through urban planning. A similar tone also characterized the statements of early proponents of the CID boom, including those at the Urban Land Institute, who contended that "the homes association is an ideal tool for building better communities." "The explosive growth of our cities, their trend to gigantism, and the high mobility of their residents are rapidly destroying a sense of community among individuals in urban America. Constructive forces are needed to counteract these negative aspects and to utilize the opportunity that growth offers to build better communities. The best possible way to bring about—or to revive—a grass roots sense of community is for home owners to control nearby facilities of importance to them and through this to participate actively in the life of their neighborhoods."[85]

This is a statement of utopian faith: the route to community is through joint ownership of private property by an exclusive group living according to its own rules.[86] Such a conviction fits into one tradition of utopian thought. In her study of communes and utopias, Rosabeth Moss Kanter found that, historically, "the initial impetus for the building of American communes has tended to stem from one of three major themes: a desire to live according to religious and spiritual values, rejecting the sinfulness of the established order; a desire to reform society by curing its economic and political ills, rejecting the injustice and inhumanity of the establishment; or a desire to promote the psychosocial growth of the individual by putting him into closer touch with his fellows, rejecting the isolation and alienation of the surrounding society."[87]

Kanter argues that the first two themes were most prominent during the nineteenth century, and the third "emerged after World War II and became especially important in the 1960s."[88] It is this strain that best fits the CID movement, which, indeed, grew during the postwar era and most rapidly during the 1960s. When ULI claimed that CIDs were the key to bringing about, or reviving, a "grass roots sense of community," it was promoting a utopian ideology for the American middle class. CIDs are the culmination of a particular strain of utopian thought that had its roots in eighteenth-century England, emerged in Bellamy's novel, was popularized by Howard, and then was promoted by powerful real estate interests in the United States.[89]

Yet there are ways CIDs differ from the utopian schemes that were typically the result of spontaneous personal interaction rather than corporate initiative. Most significantly, communes and utopian communities such as those that proliferated in the nineteenth century and during the 1960s were voluntary in more than a legal, technical sense.[90] As Kanter points out, this distinction is critical. "These are voluntary, value-based, communal social orders. Because members choose to join and choose to remain, conformity within the community is based on commitment—on the individual's own desire to obey its rules—rather than on force or coercion."[91]

Legal fictions to the contrary notwithstanding, CID membership is not voluntary for the many residents who are there because of price, location, or limited options. Such residents may not perceive the rules as sensible or government by neighbors as legitimate. Consequently, CID governing bodies make up for their lack of moral authority by relying on the coercive power of the public legal system for rule enforcement.

At a deeper level, the privatistic utopian vision of CIDs appears fundamentally flawed and self-contradictory. This version of utopia, like so many others, reflects what Manuel and Manuel might call an "overvalued idea"—that privatism is the ultimate basis of community and the only cure for the perceived evils of modern cities.

But the argument that ownership of private property is the ideal basis for a sense of community seems inherently mistaken. Sociologists who studied California CIDs found that, instead of fostering a sense of community, CIDs have evolved "a culture of non-participation" that is "rooted in the very structure of the common-interest development." The developments are "defined by shared ownership of private property" in a culture that links ownership of private property with freedom, individuality, and autonomy rather than with responsibility to the surrounding community. Consequently, CIDs contain "an inherent contradiction . . . [and] the formal organization which embodies this contradiction will be resented, and people will generally not participate or will do so in order to protect their property rights, not out of a recognition of community interdependence."[92]

In spite of its shortcomings, the utopian appeal of CID housing remains an integral part of the intense marketing that has helped it to spread across the country at a rapid rate.

This book explores several main themes. I contend that the rise of CID housing is a unique, ad hoc form of privatization carrying with it significant social and political consequences that never have been adequately considered by government or academics. CIDs represent the de facto privatization of local government services for the few. They have enormous potential for creating divisiveness in urban areas because they tend to reinforce existing conflicts over the nature and extent of local government services and over who should pay for them. CID housing reinforces and institutionalizes the separation of suburb and city and extends that separation into the city itself; further emphasizes the existing dominance of privatism in suburbia; attenuates the sense of responsibility CID residents might otherwise feel for the city as a whole, leading to increasing demands for special tax breaks; and promotes a kind of segregation different in kind and degree from that produced by simple suburbanization.

I argue that the organizational structure of CIDs and their private governments departs from accepted notions of liberal democracy in a variety of ways. I suggest that CID housing promotes an ideal of citizenship that is limited and limiting and has significant implications in the area of civil liberties. The often-heard claim that CID housing is an expression of American traditions of local democracy is, I argue, unconvincing.

I also argue that the spread of CID housing has important consequences for politics at all levels of government. Over the past two decades, the professionals who build and service CIDs have become a significant force in interest group politics in many states. To a large extent, they have been able to shape legislative and judicial policy making, prevent meaningful regulation of CID activity, and keep the discourse on such matters largely private. There are attempts under way in some states to organize millions of CID owners into a voting bloc, raising the possibility of mass political action.

My organizational approach is basically historical, and I trace these themes in the context of describing the development of CID housing. In Chapter 2 I discuss the evolution of restrictive covenants from their inception in medieval England, when they were used primarily to prevent adjoining landowners from harming each other's property, through 1928, when they became the basis for the local private government of

Radburn in New Jersey. During this period restrictive covenants, enforced by homeowners and homeowner associations, were primarily a
way to create, market, and maintain exclusive use of open spaces and
other amenities for the wealthy.

I discuss the period from 1928 through the late 1950s in Chapter 3,
concentrating on the post–World War II housing boom. The focus here
shifts from exclusivity to exclusion. Homeowner associations, both mandatory and voluntary, were an important part of efforts by developers,
real estate agents, and the Federal Housing Administration to create
homogeneous neighborhoods segregated by race and class. When racially
restrictive covenants and segregated public facilities were outlawed,
homeowner associations became, for some, a way of maintaining segregation through private action. This era contributed a legacy of exclusion
to CID housing.

I deal with the late 1950s through the early 1970s in Chapter 4,
emphasizing the role of land economics as the primary explanation for
the boom in CID construction that began in 1964. I stress the role of an
informal partnership between the Urban Land Institute, a developer
organization, and the Federal Housing Administration in promoting CID
housing as a way to build large quantities of middle-class suburban
housing despite increasing land costs.

I continue the story from the early 1970s to the present in Chapter 5,
concentrating on the problems with CID governance and management
that began to appear as this form of housing spread, and the way the
development industry responded to that challenge. My focus is on the
creation in 1973 of the Community Associations Institute (CAI) by the
Urban Land Institute and the National Association of Home Builders. I
trace the history of CAI as it evolved from being something approaching a
public interest group, intended to provide institutional support, education and training to CID boards, to its present role as an influential trade
association and special interest group dominated by lawyers and property managers. One result, I argue, is the institutionalization of a heavy-
handed managerial focus in CID governance.

In the final three chapters I deal in one way or another with the
present. In Chapter 6 I analyze homeowner associations as private governments, discussing the concept of private government generally, showing why homeowner associations fit that description, and discussing the
ways they depart from accepted liberal democratic norms.

Chapter 7 is a case study of the relation between CIDs and the legal system, using California as the case in point. In that influential state where CIDs have proliferated so rapidly, there have been opportunities for government to come to grips with the social and political consequences of this form of housing. CID advocates have been successful in preventing the courts and legislature from treating CIDs either as private governments or businesses, however, leaving them with a special, unregulated status.

In the final chapter I consider CID housing as a form of privatization, and discuss some of the ways it differs from other privatization schemes. I contend that the unexamined consequences of a continued, unregulated spread of CID housing include a potential for radical polarization in local politics over taxation and service issues, and the literal or functional secession of affluent CID residents from the city.

The burden of my argument is not that common interest housing is inherently bad. To the contrary: I do not romanticize the mythical, idyllic American suburb or small towns like the one in which I was born, nor do I wish to return to a past that never was. I acknowledge that increased density and cooperative living arrangements are probably necessary, particularly to meet the housing needs of people with low to moderate incomes. I have no quarrel with the idea of planning entire communities nor with the belief that private land use arrangements and controls can be efficient and useful if properly applied. I think that new forms of private home ownership and rental involving common property should be explored. Certainly I have no objection to strengthening local democracy.

I am not troubled by these principles but by what has been done in their name. Where CID housing is concerned, the gap between theory and practice, and between rhetoric and reality, is enormous. This gap, I believe, is the result of inadequate participation by the public in what has so far been almost entirely a calculus of private values. My emphasis is on the fact that particular forms of CID housing with obvious deficiencies have been replicated endlessly with so little public oversight. In effect, the spread of CID housing as we know it represents a near-total privatization of the process by which urban and suburban land is converted to residential property, a process in which the public has a substantial interest. Guided by considerations of private profit, real estate developers have been permitted to decide how our cities will be laid out. In the process, they have created a new form of housing that, I argue, poses a range of significant public issues.

# 2

## Restrictive Covenants and the Rise of Common-Interest Housing

"How can a section of a town get what it is prepared
to pay for? How can part of a town carry on a more
advanced form of living than the municipality as a whole is
ready to afford?"—Charles S. Ascher, 1929

In 1928 Charles Stern Ascher—lawyer, political scientist, city planner—
had the task of finding a legal way to create a private city for the affluent
within the borders of an existing political jurisdiction. He found the
answer in what he called variously "private government," "government
by contract," or "extra-municipal administration," an entity created and

administered through a comprehensive scheme of private deed restrictions known as restrictive covenants.[1]

Ascher did not invent deed restrictions, which had long been used in England and the United States, nor did he first prescribe their use as tools of exclusion. His contribution was to coordinate and promote the work of a group of Progressive Era political scientists and public administrators who used restrictive covenants to create a privatized version of council-manager municipal government for the first American garden city: Radburn, New Jersey.

At the time Radburn was, as Ascher put it, "the most complex civic unit to which government-by-contract has been applied."[2] It was the first modern common-interest development, and its physical plan and administrative structure have been widely imitated.

Radburn was an important part of a larger historical process. The evolution of restrictive covenants has made it possible for real estate developers to offer affluent home buyers master-planned comfort, exclusivity, and a sense of security in exchange for some of their freedom to use their property as they see fit.

Over the centuries sellers of real estate have acquired increasing power to restrict how future owners use a property. Modern developers accelerated the trend, applying restrictive covenants more comprehensively, more pervasively, and with less restraint. Gradually, the power to determine the character of a community has shifted. Instead of communities evolving through decisions made by the people who live there—decisions concerning the painting of houses, the planting of trees, and the building of fences, for example—the look and feel of communities increasingly is predetermined by private developers who plan, build, and restrict from the outset.

The first stage of this shift in power toward the developers began in medieval England when agricultural land in common use was broken up into parcels, and the law devised ways to regulate the new, interdependent relationships of adjoining landowners. During this time restrictive covenants were simply owners' promises not to use their land in harmful ways.

In the eighteenth and nineteenth centuries, the beginning of suburbanization brought about a second stage in the development of restrictive covenants as pieces of large estates were sold. In England and America subdividers first began to use deed restrictions as private land-planning tools, setting aside parcels of fenced and gated park land for the exclusive use of the buyers and tenants. In some places homeowners voluntarily organized associations to maintain these parks.

In the late nineteenth century an emerging sector of the American real estate industry known as community builders began to master-plan and construct large luxury subdivisions for the affluent. During this third stage developers greatly expanded the use of restrictive covenants, creating uniformity of appearance and setting up permanent homeowner associations to enforce the restrictions.

In the fourth stage, which began with Ascher's innovations at Radburn, the homeowner associations took on the form of private governments. Created and empowered by deed restrictions and styled along the lines of the council-manager system, CID private governments were enabled to perform a wide range of public functions. However, restrictive covenants confine the activities and the discretion of the private governments to a narrow range set by the developer.

By the time Radburn was built in 1928 American community builders had become heavily reliant on restrictive covenants for the implementation of their physical and administrative community plans. State appellate courts then ratified the expansive use and enforcement of deed restrictions, clearing the way for privatization of land planning.


## ORIGINS OF THE RESTRICTIVE COVENANT

In medieval England land was regulated by a "common field" system in which land was divided into strips—some good for farming, some bad, and others designated to lay fallow. The feudal lord or village council would assign several strips, not necessarily contiguous ones, to each peasant to cultivate. Villagers would make communal decisions regarding what crops to plant on which strips.

Along with these individual assignments went common land use rights. After crops were harvested, for example, anyone could pasture cattle on the land. On nonagricultural land, everyone was free to roam at will and take *profits à prendre*—products of the land, such as game, timber, and minerals.

The common field system began to break down in the sixteenth century when landowners began to experiment with sheep farming, cattle breeding, and new agricultural techniques. The new uses required fencing in, or enclosing, the land, originally by private agreement, and later by acts of Parliament. By about 1820 the commons were gone except for small green patches in the middle of villages, and the land had been broken up into a network of closed fields owned by different people.

The transition from common to enclosed fields required the development of a new set of legal tools adapted to different relations, and a new kind of interdependency. No longer would people wander freely across an open countryside; and now, one person's use of his land could hurt or help his neighbors. The potential for harm that came with the Industrial Revolution—the construction and operation of slaughterhouses, tanneries, and soap factories, for example—greatly increased the need to regulate and restrict private land use. During the eighteenth and nineteenth centuries, courts adapted the old law of "servitudes," including restrictive covenants, to these economic realities.[3]

This did not happen without struggle, however. For some time the English courts were troubled by the idea of present land owners restricting future buyers. An agreement between the owners of adjoining property not to use their land for industrial purposes constituted a contract and could be enforced. But it was a different matter if the owners of the adjoining property purported, by their agreement, to impose the same restriction on future owners. The courts were concerned that such agreements would restrict the "alienation" of property, meaning its ability to be bought and sold readily. This concern flowed in part from the country's lack, until 1925, of a reliable recording system for public land titles that would enable prospective purchasers to find out about such restrictions before buying.[4]

Over centuries the English courts evolved several principles to apply in deciding under what circumstances land-use promises, or covenants, could be enforced on future buyers. First, the courts distinguished between the "benefit" and the "burden" of a covenant. The benefit accrued to the owner, who received something of value from his neighbor (such as a promise not to use one's land as a slaughterhouse), and the burden rested with the neighbor, who had to keep that promise. Second, the courts developed a distinction between covenants that run with the land, or travel with the property like baggage every time it is sold, and those that simply bind the person making the original promise. Third, in deciding whether or not a promise would run, the courts applied an amorphous test: Did the promise "touch and concern" the land or merely concern the relationship between the people involved? Fourth, the courts ruled that there must be "privity of estate" between the parties to the lawsuit in order for a covenant to run with the land. Privity is a complex concept with two dimensions: horizontal privity referred to the original promise between the two land owners, and vertical privity limited enforcement of covenants to those whose ownership of land could be traced to one of the original covenanting parties.

The historical roots of privity run back to fourteenth-century common law. For example, in *Packenham's Case,* in 1368, a prior had promised the lord of a manor that the prior and his convent would always sing in the lord's church at religious services. The court held that those who later acquired the land from the lord could enforce the benefit of the covenant against the prior because the covenant touched and concerned the land of the lord. Whether the burden of the promise would extend to someone who acquired the prior's land, meaning that individual would have to do the singing, would be a different matter.[5]

## RESTRICTIVE COVENANTS THROUGH THE NINETEENTH CENTURY

Early uses of covenants had to do with promises between individuals concerning use of their own land and had nothing to do with large-scale planning by real estate developers. But in the eighteenth and nineteenth centuries in England and later the United States, subdividers began to use covenants to set aside private parks and other amenities for exclusive use.

The advent of this new use of covenants coincided with the beginning of suburbanization. The earliest reported court case illustrating the use of covenants for land planning is *Tulk v. Moxhay,* decided in 1848 by the Court of Chancery.[6]

During the late eighteenth century London began to expand outward in a process of rapid suburbanization.[7] Land held in family estates by the nobility gained value under speculative pressure from those who wished to subdivide the estates into residential lots. Wealthy families sold parts of their ancestral holdings to middle-class businessmen seeking relief from congested city living. As they surrendered ownership, however, the families often tried to retain some control over how the land would be used in the future. In a number of instances they created private parks for the exclusive use of those living in the newly created lots. This was a simple form of private land planning, a conceptual forerunner of today's CIDs with their private amenities.

In 1743 descendants of the Earl of Leicester tried to preserve a fenced-in private park in Leicester Square by requiring those who leased the residential lots surrounding it to promise to pay a tax for its upkeep. In 1808, Tulk, who owned the park and several of the houses around it, sold the park to a man named Elms with a restrictive covenant attached: Elms and "his heirs, and assigns" must keep the park "in an open state, uncovered with any buildings"; maintain it, along with "the iron railing round the same"; and let Tulk's tenants on the square pay Elms for the exclusive right to use the park. It would remain fenced and gated, and the tenants would have keys.

The park was sold several times over the ensuing years, and eventually it was purchased by Moxhay. Although Moxhay admitted knowing of the 1808 covenant in the deed between Tulk and Elms, the deed by which Moxhay acquired the property did not mention the covenant, so he claimed the right to build on the park land. Tulk, who still owned houses on the square and wanted his tenants to have the use of the park, obtained an injunction preventing Elms from building. The court held that it would be inequitable for Moxhay to use the land this way, considering that he knew of the covenant when he purchased the park. As the court explained, it would be unfair for someone to pay a reduced price for land bound by a covenant and then sell it for a higher price by simply not mentioning the covenant to his own purchaser.

The idea of using covenants in this manner was transplanted to the United States in 1831, when Samuel Ruggles drained a swamp in Manhattan and "laid out a square in the London fashion, and surrounded it with an eight-foot fence, with gates to which residents in the neighborhood have keys."[8] He called it Gramercy Park, and he placed title to it in the hands of trustees for the benefit and use of those who owned the sixty-six surrounding residential lots.

A similar development known as Louisburg Square was built in Boston in 1826, but no provision was made for maintenance of the private park in the center. To remedy this, the twenty-eight lot owners signed a recorded agreement in 1844 that established the Committee of the Proprietors of Louisburg Square and bound themselves and subsequent purchasers to maintain the park. The Committee of Proprietors is generally considered the first American homeowner association.[9] Unlike today's developer-created CIDs, it was voluntarily organized by the property owners.

Most uses of restrictive covenants during the nineteenth century did not involve homeowner associations, however. The restrictions generally were more limited in number than those employed by today's CID regimes and ran for limited periods of time—five to fifteen years—so there was no need for a permanent enforcement arm, such as a homeowner association. Residents wishing to enforce a mutual restriction against a neighbor had to bring lawsuits on their own.[10] This method had drawbacks, of course, in that it depended on somebody undertaking expensive and often lengthy litigation. But injunctions could be sought if it appeared that the harm from a covenant violation would occur before a case could be resolved on its merits.

Restrictive covenants were also employed by people who wished to dedicate their land to "religion and meditation." Seaside retreats and tent revival meetings were far less profitable uses for beachfront land than was residential subdivision, so such places as Martha's Vineyard and Ocean Grove, New Jersey, became subjects of litigation as real estate speculators tried to break the covenants.[11]

Over time, however, developers began to use restrictive covenants in a systematic way to create amenities beyond private parks for affluent purchasers. This new use of covenants was the start of a gradual expansion leading to the book-length deed restrictions seen in recent years.

In St. Louis, private street associations for residential subdivisions evolved during the mid-nineteenth century. In 1986 there were still at least 427 of these associations in St. Louis County. Their legal basis is in a trust arrangement attached by the developer to the deed for each piece of property; owners are obliged to pay assessments for maintenance of the common grounds, including the private streets. The associations restrict access to the streets and control traffic volume, and they pay for their own snow removal, tree trimming, and other street maintenance.[12]

In 1843 deeds for the individual lots of the Linden Place subdivision in upscale Brookline, Massachusetts, required that the lots have thirty-foot setbacks from the street, that only residences could be constructed, and that no residence could be sold to "any Negro or native of Ireland."[13] Race restrictive covenants allowed developers to sell something many affluent buyers desired: freedom from having to live with those of different ethnicity.

Between 1852 and 1856 Llewellyn S. Haskell, an adherent of the

Perfectionist faith, acquired four hundred acres in New Jersey's Orange Mountains and retained the services of architect Alexander Jackson Davis to construct Llewellyn Park. The development pioneered the now-ubiquitous curvilinear suburban street and had a natural open space at the center, part of a deliberate attempt to create a romantic, naturalistic environment. Called the Ramble, the fifty-acre open space had no features except pedestrian walkways. It was cared for by a Committee of Management elected by the lot owners, and the title to the Ramble was held in perpetuity by three trustees. The deeds for sale of individual lots mandated that the parcels be at least three acres in size and for residential use only; fences were outlawed. The development, which remains exclusive to this day, was the home of Thomas Edison.[14]

## COMMUNITY BUILDERS AND RESTRICTIVE COVENANTS

As the twentieth century began, the emerging real estate industry, and particularly the growing sector of large developers known as community builders, began heavy promotion of restrictive covenants through their professional associations. Community builders constructed and sold houses on the land they subdivided, in contrast with the smaller subdividers who cut land into lots and sold to people who then built their own homes. Restrictive covenants became the "main method by which community builders implemented their planning and design vision."[15] Deed restrictions were the legal means by which developers were able to conduct privatized land planning and, in effect, lay out the suburbs of most major American cities. They intentionally created patterns of housing segregation by race and class that persist to the present.

### Deed Restrictions and the Rise of the Community Builders

From the 1890s through the onset of the depression, covenants became more widespread in subdivisions for the wealthy, more stringent and numerous, and more long-lived (averaging thirty-three years), with provisions for automatic renewal.[16] More comprehensively planned luxury developments were beginning to take on the uniform appearance associated with today's CIDs.

This expansion of deed restrictions was related to changes in the structure of the real estate business. This emergent industry had begun to change near the turn of the century with the "rise of the community builders" described by real estate historian Marc Weiss. These large developers became preeminent through the comprehensive use of deed restrictions, the influence of powerful national organizations, and partnership with government:

The community builders were subdividers who changed the nature of American land development during the early decades of the twentieth century. They did this initially by taking very large tracts of land and slowly improving them, section by section, for lot sales and home construction. Strict long-term deed restrictions were imposed on all lot and home purchasers, establishing uniform building lines, front and side yards, standards for lot coverage and building size, minimum housing standards and construction costs, non-Caucasian racial exclusion, and other features. Extensive landscaping and tree planting were emphasized to accentuate the natural topography and beauty. Public thoroughfares included curved streets, cul-de-sacs, and wide boulevards and parkways. Often special areas were set aside for retail and office buildings, apartments, parks and recreation facilities, churches, and schools. Private utilities and public improvements were coordinated as much as possible with present and future plans for subdivision development and expansion.[17]

Large corporate developers maximized their influence by working together through national organizations with state and local affiliates, including the National Association of Real Estate Boards (NAREB) and its Home Builders and Subdividers Division. A NAREB survey found that by 1933 about 22 percent of its members belonged to what Weiss terms "a subset of a broader group of major commercial, residential, and industrial property developers that are today simply called 'big developers.'" This caliber of builder had led NAREB from 1908 on.[18]

Community builders were different from the typical subdivider not only because they were wealthier and built houses but because they had a different attitude toward government involvement in the housing business. Many small subdividers had been openly hostile to public planning regulations. The community builders referred to them disparagingly as "curbstoners," "land butchers," or "fly-by-nighters," seeing them as perpetrators of dangerous speculation and land frauds that could discredit the entire industry and depress housing prices. Unlike the curbstoners, community builders supported public planning—a process that they themselves shaped and largely controlled.

Through their organization, political influence, and close relationship with the state regulators, the community builders "played a direct role in actively supporting and shaping the emerging system of public land planning and land-use regulation."[19] Their experience with deed restrictions became a private model for public zoning ordinances, the first of which was passed in Los Angeles in 1908.[20]

> Deed restrictions, by virtue of being voluntary private contracts, often went beyond the scope of public sector police power regulations, particularly in the earlier years. These restrictions, which might even include barring the owner from painting the house a certain color, constituted a very significant abridgment of private property rights. That they were willingly and in many cases eagerly accepted by purchasers opened the wedge for the introduction and extension of public land-use controls. Deed restrictions, an innovation of community builders and their attorneys, served as both the physical and political model for zoning laws and subdivision regulations.[21]

Among the common deed restrictions that became part of typical zoning laws were those concerning street design, open spaces and recreational facilities, setbacks, house size and shape, separation and relation of multiple uses (such as commercial and residential), underground utilities, and many other features that community builders devised and public planners later adopted.[22]

## Jesse Clyde Nichols: Dean of the Community Builders

Of the early community builders, the one with the most sophisticated understanding of the relation between private power and government was Jesse Clyde Nichols. Through his success as a community builder and his activity in professional organizations, Nichols popularized two ideas among developers: the importance of developing a symbiotic relationship with government and the value of setting up a permanent mandatory-membership homeowner association to enforce deed restrictions.

This influential builder was a Harvard graduate who built 10 percent of the housing in Kansas City between 1906 and 1953 and founded the Urban Land Institute in 1936. He created Kansas City's Country Club District, a group of developments visited and later imitated by builders from all over the world. Nichols also pioneered the modern shopping center—a planned concentration of different businesses under one management with ample parking—by building Country Club Plaza in 1925.[23]

Nichols was imaginative and dynamic, but he did not accomplish his work through the private enterprise system alone. He was an outspoken exponent of "municipal assistance": he knew that he and other private big builders could not survive without the infrastructure and services provided by the municipalities or without public regulation of the land surrounding the subdivisions. Municipal assistance would keep development costs as low as possible; promote sales by having transportation (first railroad lines, later streetcar routes, and more recently freeways) serve the subdivisions; and ensure a stable residential environment through public restrictions on nonresidential uses to augment those contained in private deeds.[24]

Although Nichols was not reluctant to take advantage of government as a supplier of costly infrastructure, he wanted the assistance to come with as little government control as possible. He pioneered the use of homeowner associations to accomplish that objective.

In 1910 he set up his first association, the Country Club District Improvement Association, which was dedicated to "general maintenance and beautifying," but he let membership be voluntary. He viewed the association as a "stopgap measure" for providing public utilities until the district could be annexed to Kansas City.[25]

Nichols became dissatisfied with the voluntary association, however, because it became too independent. He told other developers that "he knew he was going to have to do something because it was becoming increasingly difficult to work with the original Country Club District Improvement Association as it continued to grow." Although other developers relinquished control to residents soon after construction, Nichols did not. He had "too much of his own ego invested in his work to sit back and let his homeowners assume total direction of his subdivisions."[26]

To keep maximum control over the residents while maintaining independence from government, Nichols hit upon the idea of a rigidly controlled mandatory-membership homeowner association. Nichols employed his idea in 1914 when he built a development called Mission Hills in Missouri. Kansas City was nearby, and the city of Merriam was a few miles to the west, but there was no city adjacent to the new subdivision. The development needed some sort of authority to provide essential public services.

Nichols was concerned that if the subdivision became part of an incorporated city he would not have what he considered sufficient control over the development or how the city provided services to the residents. In essence, Nichols wanted to have municipal functions performed without the inconvenience and uncertainty of democratic processes or interference from an outside authority. The answer, Nichols decided, was to create a private government that he controlled. In his recent study of Nichols William S. Worley writes that

> the Mission Hills Homes Company would have to do everything a city government would normally do. Nichols wished to use a homes association instead of a political subdivision such as a village because he wanted to retain as much control for himself and his residents as possible. He influenced the homes associations greatly during the early years. . . . Nichols developed and retained the homeowners' association concept not only because he wanted his residents to do things his way in maintaining community standards, but also because he was afraid that if the subdivision were part of a larger village or town organization, the political unit would not be sufficiently responsive to the needs of his residents.[27]

Nichols incorporated the Mission Hills Homes Company on August 18, 1914. He gave it the responsibility and the power to enforce the deed restrictions he imposed, maintain vacant property, hire contractors to construct sewers and streets, install lighting, remove snow, arrange for provision of utilities, and pay taxes on the common areas on behalf of the residents. As in today's CIDs, owners became members automatically on receipt of their deeds.[28]

Nichols also set the tone for later CIDs by concealing the reality of developer control behind the rhetoric of village democracy. "On the surface, Mission Hills seemed to embody all that was desirable in residential living. The small community had lots of space, a required con-

genial architectural style, and a local government that took care of physical needs without becoming political. What a new resident might or
might not have seen was that it also had a benevolent despot in the
person of J. C. Nichols who would make sure everything stayed that
way."[29]

Presaging the inflexibility so often observed in today's CIDs, Nichols
strongly believed that developers should set up the association so that
the directors were required to enforce the developers' covenants with the
greatest strictness. Any violation might set a precedent and lead to
inexorable erosion of the developer's plan. As Nichols put it, "The ac-
cumulation of these overlooked violations may lead to the downfall of the
whole character of the property."[30]

Nichols cited one remarkable example of the lengths to which he
would go to prevent any departure from the covenants in his projects:
"We recently had a case in our office where an owner requested permission to enclose with glass a porch on the side of his house for a very sick
wife. The erection would have been a violation of the building restriction.
The case was a very pathetic one and required the most delicate handling, and yet our organization felt it was of such importance, although
all of our property had been sold in that neighborhood for many years,
that we went to much expenditure of time and money to bring about its
proper solution. We did not feel we could afford to have a precedent of
violation established even under these urgent circumstances."[31]

In Nichols' view, glassing in the porch so this sick woman could enjoy
a comfortable view of the surroundings could have started an inexorable
slide toward anarchy. Developers and homeowner association boards
have remained rigid in their approach to enforcement of restrictions,
using Nichols' rationalization: setting any precedent of nonenforcement,
however slight or reasonable, will lead to widespread disregard of the
rule.

Nichols felt that what had worked, in his estimation, for the affluent
would work equally well for all homeowners. In 1914 the American
Academy of Political and Social Science gave Nichols a forum in an
*Annals* issue that discussed housing and town planning. Nichols took the
opportunity to argue that, based on his experience with affluent subdivisions, deed restrictions should be applied to housing for the working
class. His forceful presentation of the benefits of deed restrictions inaugurated what are now perennial themes for advocates of CIDs.

Practically every city has its restricted and highly protected
residence section for the better homes; and no high class development is launched today without the control of a considerable area of land, so as to establish harmonious surroundings
and give permanency to the character of the neighborhood. . . . It
is generally conceded that this important phase of city planning
in the establishment of the residence neighborhoods for the better class of homes is creating more substantial values for such
property, and sufficiently anchoring residence neighborhoods as
to avoid in the future, in large measure, the great economic loss
suffered in the rapid abandonment of the various good residence
sections of the city. This feeling of security in such home communities, and the feeling of permanence with which every improvement is added, are creating a more interested citizenship, and a
more home-loving family. The general public interest that has
been attached to the results of the various developments of
highly restricted property throughout the country has been most
encouraging.[32]

Nichols expressly refers to the making of these private arrangements as "city planning," and that is, in fact, what Nichols and others
were doing. Master-planned luxury subdivisions were laid out as part of
a private land-planning process that set the contours of many American
cities, establishing residential patterns based on class and race that
persist today.

Nichols addresses the issue of segregation carefully, arguing that
deed restrictions will prevent "abandonment of the various good residence sections of the city," which appears to be a reference to the use of
racial restrictions as a way of preventing "white flight." The article
mentions nearly every kind of restriction except those pertaining to
racial exclusion. Nichols was well acquainted with race restrictive covenants, however. Helen Monchow studied two of his developments in
Kansas City, Missouri—Armour Hills and Sunset Hill—and found that
both had "Negroes barred" covenants.[33]

Nichols contends that the sense of "security" and "permanence" produced by restrictive covenants create "a more interested citizenship, and
a more home-loving family." These ideas are echoed to this day in CID
promotional literature aimed at attracting middle-class white Ameri-

cans to what they are told will be idyllic sanctuaries for family and children that offer a sense of participatory community free from the chaos, crime, and diversity of the city. Like today's CID advocates, Nichols doesn't emphasize that the price of entry into this haven is loss of freedom. He does, however, emphasize that deed restrictions are intended to protect property values—a rationale that remains the most common justification for the loss of freedom inherent in a development run under a regime of restrictive covenants.

Most notably, Nichols' vision of a day when restrictive covenants would be used in planned developments for the working class did become reality, though not for decades.

## DEED RESTRICTIONS IN 1928: A SNAPSHOT

By the time the Great Depression struck, community builders had constructed highly restricted luxury subdivisions from Maine to California. In 1928 Helen Monchow studied the deed restrictions in eighty-four "better-class subdivisions."[34] They included such well-known developments as Forest Hills Gardens in New York, built by the Sage Foundation; Palos Verdes Estates in Los Angeles; and Roland Park in Maryland. Her study is the best analysis of the use of deed restrictions in the comprehensively planned developments that were the precursors of Radburn and today's CIDs. (In the preface she offers special thanks to Ascher, who "read the manuscript, particularly those parts dealing with the legal phases.")[35]

Monchow found consistencies across the nation, suggesting the degree to which community builders were sharing information and learning from one another's experiences in designing regimes of restrictive covenants. The restrictions fell into categories: those pertaining to the type and use of structures; those dealing with use of the lot area; those dealing with racial restrictions; and those concerning the powers of the developer, the duration and enforcement of restrictions, and maintenance of the property.

She found that forty-eight of these developments had prohibitions or restrictions on business activity; seventy-three specified that only residences, generally only single-family ones, could be built in all or most of the development; forty required approval of building plans; sixty-one prescribed minimum costs for buildings; and most restricted the kinds of garages that could be built and prohibited such "nuisances" as livestock, signs, saloons, billboards, and factories.[36]

Sixty-one of the developments had set-back provisions, and some went into great detail regarding lot frontage, building projections (such as porches), and the percentage of the lot that could be covered by buildings.[37]

Monchow deals at length with prohibitions on the sale or rental of homes in nearly half of these luxury subdivisions to racial or ethnic minorities—the notorious "racial restrictive covenants" that were declared unenforceable in 1948 by the United States Supreme Court in *Shelley v. Kraemer*. According to Monchow, thirty-nine of the developments had such explicit restrictions, which included "Africans, Mongolians prohibited," "Caucasians only," "Negroes barred," "White race only," "Asiatics and Negroes barred," "Mongolians and Africans barred," and "Caucasians only, except business." In two additional developments the restrictions stated that the "seller [subdivider] must approve" potential buyers or renters, clauses that implicitly meant racial exclusion, Monchow explains.[38]

Monchow's findings suggest that racially restrictive covenants were the real estate industry's response to the demographic shifts that brought large numbers of black Americans from the South to the Northeast and Asian immigrants to the West Coast. Of those developments with race restrictions, Monchow notes, all but one "are found in the more recent instruments." Moreover, she observes, "the device seems to be in rather general use in the vicinity of the larger eastern and northern cities which have experienced a large influx of colored people in recent years. But the most pronounced tendency is found on the Pacific Coast where the restriction is directed primarily against Orientals."[39]

Monchow also studied the critical issue of how the restrictions were to be enforced, and by whom, and noted a new idea: the homeowner association. Only two of the deeds for the eighty-four developments provided for enforcement by a developer-created association.[40] Therefore residents of some developments, such as Louisburg Square in Boston, began to form voluntary homeowner associations that would enforce the restrictions and eliminate individual lawsuits among owners.[41] Monchow found, however, that seven of the subdivisions had developer-created associations responsible for collecting and administering maintenance fees for common areas. She observed that homeowner associations were a recent development and noted a new approach seen at several sub-divisions: automatic membership for all owners upon receiving their deed.[42]

She generally approved of this new social creation but voiced some reservations that now seem prescient: "Associations of this type seem more nearly adequate to safeguard the interests of the lot owners. Their success is dependent, however, upon the development of an active community spirit which is difficult both to develop and maintain. Furthermore, they require considerable activity on the part of the lot owners, who do not as a rule wish to be bothered with details about their residential property. It would seem logical, therefore, that the changes to be expected in the mechanics of organization of the association would be in the direction of greater simplicity."[43]

Monchow's study suggests that much of the groundwork for today's comprehensive CID covenant regimes had already been laid by 1928. Restrictive covenants were being used to strictly regulate homeowners' use of their property and to create uniform appearance in the development. Developers still had not perfected a way to ensure that the covenants would be enforced in perpetuity, however. The mandatory-membership homeowner association was still in its infancy, but Charles Ascher would soon give it a definite shape, specific duties, and real powers.


RADBURN: PRIVATE GOVERNMENT FOR SUBURBIA

In 1928, the year Monchow's study appeared, Ascher became a pivotal figure in the evolution of restrictive covenants in common-interest developments. He coordinated the work of a group of political scientists and public administrators from the National Municipal League who designed a private government for Radburn, New Jersey. Their focus was on the dimension Monchow referred to as "mechanics of organization."

This group built on the experience of such developers as Nichols and combined the power of deed restrictions with the permanence of a mandatory homeowner association to create a legally sound, self-perpetuating entity with real enforcement powers. The government was designed in accordance with principles of municipal government straight out of Progressive Era political science, using the council-manager system. Ascher then wrote a number of articles promoting this creation, which became the major model for CIDs that followed.

# CITY HOUSING CORPORATION: GARDEN CITIES FOR AMERICA?

Charles Stern Ascher was born in New York City in 1899.[44] His early education was at the Ethical Culture School; he received his undergraduate education and, in 1921, a law degree from Columbia University. He practiced law in New York City and, briefly, Washington, D.C., until 1926, when he became general counsel for the New York-based City Housing Corporation. There Ascher became so interested in city planning that he abandoned law practice. He was to spend the rest of his long career as a leading authority on private land planning, a public housing administrator, and a professor of political science at Brooklyn College.[45]

When Ascher joined City Housing Corporation in 1926, the organization was a unique combination of visionary intellectual ferment and progressive capitalism. Its president, developer Alexander M. Bing, sought to harness private economic power in the service of improving society. The intellectual impetus for these reformist efforts came through overlapping membership between CHC and the Regional Planning Association of America, a dynamic group of architects, planners, and thinkers heavily influenced by the garden city idea of Ebenezer Howard.[46] Radburn was the result of this fertile collaboration.

In 1919, during the postwar housing shortage, Bing had served on the New York Housing Committee appointed by Governor Alfred E. Smith to study the problem. On the committee with him were other individuals who were to join him at CHC, including architects Clarence Stein and Frederick L. Ackerman, and Robert D. Kohn, former director of the production division of the United States Shipping Board. The committee concluded that housing shortages for working-class people were systemic, not episodic: as long as builders expected large profits, housing prices would always be too high for working people. It was the small builder who presented the biggest problem, because his entrepreneurial spirit would not be satisfied with profits in the range of 4 to 6 percent but would push him to seek profit margins of 15 to 17 percent.[47]

Bing set up CHC in 1924 as a solution to this problem. It was intended to be a large, well-capitalized, limited-dividend corporation—one that did not offer the possibility of large returns but promised a reliable 6 percent annual return on investment. Such a nonspeculative, "semiphilanthropic" corporation, if it planned carefully, built on a large scale, and used the most efficient design and construction methods, would be able to offer housing at prices within the reach of the working class. Moreover, it was felt that this investment proposition would appeal to socially conscious but wealthy investors. The limited-dividend approach and the overall concept were based to a large extent on Ebenezer Howard's ideas as implemented at Letchworth and Welwyn. Some CHC personnel also were familiar with the efficient housing construction methods used during wartime by the U.S. government.[48]

Radburn was to be innovative in both physical layout and organizational structure. As originally planned, the development was to occupy two square miles of spinach fields in the New Jersey countryside. It would house twenty-five thousand people in three neighborhoods, each built around an elementary school and all clustered around a single high school. The neighborhoods were designed so that children could walk to the elementary schools. Radburn, with its plan for safe and separate circulation of pedestrian and auto traffic, was designed for families with children. The most famous design innovation of the development was the "superblock," a large cluster of houses that were "reversed," with living areas facing inward on a green open space and the rear of the house facing peripheral streets.[49]

Both RPAA and CHC were trying to adapt Howard's utopian vision to the reality of American capitalism, and their attempts led to Radburn becoming a series of compromises.[50] Ideally, RPAA members felt, planning should be done at the regional or even national level, but they were willing to settle for planning and building something the size of a small town.[51] The construction of housing for the less affluent was at odds with capitalist profit-taking and therefore probably the job of the government, but the members of the RPAA would try creating a "semiphilanthropic" corporation. The self-sufficient garden city, with its surrounding agricultural greenbelt and complete industrial base, was an ideal form, but physical and economic constraints led RPAA to settle for nonagricultural park areas within, instead of around, the development, and the residents would have to work elsewhere.

In the end, these compromise solutions did not work out as planned. The limited-dividend approach required continuous expansion of the project. As a private corporation, CHC had to turn a rapid profit on the first houses built in order to complete the remainder. The depression intervened, however, reducing the supply of potential buyers. Additionally, CHC had guaranteed mortgages for early buyers, many of whom defaulted and left CHC liable for their loans. Radburn ended up even smaller than intended, housing only five hundred families, and CHC filed for bankruptcy in 1934.[52]

Moreover, construction costs ran higher than anticipated, and a minimum family income of $5,000 per year was required of purchasers at Radburn; that condition effectively excluded 90 percent of urban families. Radburn became "a thoroughly upper middle class town" with a "homogeneous population characteristic of affluent, upper middle class suburbs"; up to 60 percent of the families were headed by executives who commuted to New York City to earn a livelihood.[53] Without a surrounding greenbelt, Radburn was not protected from the encroachment of adjacent housing projects. Ultimately Radburn became not a garden city but another suburban subdivision for the moneyed classes, albeit one with a number of innovative features.

## RESTRICTIVE COVENANTS AND PRIVATE GOVERNMENT AT RADBURN

Similarly, the use of restrictive covenants in Radburn's organizational structure was a compromise. Deed restrictions figured prominently in Bing's plans for Radburn before Ascher joined CHC.[54] Bing explained in a 1925 article that perhaps the greatest obstacle to constructing garden cities like Howard's was American opposition to public ownership of the land, with residents being long-term tenants instead of property owners. Owners with individual control over their lots could thwart the overall plan, and market forces could push privately owned lot prices beyond the reach of the working class. Bing saw restrictive covenants that limited the rights of individual owners as the next best thing to community land ownership. "Proper restrictions" not only would serve as land use controls, he felt, but would keep the residential land from increasing too much in value.[55]

Daniel Schaffer, however, interprets this a bit more pointedly, arguing that Bing's decision to use restrictive covenants instead of community ownership was made to mollify potential investors and buyers. "The restrictive deeds established in the romantic nineteenth-century suburbs of Roland Park, Maryland, and Llewellyn Park, New Jersey, and in the pre–World War I planned community of Forest Hills, New York, served as the precedents for Radburn's political structure. The use of such traditional methods of real estate development instead of the potentially revolutionary concept of public ownership placated possible investors and home owners."[56]

As general counsel for the CHC, Ascher wrote the restrictive covenants for Radburn, which he said were "the result of some months of study."[57] The procedure by which they were produced amounted to synthesizing community builder experience and Progressive Era political science.

Ascher carefully reviewed the experience of developers who had used deed restrictions. In the library at the Harvard School of Landscape Architecture he studied the "elaborate codes of restrictions" . He visited representatives of such affluent subdivisions such as Roland Park and Forest Hills Gardens, corresponded by mail with "forward-looking real estate developers in all parts of the country," and conferred with a number of other attorneys.[58]

The particular form that Radburn's private government took was, in a sense, foreordained by the membership of the study group Ascher assembled to design it, which included leading Progressive political scientists and public administration experts. "At meetings last year the problem was put before a group of experts in municipal government and town-building: members of the council of the National Municipal League, such as Dr. Luther H. Gulick, Dr. Morris Lambie, Dr. Harold W. Dodds, Richard S. Childs, Louis Brownlow, Harold S. Buttenheim, and Dr. Lent B. Upson; men with special practical experience such as Morris Knowles of Pittsburgh, John Colt, president of the borough council of Princeton, New Jersey; and students of community organization such as Dr. Lee Hamner and Clarence A. Perry of the Russell Sage Foundation."[59]

The scholars Ascher chose to work with were prominent in their fields. Gulick, who eventually became president of the American Political Science Association, also served on the New Deal–era President's Committee on Administrative Management, which Brownlow chaired with future APSA president Charles E. Merriam. The committee's task amounted to nothing less than proposing a redesign of the federal executive branch.[60]

In addition to being well placed, the members of Ascher's study group were heavily oriented toward the council-manager plan as the ideal form of city government. The National Municipal League was a Progressive Era organization of urban reformers established in 1894. It "reflected the ideas and interests of 'structural reformers,' who sought to improve municipal administration through reforms in city charters and in the constitutional structure of urban government," and strongly advocated adoption of the council-manager plan, including it in its Model City Charters from 1918 on. Brownlow was one of the early presidents of the International City Management Association. Richard S. Childs, in particular, is generally recognized as the father of the council-manager plan.[61]

Given the combination of developer experience and Progressive Era urbanists on which Ascher relied, it is no surprise that Radburn's covenants prescribed a mandatory-membership homeowner association designed as a privatized council-manager government:

> The important functions of architectural control and collecting and disbursing the community funds (imposed as a charge in each deed) have been delegated to the Radburn Association. Frequently the developer is content to let the residents organize a loose community association of some sort after they have moved in. At Radburn, a legally incorporated non-profit association is already in existence. Its powers include the rendering of practically every municipal service in the interest of health, safety and welfare, as well as the supplementing of existing municipal services in that behalf. . . . The Radburn Association, since its functions are so much like those of a municipal government, is organized on the city-manager plan; its administration is committed to a manager to be selected solely for his executive qualifications and to serve at the pleasure of the board.[62]

Paralleling a city council with a ceremonial mayor, Radburn had a board of nine trustees with a ceremonial president. Just as a city manager served at the pleasure of the city council, so at Radburn the "manager" was to be hired and fired at will by the trustees. Neither the manager nor the trustees needed to be residents of Radburn (of the first trustees, only Louis Brownlow lived there).

This managerial government was treated as a selling point. Radburn residents were given a summary of the deed restrictions that assured them that "the Radburn Association has been organized on the model of the best modern practice in municipal government" because "the actual administration is placed in the hands of a manager who is chosen by the trustees solely on the basis of his executive and administrative qualifications." There was one major departure from normal city government, however: the trustees were not elected by the residents but were selected by CHC.[63]

Additional "elements of the machinery of municipal government" were included. Ascher made the now-familiar claim that the government was based on "consent of the governed" because each purchaser "will acquiesce . . . by the acceptance of his deed." He also provided for noticed hearings for architectural changes, akin to those used under zoning ordinances. He established an annual budget process like that of a city, with a proposed budget and level of taxation to be prepared by the manager and presented in a noticed public hearing. Like a city, the Radburn Association was to own and administer the common property, including the "elaborate system of parks intended for the exclusive benefit of the inhabitants of Radburn."[64]

Radburn represented a significant stage in the evolution of restrictive covenants, which had come a long way from their humble origins as simple contracts between property owners. The particular covenant-based form of private government that Ascher and his consultants created for Radburn has been institutionalized in today's CIDs. They are privatized versions of the council-manager system and, in a sense, a legacy of the Progressive Era.[65]

## RESTRICTIVE COVENANTS IN THE COURTS

Because deed restrictions allowed developers to maintain permanent control over a project's appearance and operation, it was essential that the covenants be enforceable in court. Two issues were especially critical: first, the covenants had to run with the land, binding not just those who bought directly from the developer but all subsequent purchasers; second, homeowner associations created by developers to enforce restrictive covenants had to have the legal authority to do so. With these principles established, developers could guarantee that their community plans would remain in force indefinitely, with the property maintained as they prescribed. Such a guarantee would give force to their marketing argument: deed restrictions enhance property values.

During the years surrounding the planning and building of Radburn, courts in several states rendered important decisions on issues that arose from disputes over covenants at luxury subdivisions. There was little precedent, so the courts were dealing in the realm of judicial discretion and policy making. At stake was the ability of developers to continue using deed restrictions for private land planning. The decisions favored the interests of developers, contained approving comments about the benefits of restrictive covenants, and formed the legal foundation for continuing and expanding their use.

In 1923 the Maryland Supreme Court decided the case of *Wehr v. Roland Park Company*.[66] Roland Park, platted and sold between 1891 and 1911, had been set up with a provision that required lot owners to contribute to a fund to be used for street lighting and repair, trash collection, and sewer system maintenance. The city of Baltimore later annexed the development, and the developer, Roland Park Company, sold the streets, roads, sewers, and street lighting to the city. The plaintiffs were lot owners who felt that they should no longer have to pay the assessment, claiming that the streets were now public property.

The court upheld the restrictive covenants and required the residents to continue paying the assessment. The decision is foreshadowed in the beginning paragraphs, in which the court describes the Roland Park development and accepts the proposition that the deed restrictions are responsible for the quality of the development. "[I]t is sufficiently shown by uncontradicted evidence to permit us to say, without discussing the same, that it became an unusually attractive development which ranks amongst the highest to be found in this State and its reputation is well known far beyond its bounds. It is only necessary to examine the restrictions in the deeds to see that the efforts of all parties concerned were to have it a development which would be peculiarly desirable for residential purposes, and which offered more than most suburban places did at that time for the comfort, health and protection of their residents" (143 Md. 384, 386–87).

In 1925 the Michigan Supreme Court took a similar approving view of deed restrictions in *Sanborn v. McLean,* which dealt with the "residences only" restriction placed on all lots in Detroit's expensive Green Lawn subdivision.[67] The restriction read, "No residence shall be erected upon said premises, which shall cost less than $2500 and nothing but residences shall be erected on said premises." The McLeans had not purchased their lot from the developer and claimed they had not been told of the restriction. They began construction of a "gasoline filling station" on part of their lot. Sanborn sued for an injunction to prevent the building from being completed and have the portion constructed torn down.

The court found the restriction enforceable. It referred to the scheme of restrictions as "reciprocal negative easements" and held that they would run with the land. The decision meant that the restrictions could be enforced against any owner who knew they existed or should have known, whether the purchase was made from the original developer or from a subsequent purchaser. The McLeans said they had been told that the lot was unrestricted, but the court disposed of this contention by noting that Mr. McLean should have known the restrictions existed because after a look around the neighborhood he could not have avoided noticing the "strictly uniform residence character given the lots by the expensive dwellings thereon, and the least inquiry would have quickly developed the fact that lot 86 was subjected to a reciprocal negative easement, and he could finish his house and, like the others, enjoy the benefits of the easement" (233 Mich. 227, 232).

As in the Roland Park case, the court emphasized the beneficial aspects of the restrictions rather than the ways they might inconvenience subsequent purchasers, linking them to the expensive or exclusive nature of the development.

Perhaps the most influential of these early cases was *Neponsit Property Owners' Association, Inc. v. Emigrant Industrial Savings Bank,* decided by the New York Supreme Court. *Neponsit* gave developers a double victory, holding that covenants to pay assessments run with the land and may be enforced by developer-created homeowner associations. The decision was widely cited for both these propositions across the country.[68]

In 1911 Neponsit Realty Company subdivided the land and sold lots with a variety of deed restrictions, including a requirement that all owners pay annual lot assessments to a Property Owners' Association for "maintenance of the roads, paths, parks, beach, sewers and such other public purposes as shall from time to time be determined." The deeds said the covenants would run with the land until 1940, that they were binding on all owners in the subdivision, and that they could be enforced by the association. The defendant was a bank that acquired a lot at a foreclosure sale and refused to pay the assessment. The association placed a lien on the property for unpaid assessment fees and tried to foreclose.

Centuries of property law required that the burden of the covenant—in this case, the obligation to pay the maintenance fee—would only run to subsequent purchasers, like the bank, if the covenant "touched and concerned" the bank's land. The concept had always been beyond precise definition, and the court cited authorities who said, "It has been found impossible to state any absolute tests to determine what covenants touch and concern land and what do not."[69] Still, there was no precedent supporting the association. A covenant to pay money for property maintenance did not restrict the bank in the use of its own land, so how could it be said to "touch and concern" that land? Yet, from a developer's standpoint, it would be impossible to maintain the common areas without assessing future owners to pay for the upkeep.

The court found that the covenant did touch and concern the land and that the bank was required to pay assessments. Noting that the assessments were to be spent for "public purposes," the court said, "For full enjoyment in common by the defendant and other property owners of these easements or rights, the roads and public places must be maintained."[70] The court accepted the concept that the covenants were intended to have a mutually beneficial effect. Future owners could be forced to pay assessments because their property values were enhanced by the restrictions.

But the other difficult question remained: even if the bank had to pay the assessment, could the Property Owners' Association sue to collect it? There was no legal precedent for such action. The association owned no land, and the bank argued that the association was not the same as the property owners and could not represent their interests. In the parlance of ancient property law, the bank argued that there was no privity of estate between itself and the association.

Lacking any precedent, the court relied on public policy considerations, and ruled that the association could enforce the covenants.[71]

> The corporate plaintiff has been formed as a convenient instrument by which the property owners may advance their common interests. We do not ignore the corporate form when we recognize that the Neponsit Property Owners Association, Inc., is acting as the agent or representative of the Neponsit property owners. . . . Only blind adherence to an ancient formula devised to meet entirely different conditions could constrain the court to hold that a corporation formed as a medium for the enjoyment

of common rights of property owners owns no property which would benefit by enforcement of common rights and has no cause of action in equity to enforce the covenant upon which such common rights depend. . . . In substance if not in form the covenant is a restrictive covenant which touches and concerns the defendant's land, and in substance, if not in form, there is privity of estate between the plaintiff and the defendant.[72]

The *Neponsit* decision was a bold departure from rules of English and American property law that dated to previous centuries. It was an important decision by the Supreme Court of what was then the largest state in the nation. It gave homeowner associations legal standing to enforce restrictive covenants and to collect assessments for property maintenance. These private governments now had the authority to carry out the will of real estate developers in perpetuity.

Through the years real estate developers have made increasing use of restrictive covenants to create amenities for the exclusive enjoyment of their tenants and owners, to carry out large-scale private city planning, and eventually to redefine the meaning of home ownership. At Radburn this evolutionary process reached a stage where the modern CID with its characteristic form of private government is visible.

When state courts gave judicial ratification to homeowner association enforcement of restrictive covenants, legitimizing the key elements of CID private government, the stage was set for community builders to realize Jesse Clyde Nichols' dream: expanding this form of housing from the affluent to the middle and working classes.

This ambitious project was delayed by the depression and World War II. But by the time the postwar housing boom began the groundwork had already been laid. The prototypes for the modern CID had been functioning for decades, and the most important legal battles had already been fought and won. With legal precedent on their side, and having learned from experience with restrictive covenants at luxury subdivisions, community builders were prepared to build their own large-scale versions of the garden city. In the process, CID housing was to become a mass-produced consumer commodity.

# 3

# From Exclusivity to Exclusion: Homeowner Associations in the Suburban Housing Boom

If a neighborhood is to retain stability, it is necessary
that properties shall continue to be occupied
by the same social and racial classes.
—Federal Housing Administration, 1938

One thing is certain; racial housing covenants don't
just happen. They are carefully and often expensively
promoted. Two groups have taken the lead in that
activity—the property owners' and neighborhood
improvement associations, and the developers of
subdivisions. Both groups have been ably aided and
supported by the FHA and financial institutions.
—Robert C. Weaver, *The Negro Ghetto,* 1948

From 1920 through 1929 more than seven million housing units were started, more than during any previous decade in American history.[1] Flush from that decade of growth, Jesse Clyde Nichols and other major builders were eager to expand their operations by engaging in large-scale construction of homes for the middle and working classes, using the CID model developed in upscale subdivisions like Radburn. But the depression and World War II delayed that ambition for fifteen years. Housing starts plummeted to 2.7 million for the decade of the 1930s and to 2.3 million from 1940 through 1945.[2]

As soon as the war ended, the pent-up demand for housing, the high birthrates, and the application of mass-production techniques to construction combined to create a building boom that dwarfed that of the 1920s. Housing starts went from 326,000 in 1945 to 1,023,000 in 1946, reached nearly 2 million in 1950, and never dropped below 1 million in any year from the end of the war through 1990.[3] Home ownership became the middle-class norm as "dormitory" suburbs sprouted in the outskirts of America's cities. Between 1890 and 1940 the home ownership rate increased only moderately, from 37 percent to 41 percent; by 1960 it had leaped to 61 percent.[4]

This explosion in the building and ownership of homes did not benefit all sectors of society uniformly. Observers of today's CIDs and suburbia commonly note the striking homogeneity of their residents. In discussing what he calls the coming "suburban century," political scientist William Schneider points out that "the middle class is who lives in the suburbs" and describes suburbia as "home-owning, homogeneous, and largely white."[5] Michael Danielson begins *The Politics of Exclusion* by observing that "to a greater degree than in other modern societies, urbanization in the United States has separated people spatially along economic and social lines."[6]

Recently, CID designers have accelerated this trend toward separation, balkanization, and homogeneity, using elaborate deed restrictions to mandate distinct lifestyles. Richard Louv calls these boutique CIDs "single-interest neighborhoods," designed just for seniors, singles, golfers, boat fanciers, or other specific population segments. Community designer Wayne Williams terms this single-interest approach "positive ghettoism."[7]

Williams' choice of words is historically resonant. Developers originally learned about marketing homogeneous neighborhoods by excluding racial, ethnic, and religious minorities from suburbia. Restrictive covenants are used to create Williams' positive ghettos just as they were used to confine minorities to inner-city ghettos.

Before and during the post–World War II housing boom, large-scale developers used homeowner associations and restrictive covenants in middle-class housing to market exclusion rather than exclusivity. As millions of African-Americans and other minorities relocated in Northern and Western cities, community builders and the Federal Housing Administration responded by promoting the creation of one-race, one-class neighborhoods in cities and newly constructed suburbs. In essence, the black American was treated as a threat to property values, like a soap factory or a slaughterhouse.

From the early twentieth century until 1948, when the U.S. Supreme Court outlawed the practice, developers used covenants to exclude African-Americans, Asians, Jews, and other minorities from buying or renting homes in specific neighborhoods or developments.[8] They did this with the encouragement of the Federal Housing Administration, which actively promoted suburbanization and segregation on the theory that both were good ways to maximize property values.

Homeowner associations functioned for decades as the primary mechanisms for the enforcement of segregation through restrictive covenants. Some were associations set up by developers in new subdivisions, and others were organized by residents in older neighborhoods but manipulated by real estate interests. Their efforts occasionally included intimidation and violence.

Although racial covenants were declared invalid, developers' experience with selling and enforcing racial exclusion laid a foundation for more sophisticated efforts to a similar end. During the early 1950s deed restrictions concerning minimum housing cost, maximum occupancy, and property maintenance were suggested as ways to accomplish the same purpose as racial covenants. Such devices enable developers to continue using homeowner associations to establish lasting patterns of housing segregation, producing a largely white suburbia. This process has heightened racial sensitivities, especially the belief that the presence of minorities threatens property values. That concept has evolved into a more general philosophy that communities should be homogeneous rather than diverse. Today's CIDs, with their elaborate lifestyle regulations, reflect and amplify the principle adopted during decades of legalized racial segregation: restrictive covenants can be used to create homes for certain people and to exclude others.

## "FORBIDDEN NEIGHBORS" IN THE CITIES

America's suburban housing was constructed during and, to some extent, in response to decades of large-scale demographic change that brought millions of immigrants and nonwhite Americans into the cities.

From the late nineteenth century through 1930, immigrants entered the United States in large numbers; more than 1.2 million arrived in 1914 alone. The bulk were Jews and Catholics from Southern and Eastern Europe who sought better economic conditions, as had the Northern and Central Europeans who preceded them.[9]

By World War I, however, the descendants of earlier generations of immigrants had begun to perceive the newer entrants as a threat and to react in both extreme and moderate forms. Some nativists expressed themselves through such organizations as the Ku Klux Klan, which was responsible for killings, floggings, tar-and-feather parties, parades, and cross-burnings; it attained a membership as large as six million.[10] Others worked through the political process. Progressive Era electoral reforms, such as the Australian or official ballot, personal registration requirements, primary elections, and the replacement of patronage with civil service were designed to undermine the political power of urban machines that were supported by blocs of immigrants.[11] The flow of European immigration was slowed dramatically, first by World War I and again in 1924 when Congress adopted the McCarran-Walter Act, which established immigration quotas based on national origin.

As their numbers dwindled, European immigrants were replaced in the northern urban market for industrial jobs by African-Americans migrating from the rural South, where mechanization of agriculture, particularly in the cotton industry, had reduced the need for laborers. Beginning in 1910 and encouraged by the industrial demands of two world wars, millions of black people left Virginia, the Carolinas, Georgia, Alabama, Arkansas, Louisiana, and Mississippi and moved to New York, New Jersey, Pennsylvania, Ohio, Indiana, Illinois, and Michigan. In the West, California was the primary recipient of these migrants. The flow was slowed by the depression, but it resumed and even increased during the 1940s.[12]

The total size of this migration has been estimated at 6.5 million between 1910 and 1970, making it "one of the largest and most rapid mass internal movements of people in history—perhaps *the* greatest not caused by the immediate threat of execution or starvation" (emphasis in original).[13]

Most of these primarily rural black Americans settled in the large cities of the North and West. Their arrival in large numbers elicited a social backlash from elements of the white population, similar to that which had greeted the Eastern and Southern European immigrants on the East Coast and the Japanese and Chinese on the West, but this one was more intense and lasting.[14]

Black families newly arrived in large cities typically were concentrated in crowded, poor neighborhoods with substandard living conditions. As population pressure built within these "black belts," and as some of the migrants began to accumulate sufficient wealth to move elsewhere, white resistance to the prospect of integrated neighborhoods began to take various forms, ranging from political activity to violence.[15]

One can attribute this resistance to personal racism in elements of the white population, but there is substantial evidence that institutional racism was a more significant factor. Racial prejudice—specifically the fear that integration would destroy neighborhoods and lower property values—was actively promoted by the real estate industry, community builders, mortgage bankers, and the Federal Housing Administration.

## THE REAL ESTATE LOBBY AND RACIAL SEGREGATION

By the time the Great Depression began in 1929 real estate development had become a well-organized, influential industry. Under the leadership of the National Association of Real Estate Boards (NAREB), founded in 1908, an alliance between real estate agents and builders was formed.[16] NAREB was the main voice for the home-building industry until the post–World War II boom. At that point large-scale builders went their own way, finding representation in national policy making through two NAREB spin-off organizations that "supplanted the realtors' association as the primary spokesmen for community builders."[17] One was the Urban Land Institute, founded in 1936 as an "independent research agency."[18] In 1944 Jesse Clyde Nichols became the first chairman of the elite Community Builders' Council of the ULI. The other spinoff was the National Association of Home Builders, formed in 1942 when the Home Builders and Subdividers Division of NAREB, which consisted of 105 community builders, split from NAREB.[19]

From 1908 to 1944, when it acted as "the principal, indeed the only, organized voice for the homebuilding industry in the U.S.," NAREB established professional standards, licensing requirements, and codes of ethics; educated members; and worked closely with government from the local to the national level.[20] Above all, NAREB endeavored to convince the public that buying real estate was a safe, conservative investment. The public had been justifiably fearful of the unregulated real estate profession, seeing it as a risky enterprise run by fly-by-night agents and subject to the vagaries of speculative bubbles and boom-bust economic cycles.[21] To expand private home ownership it was necessary to establish a sense of security about property values. The industry used its resources and influence to eliminate or minimize factors that appeared to make the value of residential property unstable.

Among those destabilizing factors, according to NAREB, were racial and ethnic minorities. Until 1950, NAREB's Code of Ethics contained the following provision: "Article 34. A Realtor should never be instrumental in introducing into a neighborhood a character of property or occupancy, members of any race or nationality, or any individuals whose presence will clearly be detrimental to property values in that neighborhood." The code further provided that any member board that failed to maintain and enforce the code was subject to expulsion from NAREB.[22]

In his detailed analysis of real estate texts and professional policies, Charles Abrams shows that the national real estate lobby, led by NAREB, displayed an "anti-racial policy that has permeated the philosophy of many of its members. The anti-racial slant became apparent in the 1920s and was accepted without resistance or fanfare. Then, like Topsy, it just grew. Unlike Topsy, however, it was anti-Negro, anti-alien, and anti-anybody-who-was-different."[23]

This anti-racial philosophy was reflected in the textbooks and other materials used to train real estate brokers. NAREB prepared a textbook that it issued originally in 1939 "for exclusive use of its member boards as a text in evening classes attended by real estate agents and their employees."[24] This how-to manual for agents, titled *Fundamentals of Real Estate Practice,* deals at some length with ethnicity and property values, setting out the accepted philosophy that neighborhoods should be kept homogeneous and that some racial and ethnic groups are by nature better for property values than others:

The tendency of certain racial and cultural groups to stick together, making it almost impossible to assimilate them in the normal social organism, is too well known to need much comment. But in some cases the result is less detrimental than in others. The Germans, for example, are a clean and thrifty people. They take pride in keeping their property clean and in good condition. They are commonly accepted as "good neighbors." The German sections in our large cities are almost invariably substantial and respectable. Unfortunately this cannot be said of all the other nations which have sent their immigrants to our country. Some of them have brought standards and customs far below our own levels. . . . Like termites, they undermine the structure of any neighborhood into which they creep.[25]

Elsewhere, the manual lists ethnic and racial homogeneity among the "factors that influence rentals," noting that "as a rule, the greater the conformity in these respects, the easier rent levels are maintained."[26]

The text emphasizes the value of race restrictive covenants by setting out a hypothetical situation in which an appraiser has "acted too quickly." Based on the values of comparable properties, he mistakenly thinks a property is worth thirty-eight thousand dollars when in fact it is worth only twenty-eight thousand dollars. Why? Because "the subject property was in a section of two blocks not protected against racial blight. The type of tenants, therefore, was considerably lower than those found in the other buildings."[27]

In offering helpful suggestions regarding "How the Broker Gets Properties to Sell," the book includes a prescription for instigating "white flight": "When a neighborhood is changing character by reason of the fact that it is being encroached upon or into by another type or class of occupancy, such as infiltration of racial groups or business property into unzoned residential areas, owners of property in that neighborhood are good prospects for listings. It will pay you to make a continual study of neighborhood trends in your area."[28]

This text was not an aberration but a reflection of the standard position of the industry nationwide. Abrams' study in 1955 found that not a single textbook in the real estate sales and appraisal industry disputed this "racist gospel."[29]

## PARTNERS IN SEGREGATION: REALTORS, BUILDERS, AND FHA

Along with increased national-level organization, perhaps the most significant development for community builders during the depression was the entry of the federal government into partnership with the real estate business. This partnership resulted in the national government adopting the industry's belief in segregated, homogeneous neighborhoods as official policy.

On June 27, 1934, the National Housing Act was adopted and the Federal Housing Administration was created. It was conceived as a way of relieving unemployment in the construction industry, but it soon became much more than that. One of its designers and the director of its Technical Division was Miles Colean, who said, "The idea had grown from the President's stated desire to have at least one stimulative agency that did not require spending by the government but would instead rely on private endeavor."[30]

The reliance on private endeavor soon became a matter of dominance by private real estate and banking interests. At the inaugural meeting of the FHA's Housing Advisory Council Planning Committee in January 1935, Colean articulated his understanding of the relation between government and business, which essentially made the former a servant of the latter. "The function of government is to make it possible for private enterprise, both from a capital and construction point of view, to produce the best results. I think we have an instrument here that if followed through to its ultimate end, can pretty well do that."[31]

Real estate historian Marc Weiss contends that, from its inception, "FHA was largely run by representatives of the real estate and banking industries."[32] Key positions were held by NAREB figures, and staff members were recruited almost entirely from the private sector.

Weiss emphasizes that Colean and others at FHA advocated an intentional process of governmental, institutional, and technological changes geared to promoting large-scale residential development.[33] FHA literature from the mid-1930s establishes that it self-consciously promoted big builders. "The Administration seeks to encourage that type of operative builder who looks upon the production of homes as a manufacturing and merchandising process of high social significance and who, preferably, assumes responsibility for the product from the plotting and development of the land to the disposal of the completed dwelling units."[34]

This is essentially a description of the large-scale community builder, who combined the roles of subdivider, house builder, and real estate agent, constructing and selling entire subdivisions. "FHA," Weiss says, "had adopted the full agenda of the community builders and was determined to make this still embryonic institutional form the preeminent approach to housing production."[35]

FHA was designed to stimulate building indirectly, not by providing money for construction or by making loans but by insuring residential mortgages against loss. If the U.S. Treasury bore much of the risk of default, private lenders presumably would be more willing to make long-term, low-interest loans to people wishing to buy homes.[36]

But the long-term effects of FHA policies went far beyond reducing unemployment in the construction industry. Historian Kenneth Jackson contends that "no agency of the United States government has had a more pervasive and powerful impact on the American people over the past half-century than the Federal Housing Administration."[37] FHA policies fueled both the rapid suburbanization of America and the segregated housing patterns that went with it.

Large-scale developers who had been building suburban housing since the nineteenth century wished to expand their operations. FHA supported this goal by emphasizing its willingness to insure loans for new single-family housing rather than loans for modernizing older homes or building multifamily housing. These administrative preferences promoted the rapid suburbanization of America and the flight of people, business, and capital from cities. As Jackson puts it, "FHA programs hastened the decay of inner-city neighborhoods by stripping them of much of their middle-class constituency. In practice, FHA insurance went to new residential developments on the edges of metropolitan areas to the neglect of core cities."[38]

One of the guiding principles behind this process of federally insured suburbanization was the "racist gospel" that the presence of minorities threatened property values and that neighborhoods should be kept homogeneous. FHA adopted the industry's idea that restrictive covenants, enforced by homeowner associations, were one way to preserve those property values, and it set about promoting the creation of "homogeneous" neighborhoods, using racial covenants to exclude minorities.

The FHA published a manual for its underwriting staff to use in determining whether to insure mortgages on a piece of property or subdivision. The manual created a quantified rating system that "allowed personal and agency bias in favor of all-white subdivisions in the suburbs to affect the kinds of loans it guaranteed—or, equally important, refused to guarantee."[39]

The 1938 *Underwriting Manual* reflected this bias. The rating system explained that "Protection From Adverse Influences" was "one of the most important features in the Rating of Location." Among these "adverse influences" were to be found racial and ethnic minorities: "Areas surrounding a location are investigated to determine whether incompatible racial and social groups are present, for the purpose of making a prediction regarding the probability of the location being invaded by such groups. If a neighborhood is to retain stability, it is necessary that properties shall continue to be occupied by the same social and racial classes. A change in social or racial occupancy generally contributes to instability and a decline in values" (sec. 937).[40]

The manual prescribed the use of restrictive covenants as the best way to deal with such "adverse influences" (sec. 934). Going beyond merely extolling the virtue of deed restrictions in general, the manual expressly advocated race restrictive covenants: "Recorded restrictive covenants should strengthen and supplement zoning ordinances and to be really effective should include the provisions listed below. The restrictions should be recorded with the plat, or imposed as a blanket encumbrance against all lots in the subdivision, and should run for a period of at least twenty-five to thirty years. Recommended restrictions should include provision for the following: . . . . g. prohibition of the occupancy of properties except by the race for which they are intended" (sec. 980 [3]).

Under the heading of the location's "Appeal," FHA set forth as government policy the real estate agent's gospel of homogeneity: "Satisfaction, contentment, and comfort result from association with persons of similar social attributes. Families enjoy social relationships with other families whose education, abilities, mode of living, and racial characteristics are similar to their own" (sec. 973).

In rating borrowers, the underwriting staff was cautioned about people who sought to buy property near those not of their own race or class. The manual assumes they will soon become dissatisfied. "The borrower who acquires property for occupancy in a location inhabited by a class or race of people that may impair his interest in the property—and thereby affect his motivation—should be ascribed a lower rating in this feature to reflect the diminishing importance of the property to the borrower" (sec. 1032).

For many years FHA continued to promote race and class separation. It responded to criticism of this policy by rewriting the explicitly racial sections in euphemistic terms but without abandoning the underlying philosophy. The 1947 *Underwriting Manual* included provisions for rating locations in terms of "Physical and Social Attractiveness." This was to be evaluated in part according to "Compatibility Among Neighborhood Occupants":

> The tendency of user groups to seek compatible conditions can sustain and enhance, diminish or destroy neighborhood desirability. Neighborhoods constituted of families that are congenial, physical conditions being acceptable, generally exhibit a strong appeal and stability. Consideration of these attitudes is essential in the evaluation of the feature Physical and Social Attractiveness. . . . If a mixture of user groups is found to exist it must be determined whether the mixture will render the neighborhood less desirable to present and prospective occupants. If the occupancy of the neighborhood is changing from one user group to another, or if the areas adjacent to the immediate neighborhood are occupied by a user group dissimilar to the typical occupants of the subject neighborhood or a change in occupancy is imminent or probable any degree of risk is reflected in the rating. It is to be noted that additional risk is not necessarily involved in such change (sec. 1320 [1], [2]).[41]

In 1947 FHA was still promoting use of what it was calling "protective covenants" to guard against "inharmonious land uses." By that time deed restrictions had become sufficiently important to have five pages devoted to them (secs. 1354–1365). They were "essential to the sound development of proposed residential areas" (sec. 1354 [1]) and should be recorded and "superior to the lien of any mortgage" (sec. 1354 [3]). Explicit references to race restrictive covenants had by then been dropped after protest, but the agency carefully advocated covenants that would "maintain neighborhood character and values" (sec. 1354 [4]); provide for "prohibition of nuisances and other land uses that might affect the desirability of the area"; and ensure that "no other lot owner within the protected area can use his property in a way that will destroy values, lower the character of the neighborhood, or create a nuisance" (sec. 1354 [3]). Seen in the light of the manual's emphasis on "compatibility among neighborhood occupants," the inference seems to be that racial covenants are desirable.

The 1947 manual also provides for homeowner associations to enforce restrictive covenants. FHA says "property-owners' maintenance associations" should have power to levy assessments, maintain common property, and "enforce other protective covenants established in a development" (sec. 1365 [4]). This would include race restrictive covenants.

The language used by FHA in 1947 shares the tone of a 1946 publication of the Urban Land Institute that extols the virtues of "homes associations." The preamble hits the same careful note, using euphemisms for racial segregation: "stability," "character," "integrity," and "solidarity." "Homes associations have proved to be one of the most stabilizing factors in preserving the character and integrity of the community, in preventing depreciation, and in maintaining a high degree of community pride and solidarity."[42]

This private-public partnership between the real estate industry and FHA had enormous and lasting consequences for American society. Jackson concludes that "FHA . . . helped to turn the building industry against the minority and inner-city housing market, and its policies supported the income and racial segregation of suburbia. For perhaps the first time, the federal government embraced the discriminatory attitudes of the marketplace. Previously, prejudices were personalized and individualized; FHA exhorted segregation and enshrined it as public policy."[43]

This national policy filtered rapidly to the local level, where cities were confronted by massive social and demographic change. During the crucial years when the biggest wave of housing construction in American history was taking place, cities were heavily influenced by segregationist policies established by NAREB, community developers, and the FHA.

## RACIAL ZONING LAWS

Early in the century, many city governments responded to white segregationist pressures by enacting racial zoning ordinances under the Tenth Amendment police power. San Francisco adopted such a measure in 1890 to segregate the Chinese.[44] In 1910 Baltimore led a number of other cities in states on the periphery of the deep South in prescribing racial zoning for black Americans. Cities with such ordinances included Winston-Salem, North Carolina; Birmingham; Richmond and Norfolk, Virginia; Louisville, Kentucky; Atlanta; St. Louis; and Dallas.[45]

The Richmond ordinance provides an example of the nature of these proscriptions and their stated rationale: "In order to preserve the general welfare, peace, racial integrity, morals, and social good order of the city of Richmond, it shall be unlawful for any person to use as a residence any building on any street between intersecting streets, where the majority of residences on such streets are occupied by those with whom said person is forbidden to intermarry."[46]

This ordinance, like nearly all the others, employed euphemisms to obfuscate its purpose.[47] Instead of stating that it was designed to keep blacks from moving into white neighborhoods, the ordinance is drafted to apply, ostensibly, to people of all races, and it is phrased in terms of preserving the public peace and "racial integrity" rather than promoting segregation of blacks in ghettos.

In 1917 the U.S. Supreme Court declared the Louisville ordinance unconstitutional, ruling that racial zoning ordinances violated the privileges and immunities, due process, and equal protection clauses of the Fourteenth Amendment.[48] The decision spelled the beginning of the end for these ordinances, though cities continued to pass them in revised form, despite clear judicial disapproval, as late as 1926.[49]

## RACE RESTRICTIVE COVENANTS, THE REAL ESTATE INDUSTRY, AND HOMEOWNER ASSOCIATIONS

The Supreme Court decision to invalidate racial zoning coincided with the entry of the United States into World War I. The war created a demand for industrial workers, stimulating the migration of African-Americans to Northern and Western cities. The generalized housing shortage that resulted aggravated the social conflict over integrated neighborhoods. When it became clear that local government could not use zoning or police power to maintain segregation, a new approach was needed. That new approach was the race restrictive covenant, put in place and enforced by private action that was beyond the reach of the constitution. As Robert Weaver put it in his study *The Negro Ghetto*, "In order to accomplish the same end [as racial zoning] and still not run afoul of the law, race restrictive covenants were hit upon."[50]

The era of race restrictive covenants lasted from 1917 until 1948, when the Supreme Court held them unenforceable.[51] For more than thirty years these covenants were the primary mechanism for excluding black Americans from urban and suburban housing. Weaver and others writing while these restrictions were still valid emphatically described the invidious nature of racial covenants and the rapidity with which they

were adopted across the North and West after racial zoning was outlawed. "The menace of the covenant is that it has become a vogue in
conveyancing. Subdividers exalt it as a guarantee of a lastingly exclusive
neighborhood. Its use is increasing to epidemic proportions. Once filed,
there is no practical way for removing it from the record. Legalization of
the private covenant is a greater barrier to race harmony than segregation laws, for the latter are at least subject to the play of educational
processes and to repeal, while covenants once filed are apt to entail the
land forever against use by the races proscribed."[52]

In 1932 the Committee on Negro Housing of President Hoover's
Conference on Home Building and Home Ownership produced a report
entitled *Negro Housing,* which drew a similar parallel between racial
covenants and Southern segregation: "What custom accomplishes by
way of controlling racial residence sites in many cities of the South, and
the segregation ordinances sought to do for the border states, the practice of entering into covenants to exclude Negroes from certain areas
accomplishes in areas of the North. For whereas it is now unconstitutional to legislate against one element of citizens, the law permits individuals to enter contractual relationships and offers machinery for
punishing violators of contracts. Thus, these covenants have become
widespread through the North, and these exclusion methods have been
reinforced by violence in Chicago, Detroit, White Plains [in New York],
New York, Washington, and Philadelphia."[53]

Racial covenants were widespread in cities from coast to coast. They
were especially prevalent in Chicago; Los Angeles; Washington, D.C.;
Columbus, Ohio; and Detroit, where vast sections of urban and suburban
land were off limits to black Americans, especially in areas close to
neighborhoods already occupied by blacks. In a 1947 Chicago study
undertaken in connection with litigation, it was found that "over half the
residential area not occupied by Negroes [was] covenanted against colored people."[54] John P. Dean's 1947 study of more than three hundred
New York subdivisions found that "no less than 56 percent of all homes
checked were forbidden to Negroes."[55]

There was a pattern in how racial covenants were applied. They
appeared in two kinds of properties and were sponsored by different
groups in each. They were implemented by developers in new suburban
subdivisions and by homeowner associations in older neighborhoods bordering on black-occupied areas.

Developer-Created Covenants in New Suburban Housing

In new developments created by large-scale community builders, racial covenants were applied to all the land in the subdivision before houses were constructed. Dean's study, which dealt with new subdivisions, found that "most race clauses took on a rather standardized form" which' he rendered as follows: "No race other than the Caucasian race shall use or occupy any building or lot, except that this restriction shall not prevent occupancy by domestic servants of a different race employed by an owner or tenant."[56]

There was an economic motivation at work in the use of racial covenants in new subdivisions. As Charles Abrams has noted, "Unlike the tiled bathroom, venetian blinds, and television outlets, the promise of racial exclusiveness cost the builder nothing," so developers "vied with each other in their quest for more groups they might exclude."[57] This allowed builders to sell segregation, at no additional cost, to white buyers eager to escape the potentially integrated city for newly created white suburbs.

Evidence suggests that racial covenants were most popular among large-scale community builders who were building entire neighborhoods that they wished to make all white. Dean's study of New York covenants in 1947 found that 63 percent of developments with twenty or more homes had race restrictions, and 85 percent of the subdivisions with seventy-five or more homes were restricted to whites. Only 8 percent of the subdivisions with fewer than twenty parcels were racially restricted. He concluded that "their prevalence is best judged by the 71.6 percent of homes in prewar developments of twenty or more homes which carry race covenants," and he ventured this explanation: "These figures suggest that in the larger subdivisions where new properties are numerous enough to create their own new neighborhood, race restrictions are considered necessary to guarantee the uniform racial character of families moving in and to maintain uniform occupancy thereafter. But where just a handful of houses are constructed in an already-built-up neighborhood, interlocking friendships, mutual loyalties, and existing social pressures can be depended upon as an adequate barrier against Negroes."[58]

Dean clearly identified large-scale builders as the major perpetrators in this exclusion of nonwhites from the burgeoning suburbs. "This practice casts a long shadow on the trend toward large-scale building operations. One builder consistent in the use of race covenants is identified by *Architectural Forum* as 'for twenty-five years one of Long Island's most prolific builders.' His past and present building program involves 11,300 dwelling units—the equivalent of a city of 40,000 to 45,000 people."[59]

The builder Dean referred to appears to be the Levitts, described by Kenneth Jackson as "the family that had the greatest impact on postwar housing in the United States" through the application of mass-production manufacturing techniques to large-scale housing construction in their "Levittowns." Abraham Levitt, and his organization "publicly and officially refused to sell to blacks for two decades after the war. Nor did resellers deal with minorities. As William Levitt explained, 'We can solve a housing problem, or we can try to solve a racial problem. But we cannot combine the two.' Not surprisingly, in 1960 not a single one of the Long Island Levittown's 82,000 residents was black."[60] Jackson notes that the Levitts were "no more culpable in this regard than any other urban or suburban firm."[61]

## Property Owners' Associations and the Fight Against Integration

In older neighborhoods bordering "black belt" areas, the use of racial covenants and other resistance to integration came about through different but related means. The "neighborhood improvement associations," "property owners' associations," "civic clubs," or "homeowner associations" in neighborhoods near black-occupied areas became active to counter the "threat" of black home-buyers. Real estate agents were heavily involved in promoting these sorts of enterprises.

The organizations are an integral but rarely mentioned part of the history of today's homeowner associations. David Handlin, in *The American Home: Architecture and Society, 1815–1915,* documents the existence of voluntary "village improvement societies" as early as the seventeenth century and writes that they proliferated in the years following the Civil War. These societies took steps to beautify and improve their communities and property, pressured local government for public works projects, and generally tried to deal with challenges to their towns.[62] William S. Worley's study of developer Jesse Clyde Nichols argues that Nichols and others in the industry used these associations as their historical precedent for creating mandatory-membership associations in their developments.[63] The two kinds of associations—voluntary and mandatory—have much in common: an interrelated history, a shared emphasis on property values and covenant enforcement, and close ties to the real estate industry.

During the early twentieth century many voluntary associations came under the influence of developer and real estate interests who used them, much as the mandatory associations they created in new developments, to confront a "threat" to property values in the form of black home-buyers. The links between voluntary associations and real estate interests are manifest.

Developers and real estate agents promoted and manipulated racial fears in white neighborhoods in order to sell new suburban homes and resell old ones at substantial profit. Residents were encouraged to believe that the arrival of a single black family would cause a decline in property values as white owners sold in a panic and that the neighborhood would quickly become predominantly black.[64] Once a black family or two arrived in a neighborhood, real estate agents often encouraged panic selling by whites at low prices, relocated them in new suburban housing, then sold the old houses at high prices to new black residents.[65]

Moreover, neighborhood residents who used voluntary homeowner associations to spread and enforce race restrictive covenants were simply imitating the practice inaugurated by community builders in new subdivisions. There was a sense in which the use of racial restrictions in newly constructed, affluent, suburban neighborhoods had made racial segregation seem a mark of social status. As Charles Abrams noted, "Buyers liked the idea of being accepted into an 'exclusive' neighborhood. To be discriminating, they were told, you must be discriminatory. The dream of the warm fireside, of the security and pride of ownership would be enlarged to include a whole community of neighbors, friendly, similar, socially acceptable, interesting, and white."[66]

Similarly, Weaver's study noted a trickle-down effect as racial exclusiveness spread from upper-income neighborhoods to poor ones. Weaver observed that "soon after instruments to effect enforced residential segregation had become prestige-laden in the more desirable areas, color consciousness and prejudice spread to the blighted areas."[67]

Additionally, there is persuasive evidence that these neighborhood organizations did not take up the cause of segregation spontaneously but were actively encouraged by people associated with the real estate business. A 1951 study of these associations in Chicago documented the connection, concluding that "realtors, builders and mortgage bankers do hold a great deal of interest in and control over the activities of the neighborhood improvement and property owners' associations. . . . Policy which appears to have been made by small home-owners of which there are many, is actually originated by those who have a business interest in real estate, of which there are comparatively few."[68]

Specifically, this study found that business interests took the lead in promoting the restrictive covenants that were circulated through neighborhood associations. In St. Louis the covenants were virtually uniform and were prepared by the St. Louis Real Estate Exchange. In Chicago the racial covenants were actively promoted by the Real Estate Board and the Title and Trust Company. In Los Angeles, following the 1948 Supreme Court decision holding the covenants unenforceable, the Los Angeles Realty Board went so far as to petition the National Association of Real Estate Boards to sponsor a constitutional amendment to reverse the Court's decision.[69] In Washington, D.C., the Real Estate Board and related interests were allegedly using neighborhood associations as front organizations to perpetuate segregation.[70] Other organized efforts by local real estate boards to maintain segregation have been documented in Milwaukee, New York, and elsewhere.[71]

Weaver reached a similar conclusion. "It seems apparent, in retrospect, that the rise of racial covenants and other instruments of enforced segregation was more the result of manipulation than the reflection of a spontaneous movement. Intense resistance to the concept of Negro neighbors was usually concentrated in given neighborhoods. It became widespread only after the professional advocates of enforced segregation had spent much time and money to propagandize its necessity and desirability."[72]

Homeowner associations determined to resist integration engaged in a range of activities. Typically, they would hold meetings and go door-to-door soliciting residents to sign restrictive covenant agreements by which all would promise not to sell their homes to blacks. As with developer-drafted covenants, these agreements were recorded and would "run with the land" to bind all future owners, permanently preventing integration of the neighborhood. The association would then sue to eject any black buyer from a residence covered by a covenant.

Homeowner associations also tried to prevent real estate agents from defying official policy and selling to blacks, and they did their best to discourage prospective black buyers. Their persuasive methods included warnings, threats, and, in some cases, violence.[73] One study by the Committee on Negro Housing reported 1922 data showing that "in Chicago, following the protests and agitation of the Hyde Park Property Owners' Association, the homes of fifty-eight Negro families were bombed within a period of less than four years" and documenting other violent incidents in Cleveland, Pittsburgh, White Plains, New York, Kansas City, Louisville, Baltimore, Memphis, and "in practically every state from Virginia to California."[74]

The Chicago Commission on Race Relations conducted a study of the 1919 Chicago race riot, in which 23 black and 15 white people were killed and 537 people were injured.[75] The commission drew a connection between real estate agents' activity, neighborhood associations, and racial violence. "Recently . . . there have been conspicuous instances of open and organized efforts to influence the minds of whites against Negroes. Ignorance and suspicion, fear and prejudice, have been played upon deliberately. The stated purpose of the propaganda was to unite white property owners in opposition to the 'invasion' of other residential areas by Negroes, but in the actual carrying out of the propaganda it was extended to all Negroes, and many methods were employed which could have no other effect than to arouse bitterness and antagonism leading to clashes. The *Property Owners' Journal,* the organ of an association of real estate men, became so violent in its preachments that the protest of whites forced its discontinuance."[76]

The segregationist activities of developers, real estate agents, and homeowner associations had lasting impact in at least two ways. First, segregated housing patterns were established during the construction of suburbs around many major American cities, and these patterns have persisted. Second, these activities aggravated racial animosity rather than ameliorated it—promoting the erroneous stereotype that integration leads to declining property values—and transferred from the real estate industry to the public a taste for homogeneous neighborhoods.[77]

## HOMEOWNER ASSOCIATIONS AND ALTERNATIVES TO RACIAL COVENANTS

As early as the end of World War II it had become clear to some observers that developers were balkanizing suburban America not only by race but by class. Catherine Bauer, who had been part of the Regional Planning Association of America, wrote in 1945 that an atmosphere of "domestic isolationism" had taken hold in the building industry and related govern-ment agencies. "For the past generation practically every effort in the field of city planning and housing, whether profit-minded or welfare-minded, has been pushing us toward enormous one-class dormitory de-velopments as completely separated from one another and from work places as possible."[78]

Robert Weaver noted the same trend in 1948 and expressly linked it to developers' experience with race restrictive covenants. "Evolution and perpetuation of racial residential segregation cannot be separated from the growth of 'exclusive' one-class neighborhoods in American cities. Both are part and parcel of a recent development in urban land use—a tendency of the economically secure and favored to move away from the problems of large cities, establish homogeneous colonies, and exclude 'undesirable' elements. It is a process which the land speculators and subdivision developers have promoted with great zeal."[79]

Homeowner associations were integral to the process by which ex-plicit racial discrimination came to be translated into more sophisticated forms of segregation based on social class. Until 1948 homeowner asso-ciations, voluntary and mandatory, were the primary mechanisms de-velopers used to enforce race restrictive covenants. After 1948, when those covenants became unenforceable in court, real estate interests invented variations on the theme of using private, contractual mecha-nisms to enforce segregation. The link between these substitute devices and today's CID lifestyle covenants is apparent.

Plans for getting around the law against race restrictive covenants were widely discussed in the wake of *Shelley v. Kraemer*. A *U.S. News and World Report* article written in May 1948, immediately after the decision came down, helpfully listed a variety of such evasions:

> Plans that have the effect of restricting neighborhoods and that apparently are within the law, under the ruling of the Supreme Court, already are in use here and there. . . . Any of these plans that prove practical as well as legally valid are expected to come into more general use. . . . Self-enforcement of a covenant that limits property ownership in a neighborhood to the members of a racial or religious group is one such plan. . . . Requiring member-ship in a club or a co-operative as a condition for owning or occupying property is a second plan, already in use, by which sale of property is restricted to certain groups. In one type of

club, the property is owned by the club itself. The householder-member simply owns shares of stock and is assigned certain property for occupancy. . . . Meanwhile, many real estate subdivisions probably will be platted and sold in connection with golf clubs, tennis clubs, gardening clubs, and a great variety of other clubs based on some common activity or interest.[80]

The option of finding different means to enforce racial covenants, such as lawsuits against white sellers for breach of contract rather than against black buyers to eject them from the development, was effectively outlawed in 1953.[81] The cooperative became a popular form of CID, with some seven hundred eighty thousand housing units taking that form by 1987.[82] The concept of creating voluntary organizations, such as homeowner associations, to implement segregation through more devious means was widely discussed in the real estate industry. Charles Abrams quotes an attorney for the California Real Estate Association who proposed using homeowner associations to privatize racial discrimination and obviate the need for judicial enforcement:

A homes association could be formed, the members of which are the owners of building sites within the residential tract, and prohibiting the occupancy except to those persons or families, who hold an occupancy permit issued by the homes association. The issuance of the permit is discretionary and without reference to race or color but based entirely upon personal qualification as a good neighbor or in other words, cultural status. This is an extension of the idea that any club may regulate admission to its membership. Many a country club restricts occupancy of home sites on its grounds to its members. Religious colonies have long been established upon the same basis. This arrangement would likewise operate against undesirable Caucasians as prospective buyers.[83]

One other way for homeowner associations to exclude most people of color and other "undesirables" perceived as bad for property values was to enforce private restrictive covenants that were not explicitly based on race but would target the poor by prohibiting specific behaviors. This approach may have grown out of a proposal by Robert Weaver, who was executive director of the Mayor's Commission on Race Relations in Chi-

cago in 1944. At that time Weaver had suggested replacing racial covenants with those that targeted certain objectionable practices. He did
this not to maintain segregation but to help protect property values
without discriminating on the basis of race. "If, instead of restrictions on
account of race, creed, and color, there were agreements binding property
owners not to sell or lease except to single families, barring excessive
roomers, and otherwise dealing with the *type* of occupancy, property
would be better protected during both white and Negro occupancy. This
would afford an opportunity for the Negro who has the means and the
urge to live in a desirable neighborhood and it would protect the 'integrity of the neighborhood.' It would also prevent, or at least lessen, the
exodus of all whites upon the entrance of a few Negroes. But it would do
more; it would become an important factor in removing racial covenants
in other improved and vacant areas" (emphasis in original).[84]

Ironically, Weaver's idea was viewed by others as the next best thing
to race restrictive covenants. The same 1948 *U.S. News and World Report* article quoted above described that approach as a way around the
law against racial covenants. "High occupancy standards, now in effect
in many communities, are being used as a means of maintaining the
general character of a neighborhood and of indirectly achieving, to a high
degree, the same ends sought by racial restrictions. Such requirements
as the minimum cost of dwellings and number of occupants per room are
considered legal and enforceable without any question."[85]

A separate article in the same issue amplified that point by emphasizing that "the courts can still enforce covenants that are based upon
other things than race and color. These might be covenants that limit the
type, size and cost of homes built in a neighborhood, or the amount of
ground around the homes."[86]

Zorita Mikva's 1951 study of neighborhood associations showed
that "occupancy standards and other substitute measures" were being
adopted by neighborhood associations in 1948 because "they could be
substituted for racially discriminatory agreements":

> Generally [the] purpose [of such measures] is to introduce cer-
> tain limitations on the use of property, such as limiting the num-
> ber of persons per room, preventing conversions which create
> crowding and/or agreeing to certain maintenance standards for
> all buildings. . . . Conservation agreements have tried to meet
> the same problem [as race restrictive housing covenants] by

imposing limitations on the use of property, without regard to the race, religion or nationality of the property owners. Though this plan has been criticized for resulting in "one-class" neighborhoods, these agreements would, some believe, lower the racial barriers to an extent. . . . Conservation agreements and strict enforcement of building and zoning laws would, it is believed, allow wealthier Negroes to purchase homes in white communities, but would prevent the entrance of slum dwellers.[87]

In this manner, homeowner associations and restrictive covenants shifted their emphasis to class discrimination, which is legal, from race discrimination, which is not. Less affluent families, who might be able to afford a house only by pooling resources or renting out rooms, would be prohibited from buying. Lifestyle restrictions were justified with such familiar euphemisms as "preserving the character"—or "integrity" or "stability"—of a neighborhood rather than by referring to race or class. Nonetheless, the principle is still the same: certain groups of people are considered a threat to property values and are excluded. The result is still increased homogeneity, and, given economic disparities between white and nonwhite Americans, this approach inevitably contributes to continuing racial segregation.

# 4

## The Expansion of Privatopia: Land Economics and the Legacy of Ebenezer Howard

> Within the past decade, rapid urbanization has intensified
> a new need—the provision of an economical single-family
> living unit adaptable to urban densities, yet keeping
> many of the attractive features of the suburban home.
> —Federal Housing Administration, *Planned-Unit
> Development with a Homes Association,* 1964

> It might have been more entertaining, for the reader
> (and ourselves) if this chapter had woven a tale of dark
> complicity between community builders and public
> officials. Bribery, rigged elections, and the harried
> supervisor tantalized by expensive wine and mysterious
> women are the stuff of political fiction, and often political
> fact as well. Fortunately—or unfortunately, depending
> on one's taste—there has been no sign of such behavior.
> The participants have simply not found it necessary.
> —Edward P. Eichler and Marshall Kaplan,
> *The Community Builders,* 1970

Common-interest housing first was used to create exclusivity, and later it became an instrument of exclusion. A boom in CID housing construction that began in the 1960s built on those dynamics but was fueled primarily by the impersonal forces of land economics. An examination of these forces is critical to understanding why such a venerable housing concept suddenly became so popular among builders, and why we may expect

79

CIDs to be the predominant form of new housing for the foreseeable future. Put simply, CIDs have become a way of squeezing more people onto less land.

By 1960 a consensus was forming in academia, government, and the building industry that America needed new approaches to residential housing construction. Those who expressed that opinion came from widely different perspectives, but they shared a focus on the shortcomings of postwar suburban subdivisions.

Some critics argued that the internal dynamics of suburban life were contributing to large-scale undesirable social change and possibly creating a new kind of American. William H. Whyte's *The Organization Man* examined the social and psychological life of corporate employees living in the suburbs. Whyte saw "the new package suburbs" as the preferred home of the "organization man," typically a corporate employee who subscribed to a "Social Ethic," a sort of "bill of no rights" that "rationalizes the organization's demands for fealty and gives those who offer it wholeheartedly a sense of dedication in doing so."[1]

Other critics were more acerbic, arguing in substance that "suburbia was intellectually debilitating, culturally oppressive, and politically dangerous, breeding bland mass men without respect for arts or democracy."[2] Many saw suburbia as an architectural wasteland of unending sameness, with gridiron streets leading nowhere and identical "ticky-tacky" houses squatting on rectangular "cookie-cutter" lots. It was argued that suburbs encouraged an "ideological retreat" to a kind of neoprovincialism.[3]

Other writers, including Charles Abrams in *The City Is the Frontier,* focused on the suburb's effect on society, examining problems created by the spatial and social separation of suburbs from urban centers. These included the relation between inner-city poverty and suburban affluence, sprawl, traffic congestion, pollution, and political fragmentation.[4]

Although concerns over the effects of the suburbs were being expressed in academic and governmental circles, the home-building industry, which by 1960 was increasingly dominated by corporate builders, anticipated another kind of problem arising from land economics. The builders could foresee a time when they might no longer be able to build "big-lot" suburban homes to sell at prices the middle class could afford. Much of the profit in building suburban housing was realized through buying inexpensive, unimproved land and subdividing it into lots suitable for building. By 1960 it was becoming apparent to builders that land suitable for suburban housing was becoming scarcer and more expensive.

If the cost of homes rose to reflect the growing cost of land, and if profit levels were maintained, fewer Americans would be able to buy houses. Consequently, if home ownership was to remain within reach of the middle class, some way had to be found to build suburban housing that placed more people on less land.

The difficulty of increasing the population density of suburbia should not be underestimated. Low density was part of what made suburbs into what Robert Fishman calls "bourgeois utopias."[5] The attraction of suburbia, from its origins in late-eighteenth-century England, had been the chance for the middle class to flee high-density urban living, the "corruption" of the city, and the constant press of contact with the city's heterogeneous population. Suburbs catered to an arcadian fantasy in which the nuclear family would be plucked from the social fabric of the city and placed in purifying contact with nature.[6] The suburban prescription for social health was a single-family house surrounded by a large yard planted as a vast expanse of green lawn. It promised privacy, autonomy, and self-determination for the middle-class family. Fishman writes, "Suburbia, I came to believe, must be understood as a utopia in its own right. Its power derived ultimately from the capacity of suburban design to express a complex and compelling vision of the modern family freed from the corruption of the city, restored to harmony with nature, endowed with wealth and independence yet protected by a close-knit, stable community."[7]

Throughout the postwar housing boom the building industry had made enormous profits by catering to this arcadian yearning, promoting suburban single-family houses surrounded by large private yards. But by 1960 this strategy was becoming a victim of its own success as land suitable for new suburbs became scarcer and more expensive to buy and develop. The harsh mathematics of land economics threatened to make the carefully cultivated middle class taste for expansive yards a liability rather than an asset.

The challenge facing the building industry was to find a way to build suburban housing on smaller lots and still satisfy the demand for bourgeois utopias. Developers solved this dilemma—and answered the critics of suburbia—by turning once again to common-interest housing.

Builders began to move away from big-lot development, in which each family had a large yard, to smaller individual lots supplemented by common areas for recreation and other activities. To provide for owner-ship and maintenance of these commonly owned areas, builders returned to the CID concepts perfected in luxury subdivisions like Radburn, including restrictive covenants, homeowner associations with managerial governments, and common property ownership.

Builders experimented with a number of new architectural approaches to common-interest housing.[8] They designed "cluster" subdivisions, and reinvented row houses, calling them townhouses. The highest densities were achieved by introducing to the United States condominium ownership, a form of housing that had been in use in many nations for decades. Developers also offered city-sized, master-planned CIDs known as new towns.

An ideological dimension to CID housing began to emerge out of the marketing strategy employed to sell it. Because CIDs departed significantly from what most middle-class families expected from home ownership, community builders and the Federal Housing Administration began a sustained effort to convince the public that what might be seen as detriments were really advantages. These included sharing property with neighbors and submitting to neighborhood governance by amateurs, who were enforcing rules written by developers. Industry and government publications told the public that it was participating in exciting new variations on the time-tested legacy of Ebenezer Howard and that they would enjoy better living through planning. Moreover, CID residents were said to be at the cutting edge of a return to traditional American "town meeting" democracy based on ownership of their own community.[9]

With the impetus of heavy promotion by community builders and the federal government, there was an increase in the number of CIDs from only five hundred in 1962 to twenty thousand by 1975.[10] But by the early 1970s it was becoming apparent that a whole new set of serious problems had developed. The increased interdependency and new responsibilities that characterized CID ownership were leading to mismanagement and even fraud on the part of developers and homeowner associations. Shoddy construction led to costly lawsuits against developers. The condominium market was shaky, and the new town movement ended when the federal government withdrew its support.

In 1973, facing the possibility of collapsing consumer demand for common-interest housing, the National Association of Home Builders and the Urban Land Institute established a new organization, the Community Associations Institute. The mission of CAI is to professionalize the governance and management of homeowner associations and convince the public that CIDs are a better way to live. It has functioned as a life-support system for common-interest housing, attempting to maintain demand for a kind of housing that makes a great deal of supply-side sense for real estate developers. Largely because of land economics, CID housing became not just a novelty or an option, but increasingly the standard form in which the consumer product known as housing is now supplied.

## THE SHRINKING SUBURBAN FRONTIER

For housing to be built at a profit, the land, construction materials, labor, and other expenses must add up to a per-unit cost that is lower than the projected selling price of the house, and that price must be within the anticipated buyer's reach. During the postwar construction boom land gradually came to represent an increasing percentage of the builder's total cost. Martin Mayer described it in this manner: "In 1948, developed land for housing—bulldozing completed, roads built, pipes installed to bring in water and take out sewage—cost the American builder, on the national average, 11 percent of the price of a housing unit; by 1959, it was 15.5 percent; in 1966, 19.6 percent; in the late 1970s, at least 25 percent, frequently 30 percent of the total bill."[11]

This gradual rise in land costs was in large part a result of suburbanization itself. Subdivisions sprouted on the most suitable land first—in flat, stable locations close to cities and existing infrastructure. But as time went by, fewer such sites were available. Developers increasingly found themselves forced to pay higher prices for remaining good land or to expend substantial sums to prepare less desirable land. This preparation might involve costly geotechnical studies and repairs, like massive earth-moving operations to turn hillsides or canyons into flat, stable sites; excavation of rock formations; stabilization of potential landslides; or elaborate drainage systems to remove water from floodplains. It might require bearing all or part of the cost of extending utilities and transpor-

tation links over great distances if local governments exacted such con-
cessions as the price for permitting construction.[12]

Increases in land costs encouraged builders and planners to find
ways to place more houses on less land. Developers were also keenly
aware that preserving open space was becoming important to the local
government agencies that granted construction permits, as the countryside was being gobbled up by one subdivision after another. Some jurisdictions even prohibited development in certain areas through down-zoning.
The prohibition was a genuine threat to the building industry.[13]

Common-interest developments offered a way to shrink lot sizes, and
they allowed builders to satisfy the need felt by home-buyers and public
agencies to preserve some ambiance of nature. Using smaller lots and
commonly owned open spaces managed by homeowner associations,
builders could create low-cost amenities like parks and tennis courts
without increasing the size of the overall development. But the increased
density and common ownership would make homeowners more interdependent than typical suburbanites. Just as the English had to develop
new rules and ways of life as they abandoned the common field system
centuries earlier, Americans would be forced to change some of their
assumptions about home ownership.

The economic logic by which CIDs came to be so popular with builders
was summarized in 1978 by David B. Wolfe in a joint Urban Land
Institute/Community Associations Institute volume:

> The common-interest community is fundamentally a creature of
> land economics, and of man's preference for owning his own
> territory. In any locale only so much land is available for settle-
> ment; and as this land inventory decreases, costs go up, lots for
> shelter become smaller, and houses are eventually built on top of
> one another. When this condensing or stacking takes place, the
> means of owning one's own territory must also be modified.
>
> A result of diminishing lot sizes has often been the require-
> ment by public agencies of open, undeveloped space to compen-
> sate for the greater residential density. . . . Ownership of this
> open space generally resides in the community through a non-
> profit, usually nonstock corporation to which all owners belong.
> . . . These reciprocal rights and obligations are the basis for the
> tie between individual titles—the common-interest aspect of the
> title.[14]

# THE CAMPAIGN TO INCREASE DENSITY

In 1960 the American Society of Planning Officials (ASPO) prepared a report, "Cluster Subdivisions," that proposed CIDs as a solution for the monotony of traditional "gridiron" subdivisions and for "two problems that plague almost every rapidly growing community on the expanding fringes of our metropolitan areas. The first problem is the disappearance of the open countryside; the second, the high cost of big-lot land development."[15]

To address these concerns, the report described a new concept known as the cluster subdivision, which had two essential characteristics: "The first is a characteristic of design and site planning in which several houses are grouped together on a tract of land. Each cluster of houses serves as a module, which is set off from others like it by an intervening space that helps give visual definition to each individual group. The second characteristic of the cluster subdivision, as it is often proposed, is the presence of undeveloped land that is held for the common enjoyment of the neighboring residents or the community at large" (p. 2).

By grouping the houses on small lots, a developer could either leave part of the land in its natural state, saving development costs, or build some relatively inexpensive amenity on it. The report notes that most cluster designs provided for special features—parks, swimming pools, golf courses, or tennis courts—on common land (p. 15).

Although it notes that such areas can be dedicated to public ownership, the report observes that this "may destroy the exclusiveness of the common open space, as well as the feeling of seclusion." Instead, the report explains, the common property could be privately owned by "a nonprofit community corporation," such as that used at Radburn, in which "restrictive covenants were used in conjunction with privately held common land" and "arrangements were made for a property owners' association to operate from the beginning" (p. 25).

Even though CIDs appeared to offer a legal mechanism by which economical and innovative small-lot developments could be organized, existing zoning and subdivision regulations were obstacles to cluster subdivisions. The laws prescribed minimum lot sizes, setbacks, and maximum densities incompatible with the cluster concept. So builders began a campaign to change the laws. In its report ASPO notes that already "efforts are being made to develop regulations which will permit these new developments without cumbersome and uncertain review procedures" (pp. 28–29).

Soon builders and planners would succeed in redefining the meaning of *density*. Residential zoning laws and subdivision regulations typically regulated density by prescribing minimum lot sizes, as well as specific minimum setbacks for front, back, and side yards. The restrictions focused on the size of each lot and the location of the house on the lot. Builders launched a campaign to change that premise of public land-use law. They argued that public agencies should consider not the size of individual residential lots but the number of people living in the entire development—including undeveloped open space where nobody would ever live and on which the builder would expend little or no development cost. The focus should shift, they contended, from the size of the individual lot to the overall population density of the project.

A 1961 report entitled "New Approaches to Residential Land Development," funded by the Urban Land Institute and the National Association of Home Builders, launched a frontal assault on the "single-lot" focus of zoning and on other public land-use controls. The report artfully phrased its demand for smaller lots, blaming public authorities—not the builders—for the deficiencies of suburbia, condemning "the engineering and mechanical approach to the subdivision and partitioning of land, as reflected in most of the subdivision standards and regulations now in effect. . . . The objective of this study has been to look beyond the stereotyped and often sterile developments that have resulted from this approach, and to explore new possibilities or re-explore old ones that show promise of satisfying the physical, economic and esthetic requirements of modern urban and suburban living within the realistic limits of value and cost."[16]

The new approaches illustrated by proposed or actual developments in Canada, Alaska, Cuba, Brazil, and elsewhere included planned-unit developments, cluster subdivisions, and town houses that used smaller lot sizes. But none of these arrangements could be realized in most American jurisdictions, given the "arbitrary public controls" in existence. Accordingly, the report promotes "flexible zoning controls" and "improved subdivision regulations" that will permit what would otherwise be impermissibly high residential densities (p. 7).

Under the ULI proposal, planned-unit developments would feature lots as small as three thousand square feet, but "lot dimensions and areas do not have to meet specific ordinance requirements" as long as the entire development, including the open, undeveloped land, conforms to "basic overall density requirements of the zoning district" (pp. 9–10).

"Cluster subdivisions," the report notes, "are just one form of residential development that will emerge when 'minimum lot size' zoning is
replaced by density control." Citing Radburn as a cluster development,
the report calls for small lots and common open spaces that would be "for
the exclusive use of property owners within the created community" and
run by neighborhood associations. Because "the standard zoning ordinance makes no provision for the unusual cluster method, new regulations are required." Such regulations would, again, involve counting the
undeveloped land in calculating density, not just the tiny lots on which
people actually live (pp. 23–25).

ULI frankly admits that so-called town house developments are
really just row houses, noting, without irony, that "anyone who is accustomed to apartment living is a good prospect for row houses." The
report argues that the absence of any yard worth mentioning is really an
advantage over the single-family detached house: "Specifically and as
one of its dominant assets, the town house enables the family to occupy
most of the land within its own property lines." To evaluate this argument, one need only imagine suburbanites being jealous because their
2,500-square-foot detached house covers only 42 percent of their 6,000-
square-foot lot while the neighboring town house occupies 90 percent of a
2,500-square-foot lot.

To illustrate cost savings, a table shows that a hypothetical town
house development with a density of twelve families per acre would yield
a relative land value of forty-eight thousand dollars per acre. All else
being equal, a development of single-family houses with a density of five
families per acre would produce a land value of only twenty thousand
dollars per acre (pp. 37–39).

In proposing the "flexible zoning controls" that would permit Americans to enjoy this increase in density, the report emphasizes the need to
attack the "status quo of zoning" in government and in the court of public
opinion. It is made clear that the public must be convinced that increased
density will bring better living. "Such revisions of zoning as may be
accomplished to effect increased densities and other objectives will come
about largely by mobilizing public opinion. Without the support of public
opinion for new and better concepts of urban growth, nothing will happen. If better use of the land is to be gained an increase in density is
demanded. With such increase will come savings in land, money, and
services and a much better physical environment" (p. 59).

Major changes in public land use controls are required, ULI argues, so that "the fresh thinking among designers should not be burdened with antiquated and outmoded subdivision regulations or with closed minds in public agencies" (p. 83). ULI provides samples of such proposed changes in laws and government attitudes in appendices, one of which is a letter from Charles Ascher in which he emphasizes the need for maintaining exclusivity through homeowner associations. Ascher argues that open spaces in cluster developments should be not be dedicated to the public but should be privately owned and maintained by homeowner associations, as at Radburn, because "if a municipality takes over the common spaces, they become public parks accessible to all residents of the municipality. . . . Let's not spawn gardens that look beautiful in a promotional brochure, but that are destined to become unkempt dumps" (p. 132).

In a follow-up report in 1963 ULI provides detailed comparative cost, area, and design figures for a variety of specific designs. This report, entitled *Innovations vs. Traditions in Community Development*, carries forward the argument for increased density. "Higher density developments have a number of advantages. For the developer, the principal advantage is the reduction of per unit costs. For the inhabitants, both public and private open space is created and depending on the development, a choice of dwelling unit types can be provided. For the municipality, operational economies as well as a more livable community environment can be achieved, providing municipal regulations permit design innovations."[17]

The report then shows how land costs on a hypothetical one-hundred-sixty-acre subdivision can be reduced by cutting lot sizes, lot width, or side yard requirements; how building costs can by reduced by constructing town houses and patio houses; and how clustering houses can reduce the cost of building roads and installing utilities.

In discussing how open spaces are to be maintained, ULI again argues in favor of homeowner associations. Among the advantages is the power of exclusion: "Existing as private or semi-private areas they may exclude undesirable elements or trouble-makers drifting in, youngsters who 'take over' facilities and push out residents. Those not living close by and unable to benefit from small local parks should neither be required to support such areas by public taxes nor allowed to invade the quiet and privacy of those enjoying the benefits created by private methods."[18]

The Federal Housing Administration soon joined enthusiastically in promoting a boom in CID construction, echoing the themes of developer publications of earlier decades. In 1963 FHA released an influential manual entitled *Planned-Unit Development with a Homes Association*.[19] It provided planners and developers with guidelines and standards for obtaining FHA insurance for CIDs, which FHA wished to encourage. The manual begins by emphasizing the need to "husband a valuable and rapidly shrinking commodity—land." Rapid urbanization now required an "economical single-family living unit adaptable to urban densities, yet keeping many of the attractive features of the suburban home" (p. 2). The answer, according to FHA, is "housing subdivisions which incorporate privately owned, open, common areas and provide for the creation of a means of maintaining the common properties. . . . With such a development, the benefits to be derived from the common properties will be reflected in the FHA appraisals of the homes, and thus in long-term low-interest home mortgages. This makes it economically possible for the developer to create such a development complete with improved common properties, and to offer the home properties favorably in a competitive market" (p. 1).

The common areas are to be privately owned and used exclusively by residents because "public maintenance of common properties that are readily accessible to the general public may encourage heavy public use which can adversely affect the residents of the subdivision" (p. 4).

The common properties are to be managed by private homeowner associations. The manual makes it clear that it will not approve applications for PUD mortgage insurance unless the developer creates a homeowner association with the power to enforce "protective covenants" that will "run with the land . . . and set a firm legal foundation for conserving the plan of the unit continuously into the future." The prescription reads like vintage Jesse Clyde Nichols:

There are certain legal 'musts' which FHA requires in connection with an agency approval of a planned-unit development. . . . The subdivision plat, dedication, covenants, and other recorded agreements must:

a. Legally create an automatic-membership nonprofit homes association;

b. Place title to the common property in the homes association or give definite assurance that it automatically will be so placed within a reasonable, definite time;

c. Appropriately limit the uses of the common property;

d. Give each lot owner the right to the use and enjoyment of the community property;

e. Place responsibility for operation and maintenance of the common property in the homes association;

f. Place an association charge on each lot in a manner which will (1) assure sufficient association funds, and (2) provide adequate safeguards for the lot owners against undesirably high charges;

g. Give each lot owner voting rights in the association. (p. 52)

The reader is assured that, based on ULI research, homeowner associations are immensely popular with residents. Even though only a few hundred such associations existed at the time, FHA shows unquestioning faith in the research arm of the building industry, proclaiming that "the incidence of resident satisfaction and favorable market effect is extremely high. Problems are relatively few; solutions are available" (p. 4).

In the same report FHA also echoes the position of the Urban Land Institute on the need for local governments to align with builders' new views on density by creating exceptions for PUDS. "The street-and-lot approach of the usual local standards often is incompatible with the basic approach of a well-designed planned-unit. If so, the local standards are unusable even as a limited measure of the suitability of the proposed design. . . . A planned-unit provision in the local subdivision regulations and zoning ordinance eliminates this difficulty. . . . More and more, localities are adding such planned-unit provisions to their regulations" (p. 11).

The manual announces that "FHA no longer uses density directly as a land-use measure," having substituted a new concept known as land-use intensity that would allow builders great flexibility in creating projects with what previously would have been unacceptably high densities. This amorphous standard represents "the overall relationships of structural mass and open space of a developed property or a development plan."

Maximum allowable intensity is to be "determined individually for each planned-unit development by the characteristics of the site and its relationship to the community pattern."[20]

The publication of *Planned-Unit Development with a Homes Association* was a watershed event in the history of CIDs because it announced to the building industry that the Federal Housing Administration had decided to insure PUDs. Forty to fifty thousand copies of the publication were circulated, and it was a major factor in the PUD boom that followed. The story behind this volume illuminates the private-public partnership that characterized the growth of CIDs.[21]

A pivotal figure in the CID boom was Byron R. Hanke, a Harvard-trained urban planner and landscape architect who was chief of the land planning division of FHA from 1945 to 1972. When President Kennedy took office in 1961, Richard J. Canavan, formerly of the National Association of Home Builders, was appointed assistant commissioner for technical standards of FHA and became Hanke's superior. Hanke proposed a sort of sabbatical for himself, during which he would explore the idea of CID housing. Hanke pointed out that there was general agreement on the need to create open spaces in housing developments, but local governments were not interested in being responsible for them. Who, he asked, was going to run them? Hanke argued for private homeowner associations, pointing out such examples as Reston, Virginia; the Country Club District in Kansas City; Forest Hills; Louisburg Square in Boston; and even the homeowner association at his own second home on Chesapeake Bay. He said he would like to research the idea further. Canavan agreed. After an abortive effort to carry out his research through the Senior Federal Executive Fellow program at the Brookings Institution, Hanke suggested approaching the Urban Land Institute.

Hanke pointed out that he had a "long, strong relationship" with ULI; that ULI was tied in with the building industry; and that they had a great deal of know-how. A contract was drawn up, but the FHA legal department said that the FHA could not assign a government employee to a private organization for what was then estimated to be three months (the study ended up taking the better part of two years). The attorneys were finally convinced that Hanke could go if several other government agencies would cosponsor the study; after that was accomplished, clearance was given to proceed with the contract.

Working with attorney Jan Krasnowiecki and urban sociologist William C. Loring of the Public Health Service, Hanke went on full-time assignment to the Urban Land Institute. The study, which began in 1962, would culminate in 1964 with the publication by ULI of a massive, authoritative volume that became the most influential document in the CID boom. The *Homes Association Handbook* spends some four hundred pages telling developers and planners in minutest detail exactly how to set up a homeowner association; it includes widely imitated model forms of restrictive covenants, articles of incorporation, and bylaws. The handbook is a compendium of the community builders' experience with CIDs and is notable for setting out a carefully edited, often-cited history of homeowner associations and their activities that avoids reference to race restrictive covenants. Although it acknowledges that there have been "various difficulties and problems in some associations, such as establishing legal agreements, keeping active and collecting assessments," the handbook is overwhelmingly enthusiastic about CID housing.[22]

Hanke's important activities in promoting CID housing continued while the handbook project was in preparation. In 1963 Hanke became aware of a new "townhouse-on-the-green" development built by Kaufman and Broad in Orange County, California. It "hit the market fantastically," and other builders wanted to imitate it.[23] They were unable to do so, however, because FHA would not issue mortgage insurance for this new kind of common-ownership property. The Orange County development received insurance only because Hanke, as head of the land planning division, specifically recommended it. But the no-insurance policy remained in force for other properties.

To remedy the insurance problem, Hanke persuaded Canavan to send him and three other high-level FHA employees to study the project on site.[24] After a one-week study they recommended that FHA insure developments like the one in Orange County subject to certain requirements. A new policy, complete with standards, was produced within one month, in May 1963.

That summer Hanke called six top FHA officials to the commissioner's conference room. He spread on the table all the photos he had taken of the development in California, along with material from his ongoing ULI project. He told the officials that FHA should put the material he had developed so far with the new PUD standards and circulate them in a good publication. He said that the only way to accomplish such a task was to set up a team consisting of the four California study participants and a writer or two. But, he emphasized, the document had to be produced and published without any FHA review so that it could be ready for distribution at the annual meeting of the National Association of Home Builders in Chicago. The objective was "to sell this thing to America."

The key FHA officials agreed, and the project was approved on August 1, 1963. The deadline was met, and the document was distributed at the NAHB meeting. Its impact was enormous. As Hanke puts it, "The industry grabbed the idea, and local government accepted it, and FHA insured it, and the concept took off like wildfire." Hanke now says the publication, *Planned-Unit Development with a Homes Association*—which was called "The Green Giant" because of its color and dimensions—"really revolutionized American residential development."

Following *Planned-Unit Development,* Hanke went back to ULI to complete the *Homes Association Handbook,* which was for ten years one of the institute's best-selling volumes. He then returned to FHA, where he worked until 1972. He was again to play a critical role in the CID movement by serving as the prime mover, under the auspices of NAHB and ULI, in creation of the Community Associations Institute.

The significance of the new ULI-inspired policies concerning homeowner associations did not go entirely unnoticed in academia; at least one writer offered the sort of questioning, critical perspective that was missing from the FHA reports. Stanley Scott noted that the new flexibility of the FHA regarding housing design was a good thing, but he asked whether "private government" would "serve the public interest." Noting that what he calls "the FHA-ULI homes association policy" was based on a "meticulously researched and well-edited but distinctly partisan" report by the ULI, Scott sees a class bias. "The lower income brackets are viewed as a likely source of special problems. Policies of exclusiveness are only thinly veiled as efforts to 'maintain high standards,' or 'insure property values,' or provide a 'private community.'"

Scott argues that the FHA-ULI policy would bring about excessive control of thousands of inhabitants by private associations manipulated by developers; institutionalization of segregated housing patterns; and disenfranchisement of renters—all in the interest of maintaining property values and stabilizing residential patterns for long periods. He points out that the twin devices of restrictive covenants and homeowner associations "favor the interests of the developer and lender in almost every way," and anticipates that "uniform and national application of such policies to all FHA-supported communities built in the foreseeable future—during the crucial era of urban restructuring that lies ahead—could be most unfortunate."[25]

## OWNING A PIECE OF THE FORTRESS

The need for developers to learn how to create and manage homeowner associations became even more pressing as condominium housing made its American debut. Condominium ownership produces extremely high density and involves the smallest tangible ownership interest of any form of housing. It is essentially a legal way for people to own, buy, and sell units in an apartment building. The owner of a condominium typically has an individual ownership interest that is a legal fiction, consisting of just the "airspace" inside the unit. The entire building and the ground on which it sits are owned in common. The two interests—an individual unit and an undivided share in the whole building—cannot be sold separately. Because the entire structure is held in common there must be a homeowner association.

Condominium ownership—"horizontal ownership" in legal parlance—developed independently of other forms of common-interest housing. It has a long history in other countries, notably Europe, but was not recognized in the United States until 1961, when the building industry was searching for ways to market housing with increased density.

Writers frequently state, erroneously, that condominiums originated in ancient Rome. The word *condominium* is of Latin origin and can be loosely translated as "common ownership." The term "derives chiefly from its adoption in the Italian codes in the 1930s."[26]

But Robert G. Natelson argues persuasively that Roman law was hostile to the idea of horizontal ownership. He cites the maxim *Superficies solo cedit,* which has been translated as "An improvement yields to the soil" or "Title to things connected to the ground is vested in the owner of the ground." The maxim reflects a "vertical" concept of property ownership in which the land and the buildings on it are owned by the same person.[27]

Natelson's research suggests that horizontal property regimes originated in Germany during the Middle Ages. The Germans, Natelson argues, were comfortable with the idea that one person could own an improvement on land owned by another, perhaps because they were acquainted with living in tents and movable cabins. By the twelfth century individuals were buying *Stockwerkseigentum* ("story property"), floors in buildings. Rudolf Huebner, in his 1918 work *A History of Germanic Private Law,* describes this form of ownership, which indeed was similar to the condominium concept: "From the 1100s onward we already find extremely widespread in German towns so-called 'story' or 'room-age' ownership. . . . Houses were horizontally divided, and the specific parts so created—the stories, floors, and cellars—were held by different persons in separate ownership; this being associated, as a rule, with community ownership of the building site and the portions of the building (walls, stairs, roof, etc.) that were used in common" (emphasis in original).[28]

The reasons behind German recognition of this type of ownership offer a striking historical parallel to some modern condominiums. Many of today's large European cities once were walled enclaves into which people crowded for protection from marauding barbarians. Story-property was "a result of a quest for living space in congested walled cities struggling with a growing urban population oppressed by the limitations of fortress living."[29] The genuine "fortress mentality" of that combative age is echoed in such inner-city condominium developments as the redeveloped Bunker Hill area of downtown Los Angeles. Mike Davis vividly describes how people "live in 'fortress cities' brutally divided between 'fortified cells' of affluent society and 'places of terror' where the police battle the criminalized poor."[30] Such condominium developments are, in a sense, a return to the ancient concept of city as fortress, in which society's haves huddle to defend their lives and possessions against have-nots outside the gates.

France recognized horizontal property as early as 1804, and later Belgium (1924), Sweden (1931), Italy (1934), and Spain (1939) did so as well.[31] The concept was then transplanted to Latin America (notably Brazil in 1928) and to Puerto Rico (1951).

The Puerto Rican experience was used as supporting evidence in the builders' successful bid to persuade Congress to recognize condominiums in the United States. In 1960 builders active in Puerto Rico wished to construct high-rise, high-density, middle-income condominium housing there. They petitioned Congress to extend FHA mortgage insurance to such housing, a type that was unknown in the United States. At House and Senate hearings legislators were assured that the condominium was not a new form of housing but one with a long and successful history.[32] The following year Congress enacted section 234 of the National Housing Act, which extended FHA insurance to condominiums nationwide.[33]

FHA then issued model state condominium legislation, and state legislatures immediately began to enact laws recognizing condominium ownership. By 1967 all fifty states had laws authorizing condominium ownership,[34] and by 1987 there were more than 4.2 million units of condominium housing in the United States.[35]

## NEW TOWNS: INSTANT CITIES IN THE SUBURBS?

The most ambitious undertaking in the history of CID housing was the effort to plan, finance, and build common interest developments the size of entire cities. As many as one hundred thirty of these new towns of more than one thousand acres were built or proposed from 1960 through the early 1970s. By one accounting, those actually built had an average size of ten thousand acres; their projected populations varied from the tens of thousands to the hundreds of thousands.[36]

New towns were advertised as American versions of Ebenezer Howard's garden cities, and they drew to some extent on the experiences of the Europeans, particularly the English, who had constructed a number of planned communities.[37] Most American new towns were planned to be more self-sufficient than other subdivisions, with some provisions for community centers, shopping complexes, and often space for commercial development. None had the degree of self-sufficiency Howard envisioned, however, and they generally housed residents who worked elsewhere. This commuter population led some to argue that American new towns were really just new communities whose builders were involved in an exercise in land economics rather than dramatic social planning. Edward Eichler and Marshall Kaplan undertook a thorough study of community builders during the new town years, and they made this distinction: "A new town is an attempt to break the pattern of urban growth, and at the same time to shift development to different places and to control it. A new community is a way of ordering the business of land development at the fringe of American metropolitan areas."[38]

America's so-called new towns really fit the latter description. They offered maximum efficiency in land use because they were literally planned and built from the ground up—planners did not have to adapt the design to a surrounding community. And they allowed developers to build housing with higher density than ordinary subdivisions. Master planning also was said to be the cure for suburban sprawl, congestion, and chaos, and for the social segregation created by the rapid suburbanization of affluent white families. Common areas, including land and facilities, would be run by private governments that would foster a "return" to village democracy by permitting a level of direct participation and sense of control denied to the urban citizen.[39]

Yet beneath the democratic and egalitarian rhetoric was often a marketing strategy that targeted the affluent and emphasized exclusivity. Builders of new towns felt that the combination of rising American incomes and dissatisfaction with ordinary suburban housing had created a market for "amenity-packed" communities. These developers decided to build housing for what they saw as a growing population of upper-middle-class Americans with above-average incomes who would be willing to pay for expensive houses, supplied complete with a "lifestyle," including lakes, recreation centers, and other commonly owned amenities. Accordingly, community builders made two basic marketing decisions at the outset: "to increase the cost of the land by installing amenities, and then to effect housing prices which are even higher than those the costs necessitate."[40]

These decisions were predicated on the assumption that "people who represent the strongest source of demand for new communities . . . will react more favorably to the community, at least during its initial years of development, if it does not contain lower-priced houses."[41] Marketing studies showed that these potential buyers saw planned communities largely as a way to safeguard property values. "From the buyers' viewpoint, then, one basic purpose of 'planning' in a new community is to minimize the insecurity that surrounds such a venture. More specifically, 'planning' will prevent certain negative possibilities, and ensure certain positive conditions—for one, the 'class image' . . . created by the price of nearby homes. . . . For the buyer in a new community, the essential role of 'planning' is to maximize the potential appreciation of his investment."[42]

These buyers also saw restrictive covenants as an aspect of the planning process that would tend to keep out lower-income buyers. In a study of two new towns in California, respondents emphasized that, as one put it, "there will be restrictions. There won't be any high wires. You won't look out and see trailers, and no big trucks. It will be nice and quiet. They won't allow people to tear the place up. They will have to take care of their houses and yards. Keep it nice looking. We would have bought the house anyway but it just made it easier to make up our minds faster 'cause there will be plants and nice yards that will cause the value of this house to increase."[43]

Eichler and Kaplan evaluate this and other comments by new town buyers as indicating a view of planning that associated restrictive covenants with keeping out people of lower social class. In Foster City, a new community of eleven thousand homes, 69 percent of residents surveyed said they would oppose including a neighborhood of homes only 13 percent less expensive than those already in the development, even if it were separated from other neighborhoods by a lagoon and a row of apartments.[44] As Eichler and Kaplan explain, "It became clear that this view of 'planning' was closely bound up with the question of the degree of tolerance which residents of Janss/Conejo and Foster showed toward lower-income families. 'Planning' to these residents was a guarantee against the introduction of 'undesirable' elements close to one's house and immediate surroundings. Not surprisingly, the most undesirable were lower-priced homes inhabited by lower-income people."[45]

Builders knew such attitudes were prevalent among the buyers they chose to target, but they apparently overestimated the numbers of affluent buyers. In designing new towns primarily as exclusive havens for relatively wealthy buyers, they made a serious marketing error. Eichler and Kaplan concluded in 1967 that "community builders correctly perceived a tendency in their initial market but now have overreacted to this trend. Projections indicate that the strongest demand for housing in fringe locations will continue to be at the lower end of the current spectrum of price ranges being offered."[46]

In simpler terms, as Martin Mayer puts it, "At the root of the problem is the fact that New Towns ask too many people to buy with their house too many things they do not want, or at least do not want at that price."[47]

Even though serious flaws in the marketing logic behind the new towns were becoming apparent to some as early as the mid-1960s, the lure of potentially huge profits drew large corporations into the housing business. Soon the federal government was to become involved in an ill-fated effort to promote new town construction.

## Housing as Product: Corporations Enter the Market

New towns were enormously risky ventures, even for the large merchant builders.[48] The developer would be required to expend millions of dollars before a single house could be sold. Moreover, there was no guarantee that potential buyers would be enthusiastic about moving into a town that had no history and no identity except in the mind of a planner and where residents, like pioneers, would have to create a sense of community and social organization.

The risk was a serious concern because the economics of private community building require selling nearly all of the houses in a development. A developer's profit is realized in the sale of the last houses, after costs have been recovered on sales of the earlier ones. Consequently, a project whose sales stall at 85 percent of capacity is generally a disaster.[49]

Because the huge capital requirements of new towns exceeded the capacity of even large community builders, many of these "instant cities," as Theodore Roszak called them, were built or financed by major corporations that had never been involved in real estate development before— Gulf Oil, Humble Oil, Goodyear Tire and Rubber, Westinghouse, General Electric, and others.[50] Corporations were attracted by the profit potential of mass-produced housing and were able to finance such projects through the stock market rather than through bank loans. Uriel Reichman discussed how this turn to large-scale construction promoted takeover of the housing business by major corporations:

> The sixties marked a noticeable change in the building industry as capital-rich corporations became increasingly involved in the real estate market. Land development became big business and major corporations entered the field for the first time. Appreciating the profit potential involved, traditional money suppliers to builders, such as insurance corporations and pension funds, made huge investments and employed more aggressive policies in order to acquire a "piece of the action." Other large enterprises, not previously engaged in building and land development activities, likewise became involved in the land development market through a wave of mergers and acquisitions, through large-scale joint ventures, and through the formation of land development subsidiaries. At the same time, a growing number of building corporations went public and thus were able to tap the stock market for equity capital. The potential of the real estate market encouraged the construction of large-scale projects which, it was found, did not entail the difficulties that had traditionally hampered developers.[51]

These new "housing giants," as one writer called them, formed an organization in 1968 called the Council of Housing Producers; by 1970 it had grown to thirteen giant firms. These corporations had produced 41,729 homes in the preceding year alone.[52] They consisted primarily of subsidiaries of giant corporations that had bought out existing builders or formed their own sub-units to carry out large-scale housing construction. They included such organizations as Levitt and Sons (which had become a subsidiary of ITT); Occidental Petroleum Land & Development Corporation (a subsidiary of Occidental Petroleum); Alcan Design Homes (a subsidiary of Alcan Aluminum); Boise Cascade Building Company (a subsidiary of Boise Cascade Corporation); Larwin Group (a subsidiary of CNA Financial Corporation); Lewers & Cooke (a subsidiary of U.S. Plywood-Champion Papers); and subsidiaries of American Standard, National Homes Corporation, and Dreyfus Development Corporation.

Among the many other large corporations that entered the housing business during the 1960s were U.S. Steel, Reynolds Aluminum, ALCOA, Weyerhauser, National Gypsum, the Pennsylvania Railroad, Loew's Corporation, Avco Corporation, Chrysler, Ford Motor Company, Metropolitan Life Insurance Company, Prudential Insurance Company, and other leading insurers.[53] They brought with them billions of dollars in capital, the view that housing was just another mass-produced consumer commodity to be sold at a profit, and a penchant for the sort of highly sophisticated financing schemes used previously in other corporate enterprises.[54]

## The Federal New Communities Program

Many new towns were privately financed and constructed, including some of the largest ventures: Irvine, California; Columbia, Maryland; and Reston, Virginia. But to minimize the risk involved and to obtain the enormous capital required, in the late 1960s some builders turned to the federal government for assistance.[55]

The historical precedent for federal involvement in new town construction was the New Deal-era Greenbelt Town program, which consisted of three communities built on the Radburn model by the federal government's Resettlement Administration under the leadership of Rexford Tugwell. Heavily influenced by the Regional Planning Association of America designers of Radburn, this program, begun in 1935, appealed to the government as a way to create jobs and provide low-cost housing in the depths of the depression. For its designers, however, it was a chance to prove the worth of the "Radburn idea," which had been short-circuited by national economic collapse. The Greenbelt towns were intended to offer an alternative to what their designers saw as wasteful and unhealthy urban growth patterns; demonstrate the superiority and cost-effectiveness of master-planned communities; stop urban decay and economically segregated housing patterns; and "restore to all classes the warm community life of the rural village."[56]

Nine Greenbelt towns were planned, but only three were constructed, and none to its anticipated size. Utilities had been laid out for as many as two thousand homes, but Greenbelt, in Maryland, ended up consisting of only 890 residences; Greenhills, in Ohio, 676; and Greendale, in Wisconsin, only 572.[57] Although the government had intended the towns to be "normal American communities" with residents being local property owners and taxpayers, the federal government decided to retain ownership and act as landlord.[58] Construction costs were higher than anticipated, which led to rents being above the reach of their intended population. Instead of the towns housing the urban working class, as planned, they were populated by people with average annual incomes ranging from $1,560 (at Greenbelt) to $1,771 (at Greenhills). Tugwell acknowledged that most urban dwellers in 1936 were making less than $1,200 per year.[59]

Those who promoted the Greenbelt towns felt that a favorable public reaction to this dramatic federal housing initiative was critical so that Congress could be persuaded to expand it. But the majority of those who wrote and spoke about the program viewed it negatively. Some considered it part of a trend toward "socialistic regimentation disguised as cooperative planning." And, even though one-third of the American population was inadequately housed, others decried the way the federal government had put itself in competition with private enterprise.[60] Congress ultimately rejected the program, selling the towns off in the early 1950s, and private builders did not imitate the Greenbelt plan. Joseph Arnold, in his comprehensive study of the program, concluded that the idea of the federal government solving housing problems by building large planned communities was simply too radical for many in government and the building industry. "The failure of the Greenbelt towns to impress either government officials or industrial leaders is rather easily traceable to the program's radical challenge to fundamental patterns of urban growth and real estate practice. That the program was sponsored by the New Deal and thus became a partisan political issue only sealed its doom."[61]

It was not until the late 1960s, with population increasing, sprawl plaguing many cities, and land becoming scarce, that government and business again turned to the idea of large-scale federally assisted planned communities. This time the government was not to construct the houses, however, but would act as a guarantor for private builders, assuming much of the risk that the projects would be unprofitable.

The federal new communities program began during a time when the Johnson administration was receptive to proposals for aiding cities and influencing the pattern of urban development, and when aiding private developers of new towns seemed a logical component of an emerging national urban growth policy. The first attempt at passing a new communities bill died in committee in 1964, but two years later a revised version was passed. That bill set up a small experimental program to assist large-scale residential construction.[62] In 1968, Title 4 of the Housing and Urban Development Act authorized HUD to provide various kinds of help to new town developers, and until 1983 the federal new communities program labored under thirteen changes of leadership, several reorganizations, and the vagaries of widely different philosophies from year to year.[63]

The most important federal legislation regarding new towns was Title 7 of the Urban Growth and New Communities Act of 1970. The course of this ill-starred effort was tersely summarized in a 1984 postmortem report by HUD, which administered the program. "Under this program . . . thirteen new community developers received guarantees for their debts for land acquisition and development. By 1973, however, the financial viability of their communities had become a serious concern; by 1975, the Department decided that no further new commitments would be made under the Title VII program. Following this moratorium, there was an effort to identify and support those communities with some potential for financial viability and to dispose of others. In 1981, there was a decision to close out the program by the year 1984."[64]

The federal government guaranteed loans from private financial institutions to the developers of these thirteen new towns, which were to consist of a total of 250,000 housing units for 785,000 people and create more than 200,000 jobs. In 1974 Congress supplemented these guarantees with $137 million in block grants for some of the developers' costs.

The "serious concern" about "financial viability" arose quickly, when twelve of the thirteen developers ran out of money, most within two or three years of signing the project agreement. All but one—Woodlands, in Texas—defaulted on its loan payments. Nine of the new towns had to be acquired and sold by HUD, and the ownership of three others had to be restructured. The program eventually cost the federal government more than $561 million, of which $445 million represented repayments of defaulted loans and interest.

The Department of Housing and Urban Development concluded that, although the new communities program had "accomplished several noteworthy objectives," such as creating more heterogeneous communities, high-quality physical development, and balanced land use, it had done so in a "costly and inefficient way."[65] The agency attributed the program's failure to a recession, exaggerated estimates of population growth, poor locations, lack of expertise and resources among the developers, inadequate management by HUD, and a financing structure that did not permit the developers adequate flexibility in meeting enormous start-up costs. As HUD concluded, "The partnership between the private and public sectors, as structured by Title VII, clearly did not work."[66]

The HUD-assisted new towns were not the only failures. The experience of developers who did not participate in Title 7 ranged for the most part from catastrophic failure to modest success, and, as Martin Mayer has noted, it was not "the sort of success that would encourage rational others to go and do likewise."[67] This suggested that something other than a flawed form of private-public partnership was to blame, such as the dubious marketing strategies of new town developers.

The new town movement ground to a halt during the 1970s, but the housing industry's commitment to CID housing continued. Developers refined the early-1960s strategy of using common property as a cost-saving mechanism, and they continued building with increased density while also providing open space and other amenities. But instead of building massive projects that overestimated the number of affluent buyers in a given area, they built large numbers of smaller projects and used pinpoint marketing strategies.

By the time the boom years of the 1980s arrived, CID housing was the norm in the building industry. Builders were selling new towns in small packages and advertising lifestyles on a reduced scale. Buyers were subtly invited to ignore the fact that nothing but a concrete block wall separated their development of two hundred simulated Cape Cod clapboard houses, complete with bay windows, from two hundred quasi-Mediterranean homes covered in beige stucco, built around a patio, and crowned in red tile. As Weiss and Watts note, the most recent explosion in CID construction consisted largely of projects that contained hundreds rather than hundreds of thousands of units.[68] "Since the mid-1970s, much of the growth in condominiums and PUDs has been in relatively small projects, often infill development in built-out neighborhoods. . . . Smaller projects increasingly include common property primarily to reduce costs rather than to promote a maintenance-free or recreational lifestyle."[69]

The move toward smaller projects has permitted developers to continue realizing the profits of CID housing as they avoid some of the risks associated with large projects.

The American experience with new towns illustrates the degree to which considerations of private land economics constrain and determine the shape of our metropolitan areas. Government policies on housing and urban planning seemed largely limited to ratification of decisions made by real estate developers and driven by considerations of profit. The most activist public policies involved insuring large-scale developers against the consequences of their own mistakes so that profits remained in private hands while losses were socialized.

Carol Christensen observes that most American new towns fell far short of the claims made by their developers. No recognizable public purposes were served. Instead of being laboratories for a new kind of town, they became "leisure 'cities' which provide a pleasant environment for middle class families in a setting which assures the protection of one's investment. Although proposed as vehicles for social change, new towns in America have accommodated to the culture more than they have reformed it."[70]

Although developers of new towns routinely invoked the name and vision of Ebenezer Howard, promising to build self-sufficient and heterogeneous communities, they finished by building suburbs that were bigger and more sophisticated than the existing ones. Typically, the promised industrial and commercial base never materialized, and the residents became commuters. Rather than housing a cross section of the population as advertised, new towns were built primarily for the white upper-middle class.

The smaller developments built in recent years share these traits and reflect the growing sophistication of the corporatized real estate industry. By the early 1980s common-interest housing had become a standardized product—like cars or television sets—offered in a finite range of models. Each model is marketed to particular groups of consumers, and each packages the idea of life in a private utopia in a slightly different way.

This approach makes a great deal of economic sense to large-scale private builders, but the spread of CID housing may have unexamined social consequences that would ordinarily concern government. Public policy regarding housing is made in an increasingly privatized political environment, however, in which economic considerations are central and social issues are viewed as externalities. Today's CID housing sector is, to a large extent, a logical result of the relation between the real estate industry and government. The role of government has been largely permissive and promotional rather than regulatory or directive. Given a great deal of latitude, the real estate industry followed the path of greatest profit and created suburbia and the consumer product we know as CID housing. At the same time, the industry worked hard to create and sustain a market for that product. One aspect of that effort was the promotion among the American middle class of a utopian ideology of privatism—an ideology that overlays and reinforces sentiments favoring exclusiveness, exclusion, and isolation.

# 5

## The Community Associations Institute: The Care and Feeding of Residential Private Governments

The Community Associations Institute is the nation's
voice on community associations issues.
—CAI Statement of Core Purpose, 1992

CAI was in part a social experiment to see if disparate
interest groups could work together for the common
good. . . . CAI quickly became dominated by those in the
business, principally managers and colleagues. . . . I
sense that the Institute is headed even more surely toward
a manager and colleague trade association. While this is
the easiest way to continue, it disturbs me.
—Lincoln C. Cummings, cofounder of the
Community Associations Institute, 1992

By the early 1970s large-scale real estate developers had established the
professional and legal architecture for mass-producing common-interest
housing developments. Community builders and government officials
had agreed that CID housing was not a novelty but the preferred solution of the building industry concerning difficult problems of land-use
economics.

Through the Urban Land Institute and the National Association of Home Builders developers could obtain publications detailing exactly how to design and build standardized CIDs that would be approved by FHA, drawing on the accumulated wisdom and experience of community builders from Jesse Clyde Nichols' era to the present. ULI could provide numerous case studies of model developments around the country, presented in high-quality format with photographs, architectural renderings, and references. With little effort, a builder who knew next to nothing about CIDs could acquire what amounted to a set of "cookbooks" that would cover every aspect of their design and construction, including marketing to target audiences, obtaining government approval, drafting legal documents, retaining contractors and subcontractors, and setting up and operating a homeowner association.[1] As a result, developers began to build CID housing at a rapid rate. Between 1962 and 1975 the number of homeowner associations increased from fewer than five hundred to twenty thousand.[2]

On the government side of this partnership, the Federal Housing Administration had cleared the way for CID construction by promoting the idea of special PUD ordinances, providing mortgage insurance for CID housing, including condominiums, and by advocating on behalf of CIDs in its own publications. FHA publications and policy making on this issue were, largely, joint products of the federal government and the real estate development industry.

These favorable developments were all on the supply side of the equation, however, and by the late 1960s it was becoming clear that major problems existed on the demand side. Although it was possible to mass-produce CIDs, it was by no means certain that people would buy them.

The disappointing experience of new town developers underscored a simple point: the building industry depended on consumer acceptance of, and demand for, types of housing that made economic sense to builders. Although builders were enthusiastic about common-interest housing because of its profit potential, the early 1970s was a time of crisis for CID advocates as concerns developed about whether middle-class consumers would reject CID housing.

A number of problems presented themselves at once. The national economy was in and out of recession, with housing starts dropping rapidly from 2,357,000 in 1972 to 1,160,000 in 1975.[3] The federal government and private developers were backing away from additional new town construction. The press was beginning to focus on disturbing events that tended to undermine the public image of CID housing. Congress held hearings in connection with a nationally publicized scandal in Florida involving recreation-lease fraud by CID developers.[4] A massive federal study of condominiums and cooperatives revealed that owners were encountering serious construction defects with alarming frequency.[5]

Moreover, CID residents were reporting difficulties with the management and governance of their developments. Weiss and Watts attribute the problems to mismanagement by developers while they controlled the board of directors and developers' failure to adequately prepare and train residents to take over the board after the developer has sold all the units and moved on. Problems were widespread. "Since many developers were unfamiliar with the considerable complexities involved in managing the new PUD and condominium associations, a substantial number experienced major difficulties during the 1960s and early 1970s. A 1973 survey of 1,760 condominium residents found that [residential community associations] had become a problem for the otherwise popular condominium concept. While a sizable majority of the respondents expressed satisfaction with their overall condominium experience, 61 percent rated their community association fair or poor."[6]

The consequences of inadequate and even corrupt management by developers, managers, and owners included underfunding of reserves for contingencies and property maintenance, inadequate or improper enforcement of deed restrictions, and, in some cases, outright theft of association funds. Recognizing that widespread attention to problems like these could cause consumers to recoil from the prospect of living in CID housing, the real estate industry needed to find a way to support consumer demand.

There were two dimensions to this challenge. First was the problem of marketing. CIDs existed because they made enormous economic sense to builders, not because buyers were aching for smaller lots, shared swimming pools, and neighborhood governments. The developers' agenda of land-use economics needed to be translated into another language so that consumers would embrace the idea of CID housing. As with virtually any new consumer product—fast food hamburgers, cable television, compact discs—buyers had to be sold on the concept.

Second was the problem of educating consumers about how to operate the new product. CID housing, seen as a product, is more like a home computer than a toaster because it requires operation of something very complex and delicate: a homeowner association. Residential private government is a product that comes with a long set of instructions, does not operate automatically, and requires a great deal of learning, time, and effort to keep going. By the early 1970s it was becoming apparent to builders that buyers did not understand what they were getting into, could not be counted on to run homeowner associations competently, and needed ongoing organizational support to prevent demand for CID housing from collapsing.

## LIFE SUPPORT FOR PRIVATOPIA

At this critical juncture in the history of CID housing, Byron Hanke, who as chief of the FHA's land planning division had been the prime mover in obtaining FHA insurance for CIDs and was principal author of *Planned-Unit Development with a Homes Association* and *The Homes Association Handbook*, again played a critical role. As early as 1964 Hanke and his co-authors saw the need for an institutional support network for these new organizations. They recommended that metropolitan, regional, and national federations of associations be formed to share information and guidance.[7] Additionally, they recommended that a national private body be created to oversee the activities of HOAS.

A national clearinghouse for information concerning homes associations, and for holding regional workshops on their operation and management would be an invaluable aid in the formation and servicing of metropolitan federations and individual homes associations. It could also provide information and guidance to developers in creating homes associations and their common facilities. In view of the broad benefits of the homes association concept and its rapidly growing application throughout the country, the establishment of such a national clearinghouse should merit the financial support of a national private foundation. With such underwriting for the initial creation and establishment of the clearinghouse, existing homes associations and developers could subscribe to its services. After a few years it could be placed on a self-sustaining basis, the philanthropic underwriting being replaced by membership dues and service fees. The study strongly recommends that the federal agencies and others concerned with housing, health, and general welfare encourage an appropriate national private foundation to underwrite the initial establishment of such a national clearinghouse or council on homes associations.[8]

In August 1966 Richard Canavan attempted to follow through on this proposal. Canavan, who by that time had left his post as FHA's assistant commissioner for technical standards and returned to NAHB as staff vice-president in the Builder Services Division, wrote to the Ford Foundation for support to create "a national clearing house for property owners' associations," but he was unable to arouse interest. The Ford Foundation explained that it was interested in inner-city problems and low-income housing issues, and it declined to support a project that was, in essence, aimed at benefiting middle-class and largely suburban residents.[9]

By the late 1960s and into the early 1970s, reports were mounting of difficulties in homeowner association management. At the time, the only guide to operating an association was the *Homes Association Handbook,* which was becoming dated, and was, as Hanke puts it, "pretty heavy stuff for a guy building houses or a guy on a homeowner association board." Hanke persuaded FHA to send him to several metropolitan areas to hold public meetings or brainstorming sessions regarding the problems of association management. Out of these meetings came a sense that the national association he and his fellow researchers had proposed in 1964 might be the answer.[10]

Hanke initially toyed with the idea of running the organization through FHA, but he soon decided it should be private. He found a receptive ear at ULI and NAHB, where "they were concerned with the whole system breaking down if the operation of these things became a problem." Hanke left FHA in 1972, and in January 1973 he persuaded NAHB to put up thirty thousand dollars to create what was to be the Community Associations Institute.

## THE FOUNDING OF CAI

Hanke, Canavan, and developer David Rhame presented the Community Associations Institute idea at the 1973 NAHB annual meeting and received approval from various committees and ultimately a general meeting of the membership. The builders were especially concerned about creating a potentially troublesome organization of homeowners, whom they regarded as likely "opposition." Concerns about excessive homeowner control were to be reflected in the ultimate design of CAI, which intentionally kept them in check and contributed to a lack of homeowner support for the organization.

In March 1973 Hanke was retained by NAHB as a consultant to design and create CAI. He assembled a team representing what were to be the five constituencies, or "interest groups," composing CAI: developers, property managers, homeowner association directors (referred to by CAI as "homeowners"), professionals who specialized in dealing with homeowner associations (lawyers, accountants, landscapers, and others, referred to in CAI parlance as "professional colleagues"), and public officials. Although the impetus to create CAI came from developers, Hanke felt that the organization had to be more than a single-interest trade association; it needed to represent a consensus among all five of the groups involved in the creation and operation of homeowner associations. This consensus would permit CAI to educate all of the interest groups regarding this specialized subject matter and to take public policy positions that would reflect the interests of all affected groups. Hanke was particularly concerned that homeowner members be assured of influence within the organization so that CAI could perform the critical function of educating association directors and members.

The "design group" that set up CAI included David Stahl, executive vice-president of ULI, who represented "public officials" by virtue of his former service under Mayor Richard J. Daley of Chicago; David Rhame representing developers; David Wolfe representing property managers; Lincoln Cummings, an IBM executive from the Montgomery Village development in Gaithersburg, Maryland, representing homeowners; and others representing "professional colleagues." Canavan was also involved.[11]

Through the summer of 1973 the group met at Hanke's home in Washington, D.C. Hanke and the others discussed at length the structure of the new organization. They debated what functions the organization should perform, how it should be funded, where it should be located, and how the different interests should be represented. They eventually agreed that the new organization would be called the Community Associations Institute and that it would have a board of directors, or trustees, consisting of equal numbers from each interest group.[12] One of the trustees would be elected to serve a one-year term as president. Each interest group would have equal power, and each group would select its own representatives to the board from the general membership.

One important provision dealt with the procedure for CAI taking a position on a public policy issue or piece of legislation. The founders drafted CAI's bylaws so that a majority of the members in each of the interest groups had to agree before a public position could be taken. That is, all five groups had to agree before the organization could act on an issue. This was to apply not only to the national organization but to its chapters. Additionally, the chapters would have to confine themselves to policy positions that were not inconsistent with those of the national CAI board. The unanimity provision, it was felt, would give CAI's positions special credibility with legislative bodies, who could be told honestly that CAI was not a consumer group, developer group, or trade association but a body reflecting a real consensus among all those concerned.[13]

The founders took this vision of the organization as a quasi-public interest group seriously. As Cummings puts it, "CAI was not intended to be a trade association—it was a social experiment. It was like putting Republicans and Democrats together in the same room." The founders were intentionally creating an institutional framework within which all the potential adversaries would be forced to hammer out their differences before taking a public position. Only sound positions would survive this process, they felt. They believed that the nature of CID housing required cooperation among all the constituencies, and that CAI would be the glue that would keep the interest groups together, foster a sense of common purpose, and promote mutually beneficial public and legislative advocacy. It was a mechanism for using a private organization to represent something approximating the public interest. The founders understood this and intentionally created an organization whose policy making structure had private governmental functions, as did the CIDs it was set up to serve. CAI, in short, was itself a private government—a sort of private legislature for a nation of private governmental regimes.[14]

In September 1973 CAI was incorporated, and its first board meeting was in November. The Urban Land Institute agreed to provide a home for CAI in its building, and David Stahl's secretary at ULI became the first CAI secretary. Stahl served jointly as executive vice-president of both organizations. But CAI was to be a separate organization with its own nonprofit corporate identity. The organization's purpose and membership were stated as follows: "The Community Associations Institute is an independent, non-profit research and educational organization formed in 1973 to develop and distribute guidance on homeowner associations and their shared facilities in condominiums, cluster housing, planned unit developments, and open space communities. Membership in the Institute is open to associations and their members, builder-developers, managers, public agencies and officials, other professionals, and other interested individuals and organizations."[15]

Hanke and the others then went about raising operating money for CAI, aiming for $500,000 to $600,000.[16] At the January 1974 NAHB annual meeting in Houston they arranged three fund-raising breakfasts and raised more than $75,000.[17] They were assisted by the fund-raising skills of the first CAI president, manager representative May Russell, a former college president from Irvine, California. They also raised $25,000 from the savings and loan industry, and in late 1974 they obtained a $25,000 contract from the Veterans' Administration to produce booklets for homeowners and home buyers, and a $50,000 contract from HUD to produce two volumes.[18]

After setting CAI in operation Hanke was asked to be its executive director, but he declined. CAI then conducted a national search, and retained C. James Dowden, who ran the organization as its executive vice-president under a succession of presidents from August 1974 to 1990. He was told at the outset that the available funds were sufficient for only three or four months of operation, so he was required to make fund-raising an important part of his job.

Cummings, the founding homeowner member of the design group and later CAI president, participated in the vital early fund-raising efforts aimed at builders, along with Dowden, Stahl, and the others. He recalls that builders were told that their future depended on the success of this type of housing, which could easily bog down in litigation and discontent if institutional support was not provided for running the associations. "The early donors," he recalls, "had the vision to realize that you have to help your neighbors to help yourself."[19]

## TROUBLE IN PRIVATOPIA: THE RESTRUCTURING

In June 1975 the board of trustees was expanded to ten; in September it grew to fifteen. Eventually it reached its maximum size of thirty. By 1992 CAI had become the leading supplier of information, education, literature, and legislative advocacy regarding CID housing. For the fiscal year ended June 30, 1992, CAI had income of nearly $4 million, a staff of 29 people, 56 chapters across the country, and 12,462 members.[20]

The institute's publications became the leading source of information in the field. They included the bimonthly magazine *Common Ground* (with a circulation of more than twenty thousand), a monthly newsletter entitled *Leadership Update,* the *Community Associations Law Reporter,* and chapter newsletters. CAI also produced many bound publications directed at managers, board members, homeowners, attorneys and others on the mechanics of setting up and operating homeowner associations. Their *Community Associations Factbook,* which went into its second edition in 1993, was the main sourcebook on the subject.

The CAI was the preeminent representative organization for its field in the building industry, in the press, and before legislative bodies. When the Advisory Commission on Intergovernmental Relations produced a conference and a volume on the subject, CAI and people associated with it were heavily involved.[21] CAI representatives often testified before Congress and state legislatures in Florida, California, New Jersey, and other states with many CIDs. Under a Public Policy Committee maintained by CAI were special Legislative Action Committees in California and Florida that retained paid lobbyists.[22] In 1985, when the California Legislature decided to significantly revise its laws governing CIDs, law professor Katharine Rosenberry, an active CAI member who was to serve as president of the national group for 1988–89, was the senior consultant to the Assembly Select Committee on Common Interest Subdivisions. The resulting Davis-Sterling Common Interest Development Act was heavily influenced by the agenda of CAI.[23]

Although the organization grew rapidly and accomplished a great deal, particularly in developing CID specializations within such professions as law and property management, some saw CAI as a troubled institution. By 1991 there was concern about shortfalls in revenue and the loss of momentum. The problems of CAI, many believed, were in part a result of the way the composition of its membership had evolved. The original concept was of five equally important interest groups, yet the membership of CAI did not reflect equal representation, or equal financial and personal involvement, from the five groups. Of the more than 12,000 members of CAI in 1992, 6,476, or 52 percent, were homeowner associations. This number represented only 4.3 percent of the estimated 150,000 associations in the nation.[24]

Moreover, in other critical interest groups participation was even worse. Only ninety-four public officials belonged to CAI, constituting only 0.8 percent of the membership. Only 177 developers were members, amounting to just 1.4 percent of the membership. The bulk of the members, outside of homeowner associations, were property managers or other professionals who made their living serving CIDs. There were 1,712 management companies and on-site managers in CAI, amounting to nearly 14 percent of the membership; 610 lawyers; 375 accountants; 240 insurance professionals; and hundreds of other "associates" and "unidentified colleagues." Together, these groups—property managers and others making all or part of their living from CIDs—totaled 37.2 percent of the membership.[25]

The work of the organization was not distributed evenly among the five groups. Homeowner representatives, who serve their own associations without compensation, were often unable to bear the costs, in time and money, of attending the local and national CAI meetings. The organization's membership dues, educational programs, and publications were expensive, priced more for professionals able to deduct their cost as a business expense than for homeowners who had to pay from their own pockets, and with no tax deduction. Developers, increasingly secure about the market acceptance of CID housing, participated less and less as the years went on. Public officials never became involved to an appreciable degree. The result was that managers and other professionals became by far the most active and involved members of the organization, both at the national level and in the local chapters. Their ongoing, immediate, day-to-day economic interest in the growth and success of CID housing encouraged them to take a continuing active role in the affairs of CAI.

In essence, there was a disparity between political control of the organization, which was shared equally among the five groups, and the financial support and volunteer effort necessary to keep it going, which was disproportionately contributed by property managers and other professionals. This situation came to a head in 1991 and 1992, leading to a major restructuring that moved CAI much closer to becoming the trade association its founders were determined it should not be.

CAI was taken over by the property managers and others who felt they had been bearing too large a share of the work and financial burden for too little power over decision making. The prime mover behind the change in direction was David W. Gibbons, the 1992 president of CAI and a Dallas property manager. He pointed out that forty-seven people—or half of the ninety-four public official members—could stop a group with more than twelve thousand members from taking a public position that the overwhelming majority endorsed. "The bottom line is, the institution was going down the tubes," he said. "We were not growing. We were lethargic; we were bureaucratic. With the interest group representation, we couldn't get anything done. We couldn't react quickly enough in the legislative arena. We were emulating our industry. It's just like in some community associations, where something gets referred from committee to committee, and nothing happens."[26]

With a new governing structure, CAI shifted its emphasis toward legislative advocacy and other forms of political action, including grassroots mobilization of its thousands of members at the national, state, and local levels. To facilitate its ability to take public positions quickly, the entire concept of the five interest groups was done away with. The board of trustees was reduced from thirty members to twenty-three, of which eighteen would be trustees only and five would be elected officers. There were to be only four types of members: homeowner, affiliate, professional, and associate. Only three spots on the board were guaranteed to homeowner representatives. All non-homeowner members from the three remaining groups were subclassified by area of specialization. Although no more than five members from each specialization could be trustees at the same time, the number of specializations was far larger than the four non-homeowner interest groups originally set up. Instead of the groups electing their own trustee representatives, all were to be elected at large. Consequently, homeowner members could be elected to the board only if they were acceptable to the overall membership.

This new structure meant that the board probably would consist of twenty people who earned their livelihood from CIDs, along with three homeowners. There might, for example, be five property managers, five attorneys, five accountants, five insurance specialists, and three homeowners. Those who opposed the changes, including founders Byron Hanke and Lincoln Cummings, felt that the institute would be dominated to an even greater extent by property managers and other professionals, with greatly reduced influence for homeowners, developers, and public officials.[27]

In a letter to David Gibbons, CAI president, Cummings explained his misgivings about the reorganization:

CAI was in part a social experiment to see if disparate interest groups could work together for the common good. It worked well in the beginning as each of the founders worked diligently for its success. Everyone benefited from the pooling of knowledge and discipline. We broke a lot of new ground for the industry and set new standards which are still being followed. I still believe in the original purpose: to help the homeowner association succeed.

There was—and still is—little incentive, however, for the homeowner him/herself to be more than a passive observer. CAI quickly became dominated by those in the business, principally managers and colleagues. . . .

I believe our success to date was in large measure because we tried to balance our policy-making and leadership among the five interest groups. It was the balance of thought, not the numbers, that counted. Even so, I readily acknowledge that we have not succeeded in maintaining the active leadership involvement of homeowners, public officials, and builder/developers. It is therefore time to change.

As I read your recommendations, I sense that the Institute is headed even more surely towards a manager and colleague trade association. While this is the easiest way to continue, it disturbs me. I think there is an alternative.[28]

Cummings went on to propose that CAI take note of focus-group findings by its Washington chapter "to better understand what the homeowners really want"; that membership groups be reduced to three, including consumer, provider, and research and education; that each group select its own representatives to the board of trustees; and that the quality of educational products be improved. Although Cummings supported the new emphasis on legislation, he argued that "it is still important to maintain a balance between interest groups: that is one of our strengths, that we do not take positions that help only one segment of the industry; we speak for all. Majority vote is inadequate if all the electorate is of one party."[29]

Notwithstanding these organizational changes, CAI has no intention of abandoning its public image as something more than a trade association, and it clearly wishes to retain the credibility resulting from that perception. The organization also wishes to maintain as much control as possible over the public discourse concerning CID housing. A strategic planning committee drafted a Statement of Core Purpose in 1992 that echoes the theme of the old CAI, proclaims that "the Community Associations Institute is the nation's voice on community association issues." Its new logo is a diamond-shaped arrangement of parallel horizontal lines that gradually widen to form an arrow or wedge pointing to the right. "The parallel lines of different lengths coming together represent CAI's diverse membership working in unity," CAI says.[30]

This unity, however, is largely a matter of symbolism and public relations. CAI finds it easier to speak with a single political voice only because it has reduced the role of constituencies that might differ. For example, CAI has considered inaugurating a seal of approval to bestow on homeowner associations and developers who meet what CAI considers the minimum standards of operation.[31] People shopping for a home could look for existing associations with the seal, and, in new developments, could choose to buy from developers displaying the seal. The acceptance of such a seal as the standard of quality in the industry would enhance the institutional role of CAI. Under the old consensus rules, however, developer members might resist establishing such a certification program, fearing it would give CAI too much power, or be at odds with each other or with managers over the proper criteria for awarding the seal.

Similar disagreements could, and did, arise within CAI over laws governing suits filed by homeowner associations against developers, especially over defective construction. It would be in the immediate interest of CAI members who belong to homeowner associations to facilitate relaxed standing-to-sue requirements, to permit "strict liability" recovery without proving negligence and to expand the kinds of damages that may be recovered. Developers, on the other hand, would naturally oppose these positions strenuously. For the old CAI to take a position on such an issue it would have had to please these opposed interests, which would require compromise, or remain silent. The reorganized CAI, having done away with homeowner and developer veto power, might be able to take a strong advocacy position on such an issue, assuming the managers and other influential, but not necessarily opposed, groups could agree. But it was uncertain whether such a position would really be better for those most directly affected than the compromise or silence of the old structure.

As 1993 began, the reorganized CAI could speak of a number of recent or potential legislative accomplishments. The institute was consulted by the U.S. Department of Justice regarding guidelines for implementing the Americans with Disabilities Act, and it provided technical advice through a CAI task force to the Department of Housing and Urban Development regarding Project HOPE (Home Ownership Opportunities for People Everywhere). CAI also became involved in a joint task force working to adopt "uniform legal underwriting guidelines for mortgage approval." The institute's interest was to find a "solution to today's fundamental problems caused by outdated, excessively narrow underwriting criteria which impedes community association operations and discourages creation of new ones." CAI also offered "strong support" for a Uniform Unincorporated Nonprofit Association Act proposed by the National Conference of Commissioners on Uniform State Laws. CAI identified state legislators in all fifty states who sponsored bills affecting homeowner associations "in a major research project that will allow CAI to monitor and respond to statewide legislative actions."[32]

The new structure facilitated political action, but at the price of reduced representation. Moreover, CAI's claim to be "the nation's voice on community association issues" rang hollow. The political structure of the old CAI gave it an arguable claim to representing a privatized version of the public interest, but the new structure removed whatever special legitimacy the organization had beyond that of a typical trade association petitioning for legislative beneficence for its members.

Hanke and Cummings, as well as others, expressed concern that the reduction in homeowner, developer, and public official control might cost CAI dearly in its ability to perform the critical educational mission for which the organization was created. Hanke had seen as early as 1964 that CID housing could not function as intended without national institutional support for education of developers, CID board members, millions of homeowners, and public officials. The problems that developed in the late and early 1970s, and which spurred the creation of CAI, proved him right. The founders felt that, whatever shortcomings the old organization might have had, it was set up to reach out to, and include, these critical players. The new CAI, they feared, might well reflect a single-minded property manager perspective on CID housing that would make it even harder to reach and educate other important constituencies—groups that simply had to be reached if the entire concept was to succeed.[33]

Unfortunately, the burden of providing institutional support to those who lived in and served CIDs had fallen on the shoulders of a single organization. During the enormous expansion of CID housing and the concomitant growth in the number of private governments across the nation, public governments at all levels were essentially passive or uninvolved. In this vacuum, private organizations assumed the leadership role. CAI, and to a lesser extent ULI and NAHB, began to serve as a sort of national legislature that set policy for a nation of private communities, and it became influential in establishing priorities in this area for public legislatures.

## DIFFERENT VOICES: ALTERNATIVES TO CAI

Although CAI remained the only national organization claiming to represent homeowner associations, a number of smaller groups with a more local focus and an emphasis on homeowners came into existence.

One of these was the Maryland Condominium and Homeowner Association (MCHA), which differs from the CAI model in several respects. The Maryland group emphasizes the needs of those who reside in CIDs and permits only resident CID unit owners to vote for or serve on its board of directors. Service providers can join, but only as nonvoting members. Dues for MCHA are low —$25 per year as of 1992—and all its programs are free for members. This contrasts sharply with CAI's higher dues structure ($75 to $215) and expensive publications and programs; costs of publications range from $10 to more than $300, and seminars, such as those on legal issues, cost as much as $400. Despite a shoestring budget and differences of opinion with CAI policies, MCHA nonetheless has been effective in influencing the Maryland state legislature and the laws of Montgomery County, where an estimated one-third of the residents live in CIDs. In Montgomery County, MCHA advocated on behalf of a sunshine law for CID board meetings, special alternative dispute resolution provisions, a county Commission on Common Ownership Communities, and creation of two county task forces to propose additional laws regarding CIDs. At the state level, MCHA was heavily involved in promoting passage of the Maryland Condominium Act and appointing a task force on common-interest housing.[34]

In California, alternatives to CAI for homeowners included the Executive Council of Homeowners and the Council of Condominium and Homeowner Associations. For CID property managers, a new organization called the California Association of Community Managers was formed.

Neither CAI nor the local alternative organizations that grew up to supplement it or compete with it aims to transform CID private government. Their agendas emphasize reform rather than revolution. The basic model of CID government remains largely unchallenged, perhaps because to many people this model has seemed more than adequate in theory and has only suffered in practice. Ebenezer Howard's vision of a new kind of city, Charles Ascher's idea of "government by contract," and Byron Hanke's intent to promote and support a new kind of planned community that offered great land-use economies all had to leave the drawing board and exist in the privatized environment in which American housing is planned, built, and administered. The ideal was that of self-governing local communities living the fantasy of the New England town meeting. The reality, too often, was an undemocratic oligarchy in which an apathetic body of residents was governed by a few dedicated or overly zealous neighbors who were for the most part told what to do by property managers and lawyers. In the absence of meaningful legislative regulation or oversight, the idea of residential private government took the shape advocated originally by developers through ULI and FHA, and later by lawyers and property managers through CAI.

# 6

# Homeowner Associations as Private Governments

It is essential to remember that a [homeowner association] is a business operation, but one without a profit motive.
—Urban Land Institute/Community Associations Institute, *Managing a Successful Community Association*

Like other corporations, homeowner associations have full legal rights, limited responsibility for the individuals who operate them, a potentially infinite lifespan, and a dedication to a narrow private purpose—in this case, protection of property values. In carrying out this purpose, homeowner associations function as private governments.

Private government is an idea with a long pedigree in political theory. References to private associations as governments within a government begin at least as early as the seventeenth century, when Thomas Hobbes wrote of private "systems" within the body politic—the commonwealth—that are akin to the muscles of the body. Some of these systems, including those set up for business purposes, could bring about the disintegration of the commonwealth if there were too many of them or if they acquired too much power. "Another infirmity of a Common-wealth, is . . . the great number of Corporations; which are as it were many lesser Common-wealths in the bowels of a greater, like wormes in the entrayles of a naturall man."[1]

In modern political science the same comparison of corporations to governments, in their internal workings, appears as early as the work of Arthur Bentley, who wrote in 1908 that "a corporation is government through and through."[2]

In 1944 political scientist Charles E. Merriam argued that the study of government could not be complete without addressing the obviously political subsystems that exist outside the formal institutions of government yet exert a governmentlike authority over their members. Studying private governments is more difficult than it might appear, however, because it calls on us to come to grips with a distinction we commonly take for granted: "What is public and what is private? And how do we draw the line between them? At first blush this seems very clear, but on closer examination it is not so evident."[3]

Perhaps one of the most clearly public functions is law enforcement. Yet law enforcement is not a public end alone but a common interest of both public and private spheres. For example, if a private corporation retains a group of civilians as security guards, equips them with uniforms, badges, and weapons, and charges them with responsibility for law enforcement on the corporation's property, they are performing a private function but protecting the public to some extent as well.

If the state requires such security guards to register with a public agency after they meet state-mandated standards, these private employees are becoming less distinguishable from public police officers. If the state sponsors and conducts training programs that they must complete, the distinction becomes even less clear.

There are many other possible examples of individuals and organizations that perform what we might normally consider public, or at least quasi-public, functions, and have close ties with government. The point is simply that the words *public* and *private* may seem distinct enough—

and they are used in popular and political discourse as if they were—but they are not.

Corporations often exercise what amounts to governmental power over their employees. This has led a number of political scientists, as well as some business and legal scholars, to argue in favor of calling corporations private governments, and, some say, of holding them accountable to constitutional standards.

The difficulty of distinguishing between public and private where the corporation is concerned is reflected in academic accounts of its history. Business and management scholars Richard Eells and Clarence Walton wrote of the "two genealogical lines" of the modern corporation.[4] The lines are not harmonious with each other because one considers incorporation a privilege granted by the public while the other views it as a private right.

The first line dates from the crown-chartered joint-stock companies created by western European nations, such as the British East India Company chartered in 1600. During the mercantile era, business was essentially an instrument of government, and these corporations were chartered for purposes determined to be in the public interest. This history emphasizes the corporation as a creation of the state, a sort of privilege or concession that can be granted or taken away, as reflected in Chief Justice John Marshall's statement that it is "an artificial being, invisible, intangible and existing only in contemplation of law."[5]

The other genealogical line is the long history of implicit freedom of association for business purposes, of which Eells and Walton say, "Men formed such bodies without the sanction of a sovereign as far back as we can trace business activity under modern conditions." In this view, incorporation has been not merely a privilege to be granted or taken away but an activity undertaken without state sanction. This gives it, for Eells and Walton, the status of a right because it flows in a general sense from the freedom of association guaranteed by the constitution. They see a "historic practice of men in a free society to organize voluntarily for the pursuit of common purposes—quite independent of state action."[6] This view recognizes that people have for centuries pooled their resources for business purposes and will presumably continue to do so unless actively prevented. Moreover, the corporation, in this perspective, is seen as more than an artificial person. It is a social entity as real and material as any other group and a valued manifestation of a society based on pluralism.

Eells and Walton recognize, though, that large business corporations function as private governments in the lives of their employees, that they are undemocratic and oligarchic, and that they are often closely entangled with public government (through such connections as government contracts) to the point of being its agent. Consequently, they argue that corporations should become more socially responsible and harmonize their operations with an American way of life they see as being based on constitutionalism, individual freedom, freedom of choice, and equal opportunity.[7]

Legal scholar Adolph Berle emphasized in 1954 the ways the modern corporation "has, de facto at least, invaded the political sphere and has become in fact, if not in theory, a quasi-governing agency." He argued for a civil rights act setting up a forum for guaranteeing the constitutional rights of individuals aggrieved by corporate deprivations of liberty or property, saying that "the danger is the ancient one of irresponsible power, functioning outside the discipline of law implicit under organized government."[8]

In 1959 political scientist Earl Latham analyzed corporations as systems of private government, arguing that

one of America's most important political problems is a long-needed and now urgent redefinition of the relation between giant corporations and the commonwealth, for the growth of the corporation has produced a tension of power in which giant enterprises have at points come to rival the sovereignty of the state itself. The great corporations are political systems in which their market, social, and political influence goes far beyond their functional efficiency in the economy. Indeed, in the very culture of the American people, the influence of the larger principalities overflows the banks of their corporate jurisdiction or economic reason. In the name of free enterprise, corporate collectivism has made deep inroads upon the celebrated individualism of the economy, and corporate welfarism has gone an equal distance toward tranquilizing the historic initiative of the individual in a smother of narcotic "togetherness."[9]

More recently, John McDermott has argued that "the modern corporation is *the* central institution of contemporary society" and that the corporation has redefined the class structure and the meaning of property. "Liberal society," he argues, "is rapidly being supplanted by corporate society," with social classes now being based on position in the corporate hierarchy, and a new property system of "quasi-collective property" is emerging to replace the private property system.[10]

Of course, homeowner associations cannot rival the largest business corporations in financial resources. But many CIDs are of comparable population, with tens or even hundreds of thousands of inhabitants. Residency in CIDs requires home buyers to become part of a corporation and live according to its rules, which reach into areas of people's lives that business corporations would leave alone. In this sense, CIDs represent a tendency toward universalization of corporate values.

In the remainder of this chapter I describe the typical organization and functions of a homeowner association private government, compare these characteristics with general social scientific definitions of private governments, and examine the ways homeowner association private governments depart from basic assumptions of liberal democracy.

## HOMEOWNER ASSOCIATION REGIMES

Although the precise names and legal descriptions vary slightly from state to state, there are four basic types of CIDs: condominiums, planned developments, stock cooperatives, and community apartments.

All four forms of ownership involve common ownership of private residential property coupled with individual use or ownership of a particular residential unit; mandatory membership of all property owners in an association that governs use of the commonly owned property and regulates the use of the individual unit; and a set of governing documents providing for the financing of the association, the procedures for its governance, and the rules that owners must follow with respect to common areas and individual units.[11]

There are differences among these forms of ownership. The term *condominium* refers not to a kind of building but to a kind of ownership. The property can be apartmentlike or a detached single-family home. Condominium ownership means that each buyer purchases an undivided fractional ownership interest in the common areas in addition to his or her individual unit. The homeowner association manages the common areas.

Planned-unit developments consist of detached single-family homes or townhouses. The homeowner association owns as well as manages the common areas, which often includes streets and parks.

In stock cooperatives and community apartments the owner purchases a share of stock in the entire development. That share carries with it the right to exclusive use of an individual unit and shared use of the common areas. Developments of this sort are more common on the East Coast than in the sunbelt states, where condominiums and PUDs predominate.[12]

In a CID, everybody who buys a unit automatically becomes a member of the community association. So, although the decision to purchase may be voluntary, membership is mandatory. The association is founded on, and governed by, certain documents that are akin to a state's constitution and set of codes. Typically these include some, or all, of the following: a set of covenants, conditions, and restrictions that run with the land and are legally binding on present and future owners of the property; articles of incorporation, if the association is incorporated; bylaws; and rules and regulations.

The CC&Rs are written by the developer and are normally only subject to modification by supermajority vote of all members, not just of those who choose to vote. For example, a typical provision for amending the CC&Rs would be require a two-thirds vote of the entire membership. Amendments are therefore difficult to enact, especially because most CIDs have a number of absentee owners who rent their units and are not present to vote, even if they are interested in the issue. So the developer's idea of how people should live is, to a large extent, cast in concrete. This rigidity was advocated in the 1964 *Homes Association Handbook,* in which ULI and FHA proposed that changes in the CC&Rs require the two-thirds vote and a three-year waiting period before they would become effective.[13] This permanence was seen as an asset for mortgage insurance purposes because it tended to prevent owners from banding together to relax the developer's property maintenance standards by amending the CC&Rs.[14]

The articles of incorporation, similar to those of any other nonprofit corporation, primarily set out the purpose of the corporation, which is to maintain and protect the common areas and to enforce the CC&Rs. The bylaws and rules and regulations are also written by the developer.

These documents are every bit as enforceable as the laws, charters, and constitutions of public governments, though new owners often fail to recognize that fact. Taken together, they give a developer the power to create a distinct lifestyle in a development, which the developer can use as a powerful marketing tool. Moreover, they are the rules of the regime under which, ultimately, the residents will be living.

The documents provide for the election of a board of directors of the association from among the membership, so neighbors eventually will be running one another's lives, without any minimum requirements of education, experience, or professional competence. They are not paid for their services. At the outset, however, the developer staffs all board positions with his own employees and customarily retains three votes for every unsold unit, so the developer is effectively in control of the association until nearly the entire project is sold. The developer then presides over a transition period during which elected residents take over all positions on the board of directors and the operation of the development.

Only property owners are eligible to vote in elections, so renters are disenfranchised.[15] This ownership qualification for voting raises constitutional questions, especially considering the large number of rented units in many developments.[16] In California, a median of 20 percent of the CID units are rented; in 14 percent of the developments the majority of units are rented.[17] Additionally, only one vote per unit may be cast, rather than one vote per adult occupant.

These elected directors are responsible for seeing that the dictates of the developer's governing documents are carried out. This includes maintenance of the common areas and management of all association assets, which can range from next to nothing to millions of dollars. The funds for maintenance and the association's other functions come from monthly assessments and dues that the owners must pay, as well as special assessments for particular purposes. These payments are the "taxes" of the private government, and they can range from relatively nominal fees to hundreds of dollars each month, depending on how extensive the common areas and facilities are.

In addition to caring for the common areas, the association is charged with enforcement of the governing documents over all unit owners and occupants. This power is very real but often underestimated by new purchasers unfamiliar with CIDs, and it is the source of a great deal of acrimony.[18]

The overriding purpose of the association, as defined by its documents, is the protection of property values through maintenance of the property itself and through preservation of the project's character and appearance. In carrying out this purpose the board of directors has all the powers of any nonprofit corporation, including the power to buy and sell property. Beyond these basic requirements there is an enormous range of restrictions that the developer may have created as part of a target-marketing strategy.

The association is empowered—and required—to enforce these CC&R provisions by imposing fines. The quasi-adjudication process is typically quite informal, considering how much is at stake. Charges of violation are made and heard by the board. There are no policies that separate the roles of accuser and trier of fact or that call for the empaneling of an independent, impartial jury. In most states, failure to pay the fine authorizes the association to attach a lien interest to the individual unit, and, ultimately, to sell the unit at auction if the fine is not paid.

In addition, the association can impose certain standards of behavior on residents and anyone who visits the property. Taken as a whole, these powers permit the regulation of a wider range of behavior than any within the purview of a public local government. Among other things, the governing documents require the individual owner to maintain certain standards of repair and maintenance in his or her individual unit. Unkempt yards, peeling paint, and other indications of neglect that might affect the neighborhood's property values are subject to censure. Generally there are also restrictions on the uses to which the units can be put, such as the number of occupants permitted, age restrictions for residency, maximum lengths of stay for guests, and whether any sort of business can be conducted from the home. In addition, owners who wish to make physical alterations in the home—painting it a different color or adding a room, a patio, or even an awning—are generally required to submit their plans to the board of directors or to a committee created by the board to review such matters and approve or reject the applications.

There may be a number of committees working under the board, and the organizational structure can be quite complex, with committees for recreational matters, architectural review, liaison with city government, finances, elections, executive matters, and other issues.

Because the boards are responsible for maintenance of the common areas, their decisions can have enormous financial significance for members. They must decide when to repair or replace roofs, exterior walls, pools, and streets. These expenses can run into the hundreds of thousands, even millions, of dollars. Normally the only source of this revenue is the residents, and ideally boards should reserve funds well in advance to prepare for such expenses, calculating monthly assessments that allow for regular maintenance, as well as eventual replacement of things that wear out. Reserves tend to be lower than they should be because the political consequences of raising monthly assessments are as predictable as for a city council candidate who promises to raise taxes. One study in California showed that reserves averaged 40 percent of the annual budget, with only 28 percent of the developments reaching the 75 percent of the budget that is recommended by most industry experts.[19]

Reserves become especially critical when the unexpected happens—when roofs fail prematurely, pools develops cracks and leaks, pavements deteriorate, structural beams begin to shift, or water begins to fill basements or ruin interior walls. Recent surveys suggest that as many as one-third of all CIDs have major defects in original construction.[20] When physical problems arise, boards are faced with unpleasant and difficult choices. They have the power to raise regular assessments and to require special assessments (sometimes only after approval by the members), but this can place some members in the unfortunate position of being unable to afford the cost of their home. At times like these the board may be pressured by members to sue the developer for the funds to make repairs. These lawsuits often involve hundreds of thousands of dollars in litigation expenses and sometimes result in multimillion-dollar settlements and jury verdicts. These suits are also divisive and can place enormous stress on board members, who are responsible to the membership for supervising the association's legal counsel.

In most states, board members are protected against resident lawsuits by the business judgment rule, a legal provision governing the liability of the directors of profit and nonprofit corporations which holds that board members are not liable to the shareholders for their errors as long as they act prudently and in good faith. A typical version reads as follows: "A director shall perform the duties of a director . . . in good faith, in a manner such director believes to be in the best interests of the corporation and its shareholders and with such care, including reasonable inquiry, as an ordinarily prudent person in a like position would use under similar circumstances."[21]

One way to demonstrate prudence, and thus avoid personal liability, is to rely on the advice of experts. The law cited above goes on to provide that "a director shall be entitled to rely on information, opinions, reports or statements . . . prepared or presented by . . . counsel, independent accountants or other persons as to matters which the director believes to be within such person's professional or expert competence."[22] In the matter of covenant enforcement, this would mean lawyers and property managers. Unfortunately, the potential for conflict in CIDs is enhanced by the conventional professional wisdom regarding rule enforcement, which is purveyed by the managers and lawyers who serve CIDs. Board members are routinely advised to be extremely aggressive and inflexible in the enforcement of CC&Rs, a practice that produces enormous hostility against boards on the part of those who are censured and fined. This philosophy reflects the position taken by early builders, particularly Jesse Clyde Nichols, who endeavored to set up a structure that would require homeowners to strictly enforce against each other the builder's rules. It is still found in the pronouncements of such figures as F. Scott Jackson, CAI president in 1982–83 and coauthor of several books on CID housing, including a CAI publication on CC&R enforcement. Jackson's perspective illustrates the legalistic managerialism that is the dominant view in the industry: "Rules must be enforced uniformly, promptly, and firmly by the board. Delays can result in waivers and allow the violator a defense that he or she may otherwise not have had. Other homeowners may violate the rule and eventually you have a general disregard of the rules."[23]

This ideology is put into practice by lawyers and property managers in the advice they give to CID boards. Board members are often told by counsel and managers that failure to enforce the rules as advised can constitute a breach of their obligations as fiduciaries to the membership and could result in suits against the association and themselves personally.[24]

This pervasive industry attitude in favor of harsh enforcement is enhanced by the kinds of individuals who are drawn to serve on CID boards. Board members receive no pay for their services yet they must take on what are often heavy responsibilities. Typically the board must meet at least once every month, generally in the evening or on weekends, and difficult decisions regarding finances, assessments, and rule enforcement can generate an unpleasant and often personal reaction from their neighbors. Committee meetings make a further demand on the time of volunteers. People who willingly volunteer to undertake such tasks often are motivated by a strong sense of community responsibility. But these positions also offer obvious benefits to those who may wish to be on a board or architectural committee to enjoy the perceived pleasure of wielding power over others.[25] Those of an authoritarian bent have strong support from CAI and the attorneys and managers who advise CID boards to behave in a harsh and even threatening manner in rule enforcement. Those who wish to forbear are standing against the conventional wisdom.

Covenant enforcement litigation has become a profitable legal specialization for attorneys in states with many CIDs, as has its corollary: suit, or countersuit, by members against their boards for negligence, breach of their fiduciary duty to the members, abuse of authority, and suit under some theory of quasi-governmental liability, such as alleged violations of constitutional rights.[26] In many cases, the attorney who advises the board on whether to file suit will handle the litigation and receive substantial hourly fees, raising the question of whether legal advice in these matters is always as disinterested as it should be.

To alleviate the oppressive burden of lawsuits arising from CIDs, several states have considered or enacted special provisions for alternative dispute resolution. ADR can be mandatory or permissive and binding or nonbinding. One approach is to make it mandatory and nonbinding but require that the party who rejects the ADR outcome must pay the other side's attorney fees if he or she goes on to lose in court. A California law passed in 1992 making ADR mandatory for certain kinds of CID disputes was vetoed by the governor but was reintroduced in a modified form in December of that year. The Florida Condominium Act requires nonbinding arbitration in such disputes before either party can file suit. In Illinois, a proposed Common Interest Ownership Act included mediation provisions. Montgomery County, Maryland, where an estimated one-third of the population lives in CID, has established an ADR system within its county Common Interest Ownership Commission. In Hawaii, CAI was influential in establishing an ADR program involving a nonprofit Neighborhood Justice Center.[27]

Such organizations as CAI see ADR as a way to resolve disputes more quickly and less expensively than in courts because it does away with the need for attorneys, judges, and most of the other elements of a legal system. Some state court systems may strongly support ADR as a way to divert a flood of cases that often seem trivial but are hotly contested by the litigants. An ADR system operated by people with a CID industry mind-set could reflect the aggressive, legalistic managerialism that seems to generate disputes rather than resolve them. But an ADR system could adopt a more balanced attitude, viewing disputes as problems among neighbors that must be resolved amicably.

# PRIVATE GOVERNMENT THEORY AND THE CID

Latham uses a five-part definition to explain why he characterizes corporations as private governments, and this definition fits CIDs as well: "The corporation is a body politic which exhibits describable characteristics common to all bodies politic. In a functional view of all such political systems it can be said that there are five essential elements: (1) an authoritative allocation of principal functions; (2) a symbolic system for the ratification of collective decisions; (3) an operating system of command; (4) a system of rewards and punishments; and (5) institutions for the enforcement of the common rules. A system of organized human behavior which contains these elements is a political system, whether one calls it the state or the corporation. And state and corporation are mature political systems to the degree in which they exhibit all the essential characteristics."[28]

Latham's authoritative allocation of functions is found in the corporate articles of incorporation and other governing documents, which determine the purpose of the CID and set forth the distribution of power, including the board's power to further refine the structure by forming committees and subcommittees.

The symbolic system for the ratification of collective decisions is the annual election by which board members are selected, which establishes whatever claim to legitimacy the board may have. In some associations, especially small ones, these elections are a mere formality because there are established and recognized leaders. In larger associations the campaigns are often waged in deadly earnest, complete with promises, rumors, factions, and allegations of election fraud.

Latham's operating system of command is the board and the committee structure, including the often powerful architectural committee. In some cases, such as when development residents are predominantly of lower socioeconomic status, the committee may have no professional expertise; there may be no architects, engineers, or designers on the architectural committee. There may be a legal committee charged with supervising the association's legal counsel, who may be handling delinquent assessment suits, CC&R enforcement litigation, and even a massive construction defect case against the developer. Yet there may not be a single lawyer on the committee. It is also possible, especially in larger and more expensive CIDs, that there may be an abundance of professionals in a variety of fields, so that the committee functions in a businesslike and competent way. But because formal qualifications are not required, there are no guarantees.

The system of rewards and punishments is the board's ability to fine members for rule violation and to withhold or grant permission to do certain things. Again, this may be done in an even-handed way, according to relatively objective standards, or it may reflect the worst kind of nasty neighborhood favoritism imaginable. There is no real formal check on this sort of behavior, short of the election process and the occasional provision for recall. Advocates for CIDs have consistently argued for greater sanctioning power for these boards, up to and including heavy, punitive fines and even the authority to banish people from the development for noncompliance.

Latham's institutions for the enforcement of the common rules would be, for most public governments, an administrative apparatus, such as a court system. The purpose of the system would be to provide an objective forum where even-handed justice could be handed out. But in CIDs, as in many private governments, there is a much less well-developed judicial function. In CIDs, power is unitary. The board cites violators and holds the hearings that constitute the "trial."

Often the enforcement mechanism is the civil court system, to which boards increasingly resort for enforcement of the CC&Rs when internal mechanisms fail to produce compliance. Association lawyers use the courts to collect unpaid assessments and fines through satisfaction of liens on residents' homes, and they sometimes use the ultimate sanction of forcing the sale of the home to collect payment. Courts are also where the limits of association power over residents are tested, as boards or residents seek judicial intervention to uphold or invalidate restrictions.

Political scientist Sanford Lakoff offers definitions of public and private governments, and his conceptualization, like Latham's, would favor viewing homeowner associations as private governments:

> Public governments, on the one hand, are those general as well as special-purpose associations and agencies either to which all inhabitants of a given locality are subject or of which all citizens are members. Private governments, on the other hand, are those limited-purpose associations or organizations, usually voluntary in membership, which exist both alongside and subordinate to public governments. Private associations are considered governments when they exhibit, to a significant extent, certain

fundamental political characteristics. In varying degrees and in ways circumscribed by the ultimate coercive sanctions of public governments, private governments exercise power over both members and non-members, often in vital areas of individual and social concern. They make and apply rules affecting and limiting the behavior of members. Often they have well-developed systems of legislation, adjudication and execution, and at least rudimentary electoral and federal systems. In organizational form, they run the gamut from authoritarian to populist.[29]

The lawful powers and activities of CID boards of directors fit Lakoff's definition of a private government.[30] They are limited-purpose associations; they are ostensibly voluntary in membership; they exist "alongside and subordinate to" public governments; and, most important, they exhibit "fundamental political characteristics." That is, they exercise power over members and even nonmembers in vital areas of concern, in that their decisions govern what individuals do in the privacy of their own home and what they do with the physical structure of the house and its surroundings. Their actions touch on what is perhaps the most basic human drive: the desire to exercise control over our immediate environment. They do this with the force of law, because their edicts are enforceable, and they have more or less well-developed systems for rule making and enforcement.

The system of command in CIDs tends to be oligarchic, which is consistent with what is generally said about private governments. As noted by Berle and others, private governments—corporate and otherwise—seem to be temperamentally inclined toward oligarchy. Political scientist Grant McConnell pointed out the ways private governments, such as corporations, labor unions and political parties, tend to perpetuate oligarchic systems of authority that are at odds with the stated goals of the larger society. This, he argues, tends to confirm the "iron law of oligarchy" observed by Robert Michels, "who says organization says oligarchy."[31] Barton and Silverman, whose California study seems consistent with this line of thought, report a common perception that boards are just a small group of powerful neighbors. This impression is based on such factors as lack of member support for and understanding of board functions and activities, low attendance at annual meetings, and frequent conflict between boards and members.[32]

According to the best definitions available in social science, the CID clearly constitutes a form of private government. Yet CID advocates and the courts now resist assigning the private government label to home-owner association boards. Among those who question the applicability of the private government label for CIDs is Katharine Rosenberry, a recent president of the Community Associations Institute.[33] Rosenberry is a law professor and was the senior consultant to the California legislature during the 1985 redrafting of the state law governing common-interest developments. She also chaired the committee that redrafted the bylaws of the Community Associations Institute during the sweeping reorganization of 1992 that reduced homeowner influence.[34]

This resistance to the government label reflects a concern that constitutional limitations on municipal government activity might become applicable to homeowner associations. It represents a change of position within the industry, however, because examination of the early literature generated by proponents of CIDs and homeowner associations shows that, years ago, they clearly and explicitly understood they were creating residential private governments.

In 1973 Hugh Mields and the Urban Land Institute produced an analysis of the new town movement in which the issue of government is discussed. As a condition of giving federal assistance to these projects, the Department of Housing and Urban Development required that the residents have a means of government that included voting rights. Discussing this condition, Mields wrote:

> There are many significant questions about the constitutionality of the "private governments" a developer must of necessity establish, even before occupancy by the first residents. If they are based, as most of them are, on the home owner association concept, serious legal issues arise in terms of equal enfranchisement of all citizens, since most HOAs exclude lessees from membership. Thus these "private governments" may violate the equal protection clause of the Fourteenth Amendment. In essence, they establish the new community as a municipal corporation without ensuring that those citizens who will be governed have a voice in the decision-making process. In addition, HOAs are not voluntary associations, though they have been treated as such. The fees or assessments that they collect have been held to be a form of taxation which again is legally suspect. The crucial

legal questions regarding the extent and substance of legitimate citizen participation all relate to this problem.[35]

In 1974 CAI and ULI produced a volume entitled *Managing a Successful Community Association* that was intended to guide associations through the first few years of wrestling with the problems of self-government. This volume was intended to be read by the members of the new associations—the administrators of the new private governments and the citizens—to put the CID phenomenon into context and to explain the historical significance of the new movement. This influential and often-cited book, calling the growth in community associations a reflection of a "new trend in land development philosophies," described the associations as follows:

By their very nature, associations become mini-governments. They provide services that in many areas of the country have been provided by municipalities, including maintenance of common areas, roads, utility systems (water and sewer), lighting, refuse removal, and communications systems. Implementation and enforcement by CAs of these easements of access, architectural covenants, and use restrictions contained in land documents are analogous to police and public safety services provided by governmental bodies.

It is significant that many federal officials feel that the American people need new forms of service delivery at the local level; the public cost of providing service is too high, and services provided are often inadequate. In today's America, when numerous polls have shown that the majority of Americans have greatly diminished confidence in the capability of the nation's basic institutions to meet public needs, the CA has emerged as a new, close-to-home institution through which citizens can have a very real role in influencing those affairs that shape their lives and those of their families, as well as their environment.[36]

The unfavorable characterization of local governments illustrates that CID advocates have been competing with local governments for "citizens" and have long advertised CIDs as performing traditional governmental functions better than public governments can. Other CAI representatives echoed the "mini-government" line of thought. Wayne Hyatt, the most prominent legal advocate in CAI and a former president of the organization, wrote:

> Upon analysis of the association's functions, one clearly sees the association as a quasi-government entity paralleling in almost every case the powers, duties, and responsibilities of a municipal government. As a "mini-government," the association provides to its members, in almost every case, utility services, road maintenance, street and common-area lighting, and refuse removal. In many cases, it also provides security services and various forms of communication within the community. There is, moreover, a clear analogy to the municipal police and public safety functions. All of these functions are financed through assessments or taxes levied upon the members of the community, with powers vested in the board of directors, council of co-owners, board of managers, or other similar body clearly analogous to the governing body of a municipality. Terminology varies from region to region; however, the duties and responsibilities remain the same.[37]

Although CAI took the position that CID boards were running governments that were superior in many respects to local public governments, it tried to steer CIDs away from true political organization and toward a preoccupation with management. *Managing a Successful Community Association* suggests that if CIDs engage in politics they will be sued because they have "deep pockets":

> The important aspect of the CA lies in its basic nature as a privately owned and operated vehicle of service to a specific community. It is not, above all, a built-in civic association to be used for civic and political pressuring. The activities of the association must always take place in consideration of its status as a nonprofit organization for public service and in recognition that, unlike the typical civic association, the CA often has substantial funds which make suits against it by allegedly aggrieved parties more attractive.
>
> A civic association with nominal annual membership dues does not present as attractive a target for suit; therefore, the

community should look toward such a voluntary organization wholly separate from the CA to press the more controversial interests which occur in the context of a larger public domain. . . . [The CA] must conduct its operations in accord with sound business practices and seek to maximize service and minimize expense.[38]

It seems that CID advocates, during the critical growth years for this form of housing, tried to create a particular kind of private government without politics. Residents were urged to turn in on themselves and, in their enclosed developments, try to "maximize service and minimize expense" for the members. Any desire to organize for political purposes should find expression in organizations "wholly separate from the CA." Divorcing all internal disputes from the American political context would, of course, have the effect of rendering these disputes mere matters of management in which the issues, whatever they may be, would be personalized and trivialized—and, above all, depoliticized. There is no racism, no sexism, no social class distinction, no social injustice, no constitutional regulation—just good or bad business management practices.

This attitude is an extreme but not illogical outcome of founding modern CID private governments on the model of the city manager system, but in the form of a private corporation dedicated to the preservation of property values. A municipal government has to concern itself with more than protection of property, being charged as well with preservation of the general health, safety, and welfare. Theodore Roszak's pungent observations about Valencia and Foster City, two new towns built in California in the 1960s, cogently summarize the result of combining managerial government with the narrow focus of a corporation. "Foster City's money is earmarked for barbecue pits, sailboats, shopping on the 'flower-splashed mall,' and the usual distractions of suburban affluence. . . . A city whose sense of politics never gets beyond selfish defensiveness, and an obsessive concern for property values, is a sick city."[39]

Because social scientists have done little in the area, the study of CID private governments has been left primarily to those in private industry who would study the governments only in a nonpolitical context. In that context, issues of authority, justice, and legitimacy can be ignored in favor of a bloodless and myopic focus on how to make organizations run more efficiently. This focus, Sanford Lakoff points out, is an outcome of leaving the study of such private governments as business corporations to others, and it turns the study of what is really politics into the study of management.[40] Complementing the lack of social science research has been a steady stream of how-to publications by such organizations as the Urban Land Institute designed to promote "better management" of the developments. If CID private government has fallen short of the utopian expectations of its founders, it is in part because academics have not addressed the subject in earnest.

## WOULD LOCKE HAVE LIVED IN A CONDOMINIUM?

One way to move toward understanding CID private government is to scrutinize it in the context of basic assumptions of liberal democracy. Government by homeowner associations departs in a number of ways from the liberal model but at the same time seems to carry some liberal assumptions to an extreme. Perhaps one reason more academic writers have not examined the political nature of CIDs is that they are so hard to characterize. There are several models that fit CIDs to some extent.[41]

First, the fact that only property owners are eligible to vote is reminiscent of Lockean principles.[42] The CID concept is consistent with the notion that property ownership is at the heart of the social contract. Voting is based on a "one unit, one vote" principle, so owners of more than one unit have more than one vote.

Indeed, the entire CID is based on an explicit, written, binding contract for the purchase of a piece of property; the contract carries with it certain lifestyle restrictions deemed necessary to protect the property interest. These restrictions are equally binding on all members—all of whom, it is assumed, entered as rational persons into the relationship. Consequently, all the owners and renters have ostensibly consented to be governed by the association insofar as necessary to protect their property interest; in that sense, the association's decisions are legitimated, because the members have consented to equating "rights" with "property rights." This, it seems, is a Lockean conception.

Second, it could be said that the CID corresponds in many respects to Nozick's "protective associations," libertarian utopias that are in some respects not far removed from Locke.[43] Such associations, Nozick might say, are voluntarily entered into; have an explicitly defined relationship between association and individual; may be voluntarily left by selling;

compete with each other for membership in the sense that owners can move to from one to another; and offer due process rights but no substantive justice to members. Justice as fair procedures is consistent with Nozick's conception.

Third, it could be said that the ownership system that gives each owner an individual place to live, as well as shared ownership of the rest of the development, amounts to socialism by contract. Although there is no provision for redistribution of property on the basis of need, there is no initial inequality to correct, at least on the surface—everybody starts in relative equality, owning identical or similar units. This does not take into account the total economic picture of all residents but merely indicates that each has the basic necessity of a home, which implies the absence of poverty.

This socialism by contract analysis breaks down if a member can't make the mortgage payments, because there is no deeper commitment to social justice underlying the arrangement. There is no provision in CID documents for the association or the other residents to help the family who is about to lose its home. Such a provision could be made a part of governing documents, particularly in the large new town developments where there are financial institutions capable of making commitments to local CID residents. Conceivably a CID could enter into this business and institute economic justice within its walls.

Fourth, it could be said that CIDs have a communalistic, even cult-like, isolationist nature. They are deliberately cut off from the surrounding society and dedicated to living according to a specific set of rules. This dimension has led some in the press to characterize CIDs as a reversion to feudalism. In particular, communities for senior citizens often acquire an almost hostile tenor with respect to the larger society. They often emphasize security measures to a chilling degree. One study found that in Leisure World, in California, 92 percent of the home buyers rated security as "very important." The development is surrounded by "six-foot block walls topped with two-foot-high bands of barbed wire," and more than three hundred private security officers patrol the grounds.[44] In other developments, most notably bunkerlike security developments for the rich, there are such niceties as laser sensors, security gates with tire spikes, electronic locks, and an elaborate system of television monitors and automatic alarms linked via computer.

Residential isolation and the acceptance of seemingly oppressive security measures (coupled with withdrawal from the work force, in the case of seniors) lends an eerie detachment to the atmosphere, not unlike what one might expect to encounter in a commune.

A children's book entitled *The Great Condominium Rebellion* describes the visit of a fictional thirteen-year-old girl and her brother to their grandparents' condominium. The teenagers find themselves confronted with a bewildering array of behavioral restrictions that make adolescent life all but impossible and cause them to be the recipients of numerous disapproving stares and reproaches. To their horror, their grandparents fail to support them and instead accept the constraints as normal and necessary. In desperation, the fictional teenagers write home, "Dear Mom and Dad: Who are these people living in Grandma and Grandpa's bodies? Having a miserable time. Love and tears, Stacy and Marc."[45]

Fifth, one could regard CIDs as the corporatization of the home. The vast majorities of CIDs are incorporated, in most states as "mutual-benefit corporations," a status that gives them all the powers of a natural person.[46] All homeowners automatically become a part of the corporation and are thereby bound by its articles of incorporation, bylaws, and rules and regulations. Most CID boards have the right to enter individual homes as they deem appropriate and necessary to protect everyone's investment. The individual is subservient to the corporation, and residents must learn to accept that fact.

In addition, many CIDs are extremely wealthy. Some have made millions suing their developers for construction defects.[47] Others are composed of many affluent residents who swell the corporation's coffers with substantial dues. CIDs are permitted to invest and they do, though the profits are not distributed to the members but reinvested.

Another aspect of the corporate nature of CIDs is the increasing power of managers. It has long been noted that corporations tend toward a separation of control from ownership, with power ultimately resting with management rather than the shareholders.[48] In CIDs, management companies and other professionals (lawyers, accountants, actuaries, architects, engineers, and so forth) retained by the board of directors carry out many responsibilities, and, of course, the board itself makes the decisions. There is a pronounced tendency toward a lack of involvement among the rank and file, who seem to prefer to turn things over to the board and management company, according to Barton and Silverman.[49]

In this sense, CID residents, in their concern with property values, often behave like the stockholders in any large corporation, who neither know nor care about corporate affairs as long as their stock goes up and they keep receiving dividend checks. This sort of peripheral interest is especially disturbing when the corporate affairs in which people are uninterested are the workings of their own neighborhood.

According the Barton and Silverman study, the corporate management model seems to permeate the thinking of board members as well as residents, so that the CID is thought of as "a type of business, where efficient property management saves money and increases the value of owners' investments," an attitude that conflicts with neighborliness. As Barton and Silverman concluded, "We see a general tendency for both associations and professional managers to emphasize ease of management over member involvement and to regard 'people problems' as simply a complication of property management. This emphasis is misplaced."[50]

A more speculative matter is the long-term social and psychological effect on the American family of having the corporate model imposed on the home and its surroundings.

For example, imagine that a family sweltering through a long, hot summer decides to relieve the heat by installing a window air conditioner. The family then receives a command from the board of directors to remove the unit, which allegedly violates a common prohibition on installing anything except drapes in, on, or around the windows. This family will have to obey the command and explain it to the children. The honest explanation would be to say that the family must endure the heat because they are all part of a corporation dedicated to preserving everybody's property values, and this restriction, though it seems ridiculous and unfair, actually aims to prevent people from hanging from their windows such items as wet laundry, signs advertising cars for sale, and other undesirable things—including dripping, rattling air conditioners—all of which would tend to make the development take on a Tobacco Road ambiance and depress property values.

This rationale is different from saying "We can't do it because it's a crime" or "We can't do it because we are friends with the Jones family downstairs, and it just makes too much noise for them." The rationale is neither completely authoritarian nor one that rests entirely on cooperation with and respect for the rights of neighbors. It is a corporate, business, and property-oriented rationale. It is conceivable that children raised in CID housing may be undergoing a form of differential political socialization. Richard Louv wonders, "As an increasing proportion of middle-income U.S. families with children purchase condominiums and townhouses, will these developments be pro-child?"[51] Louv speculates about the difference between being raised in a real city or town and growing up in the artificial environment of a typical common-interest housing development:

> Whenever I drive up the freeway, looking out at all the new developments, I wonder what they're going to be like in twenty or thirty years. I wonder what kind of culture we're creating. Will the children who grow up in these places have any sense of commitment to them? Or will these developments someday become vast, soulless slums? What's been forgotten is that it is our culture that is being shaped, not just housing. People need homes; there is no question of that. But in recent years, Americans have been spending more and more for less and less. Houses should be built cheaper, say developers; let's cut corners, shave lawns, slash red tape. The developers—and their co-conspirators, the politicians—insist that we want instant colonies that look like a kind of stucco algae, faceless and grim (despite recently applied pastel cosmetics); amenity-filled private enclaves surrounded by walls and divorced from their surroundings, locked into place by strict covenants.[52]

Louv summarized his concerns succinctly: "We have a generation in this country that doesn't know you should be able to paint your house any color you want."[53]

## ONCE UPON A TIME, THERE WAS A SET OF RULES

The CID, in a strange way, embodies bits and pieces of all of these ideas— Lockean, libertarian, socialistic, feudal, and corporatist. Rather than try to pigeonhole this new social and political entity, it is more important to examine it from the standpoint of its relative legitimacy and possible effects on the meaning of citizenship.

Some of the most troubling questions arise when we see CIDs as private governments and then attempt to find a legitimate basis for their rule. The classical liberal justifications used to legitimize American government tend to undermine, rather than support, this form of private government. CID regimes are inconsistent not only with political theories of legitimacy but with the normal process by which governments are created.

For example, the Puritans who brought European ways to America in the seventeenth century had the advantage of beginning with a community of people who shared basic values—in this case, religious ones—and then proceeding to try to construct a civil society in which people could live in a manner consistent with God's laws. Homeowner associations reverse this order, and in so doing they exalt the status of rules—rules designed first and foremost to protect property values—above the fabric of the community.

The creators of CIDs—corporate developers and their lawyers—begin their projects on paper. They design the entire development, including houses, streets, and recreation facilities, complete to the last detail. Using relatively standardized CC&Rs, articles of incorporation, and by-laws, they set up a system of government complete with a set of rules. They obtain permission from the state to subdivide the land, and from local agencies they acquire the necessary building permits. Then they hire numerous contractors to build the houses and the common areas. In short, they build a sort of ghost town, with everything in it but human beings. Finally, they begin selling the project to the people who eventually will live there.

The priorities embodied in this process are clear and explicit: first, there is a plan; second, there is property; third, there are rules to protect the property; fourth, there is a physical "city"; and last, there are people to live in the city and to follow the rules that protect the property. In short, a CID is a prefabricated framework for civil society in search of a population. The population may come and go, but the property and the rules will remain, and the population will remain in service to the property.

This is a reversal of the Lockean belief that the right to own property arises in the state of nature, before the social contract is established, and is therefore largely outside the reach of government regulation, except for necessary taxation. The CID differs in other important respects from the classical liberal state-of-nature argument justifying government.

In Locke's view, it is assumed that human beings exist initially in a state of nature, with no government—what we might call the original "private" sphere in a pure sense—and that they decide to erect a civil society as the "proper remedy for the inconveniences of the state of nature."[54] They then set up a civil society whose legitimacy must be based on the consent of those it governs. This is a variation on Hobbes' famous argument that life in the state of nature is "solitary, poor, nasty, brutish and short" because people are living without civil laws and are subject to one another's selfish aggression. According to Hobbes, people are subject to strong government out of necessity, to ensure their self-preservation; Locke prefers limited government based on "consent" and arising out of "inconveniences."

In the theories of Hobbes and Locke we see the development of the distinction between private and public that, though often unclear, is with us today. The private sphere, for these theorists, is what we retain from the state of nature, and it remains ours by natural right. For Hobbes, the essential natural right is self-preservation. Locke adds to this the right to possess property. In the public sphere is the state, or government, along with the laws that regulate our behavior and are consistent with the legit-imate ends of government—meaning, for Locke, that government would protect property rights and certainly not unduly interfere with them.

This order of events is turned on its head in the CID. At the out-set there is nothing—a state of nature devoid of people except for the developer-creator, who begets the "community" and its social order to his liking and makes it unchangeable. After that is done, the people arrive at his invitation and are permitted to live there forever according to his rules, long after he has abandoned them to their own devices. This scenario is closer to Genesis than Locke, resembling the early days of the Garden of Eden more than the Puritans' arrival in the New World. It also deviates significantly from the classical liberal justification for gov-ernment.

In a variety of ways, CIDs elevate rules and legalisms above the social fabric of the subsociety. In essence, law, instead of serving the commu-nity, is elevated above it. There are three ways this priority of rules over community manifests itself, all of which relate to what it means to be a citizen of these subsocieties, and these factors tend to undermine any claim to legitimacy under principles with which Americans are familiar:

1. There is a serious question regarding whether there is any meaningful consent to the rules of these subsocieties.

2. The concept of "rights" is replaced with the idea of "restric-tions" as the guiding principle in the relationship of the individ-ual to the community.

3. The concept of responsibility to the community is defined as nothing more than meeting one's economic obligations and conforming to the rules—all of which has the ultimate stated purpose of simply protecting property values.

## Consent

In what sense can people be said to consent to the laws of the private government when they did not participate in their making and when membership in the association is compulsory? People could certainly participate in changing the rules to the limited extent possible, but in fact they did not even participate in making the rules by which the rules can be changed.

Consent is not just a logical issue, because developers routinely require a super-majority vote, such as 80 percent of *all eligible voters,* for changing the restrictions. Considering the poor turnout for city elections, one can imagine how hard it is to attain such a vote. Some states have passed laws making it possible for fewer residents than the super-majority to go to court to change these requirements, under certain conditions.[55]

Developers and other proponents of CIDs typically argue that people consent to the rules of a CID by buying and living there. If they don't move out, it is assumed that they consent. But this argument, a standard in the industry, runs aground on the facts. First, it is increasingly difficult to find non-CID housing in many parts of the country. Second, as the real estate market consolidates at the large corporate level, the opportunity for real choice among CIDs—that is, for meaningful choices among different lifestyles and regimes of rules—may be diminishing. Any diversity that exists is provided at the discretion of the real estate development industry.

## Restrictions Instead of Rights

A second way CIDs embody a different kind of citizenship by placing rules ahead of community is in how CIDs have replaced the concept of *rights* with that of *restrictions.*

These restrictions are legally known as "equitable servitudes," a legal concept that predates the constitution. In essence, equitable servitudes allow somebody to sell land but still control how that land is used.

In CIDs, the doctrine has a specific and characteristic application. The developer initially owns all the land in the development, then subdivides it and creates the document of covenants, conditions, and restrictions that goes with each parcel. So all buyers are mutually bound by the same restrictions from the moment of purchase, meaning there was never a time when they buyers were in a "state of nature," because the developer had that to himself. And there was never a time when they created civil government, reserved certain rights to themselves as inalienable, and gave certain rights to government. The developer did all that. Instead, they were bound to enforce the CC&Rs against each other and were restricted in their use of the land by those CC&Rs and the other documents. In essence, they never had rights, natural or otherwise, to begin with. The very essence of their ownership interest is that it was partial ownership, burdened with permanent restrictions on how the property may be used.

Residents in CIDs commonly fail to understand the difference between a regime based formally on rights, such as American civil governments, and the CID regime, which is based on restrictions. This often leads to people becoming angry at board meetings and claiming that their "rights" have been violated—rights that they wrongly believe they have in the CID.[56]

This absence of rights has important consequences because the balance of power between individual and private government is reversed. It could be said that, in reality, public governments try to accomplish the same thing, but the point is that in the CID it is not a subversion, or a perversion, of justice for this to occur, but quite legal and proper.

There is also an irony here. It is perhaps no coincidence that in the country in which the distinction between private and public is thought to be so clear, and the concomitant preservation of the private sphere so complete, we also find a peculiarly American form of private government in which the property rights of the developer, and later the board of directors, swallow up the rights of the people, and public government is left as a bystander.

## Social Responsibility Equals Paying Your Dues

A third indication of the new citizenship in CIDs is the assumption that a resident's responsibilities to the "community" can be satisfied by meeting one's economic obligations. This consists of making house payments, paying association dues and assessments, and conforming to a set of lifestyle restrictions that have the sole stated purpose of preserving the value of the commonly owned property.

It could be said that civil government permits a similarly detached citizenship. Citizens pay taxes, obey the law, do their jobs, vote if they choose, and serve in the military if drafted. Beyond that, any further involvement in community affairs is a matter of choice.

But cities, states, and nations have vast networks of private and public threads that tie citizens together and make them interdependent. We are linked via law, religion, the mass media, and bureaucracies in ways that encourage or compel us to be responsible to, and for, each other. These responsibilities extend far beyond maintaining property values and conformity. In CIDS, a different, more restricted model of civic responsibility obtains.

The long-term effects of these departures from liberal assumptions may be significant. Students of politics have long recognized that people learn a great deal about the meaning of citizenship from day-to-day life in their communities. Robert Dahl has written that "what Pericles said of Athens, that the city is in general a school of the Grecians, may be said of every city of moderate size: It is a marvelous school."[57] The spread of common-interest housing means that different lessons are being learned and that generations of children are "going to school" on the streets of a new kind of city.

# 7

# CID Private Governments and the Law in California

Constitutional and common law protections do not lose
their potency merely because familiar functions are
organized into more complex or privatized arrangements.
—Majority opinion of the California Supreme Court in
*Frances T. v. Village Green Owners Association*

The rapid spread of homeowner associations, and the activities of their
private governments, created a number of complex social and political
issues that needed resolution. The actions of developers in creating these
regimes were undertaken as private initiatives. Ratification of the idea
by the Federal Housing Administration, and passage of state laws that
enabled creation of condominiums and other forms of CID ownership, did

not mean that all the implications of CIDs spreading across the nation had been studied—only that FHA and the states had endorsed new concepts in land planning. To the contrary: the growth of CID housing and its implications drew little comprehensive attention from government. Yet, issue by issue, CID-related matters began to come to the attention of public policy makers.

One question that proved to be among the most troubling for courts and legislatures was "What are they?" CIDs could be seen as governments or as businesses, each of which has its own legal limitations and liabilities, or as something else entirely. Once it was determined what they were it would be possible to decide what they could and could not do. So the definitional question stood at the threshold of a host of new and difficult issues arising from the complex web of relations among the various parties, including the individual owners and renters, the association, the developer, and the surrounding community and its public governments.

Most significantly, this question had to do with the power private governments were to have over their members and the degree to which CID directors and the corporations themselves could be held liable for their actions. It needed to be determined how much public regulation of CIDs should exist and what sort of regulation that should be. In resolving these issues, the state needed to decide what kind of entity it was dealing with.

When the boom in CID housing construction began in the 1960s, the small body of law for dealing with CIDs existed primarily in the form of published appellate court opinions resulting from lawsuits. Judges were required to apply legal concepts and theories derived from areas of law that had evolved without CIDs in mind but still seemed to pertain. Common law sources from which judges could draw in adjudicating specific lawsuits included corporation law, especially the law governing nonprofit corporations; the law of servitudes, which dealt generally with restrictive covenants; tort law pertaining to the duties and liabilities of landowners and landlords; and constitutional restrictions on the powers of government over the individual. But there was no assurance that attorneys across the nation would present the same theories in similar situations, nor was there any reason to believe that judges would necessarily reach the same conclusions. Consequently, different results were reached on important issues from state to state, many even among judicial districts in the same state.

Whatever its shortcomings, common law became an important source of guidance because there was insufficient legislation to provide specific statutory direction. Legislatures were slow to grasp the overall significance of CID housing, and for the most part they acted only in response to developer abuses of homeowners as consumers. Problems such as recreation lease fraud, construction defects, and underfunding of reserves prompted investigations and legislation aimed at eliminating these particular problems. Because most of the problems seemed to involve condominiums, the bulk of regulation of CIDS was targeted at condominiums, leaving other forms of CIDS largely unregulated, and what regulation existed had a consumer-protection focus. For example, when the state of Florida, scene of some of the worst abuses of condominium purchasers, became the first state to establish a permanent government department to regulate in this area, it called the agency the Bureau of Condominiums and located it in the Department of Business Regulation.[1] Legislatures nationwide failed to come to grips with the full range of issues presented by the rise of common-interest housing.

This inaction was, in part, the result of industry lobbying. Such industry organizations as CAI were concerned about what they feared could become overregulation, and they worked to thwart federal and state measures that they considered excessive. A 1983 CAI publication reflecting on the first ten years of the organization's existence noted that "during those early hectic years, the community association form of ownership was under attack by the public sector. CAI responded to several national legislative proposals to regulate condominiums and homeowner associations."[2]

The first legislative activities of CAI had to do with federal taxation of homeowner associations: "There was one burning public policy issue as a result of several adverse IRS rulings affecting associations' tax status. As a consequence, the CAI Board, through its legal counsel, aggressively pursued corrective legislation toward establishing a unique tax status for associations, and CAI was successful in creating 'Section 528.' Later, through further efforts by CAI, the tax rate applied to associations exercising this provision of the code was lowered by one-third to a more acceptable level."[3]

In part because CAI and other industry organizations had varying degrees of success in stopping and otherwise influencing regulation at the state and national level, there was substantial variation in state laws. The effort to standardize state legislation in this area began in 1977, when the National Conference of Commissioners on Uniform State Laws adopted the Uniform Condominium Act. In 1980 the conference adopted a Uniform Planned Community Act, and the next year it adopted a model act for cooperatives. In 1982 the conference consolidated all three acts into the Uniform Common Interest Ownership Act, which it recommended for adoption by the states.[4] Wayne S. Hyatt, the most prominent advocate of CAI in legal matters and editor of its *Community Association Law Reporter,* was involved in preparation of all the acts. John P. Donohoe, a CAI trustee and later chair of the Public Policy Committee of CAI, worked on the model acts for planned communities and cooperatives.[5] By 1992 CAI concluded, some version of the four model acts had been adopted in nearly one-third of the states.[6]

The body of statutory and case law governing homeowner associations grew rapidly and became a distinct area of specialization. The *Community Association Law Reporter,* a monthly update of legal developments affecting homeowner associations nationwide, was published for CID legal practitioners. The *Reporter* summarized cases and legislation that came to Hyatt's attention through a national network of attorneys associated with CAI.

The headings under which Hyatt grouped his material for the *Reporter* gave some sense of the magnitude and complexity of homeowner association law. The headings included architectural control, assessments, association operations, contracts, condominium conversions, covenant enforcement, developer liability, developmental rights, documents, federal law and legislation, mechanic's lien foreclosure, municipal relations, powers of the association, risks and liabilities, security, state and local legislation, taxes and tax legislation, timesharing, use restrictions, and warranties.

Along with a substantial body of law review articles were legal textbooks, treatises, and practice guides for attorneys practicing in the area.[7] Hyatt coedited a treatise on homeowner association litigation and wrote a number of law review articles regarding CID housing.[8]

Although it might have been possible in 1960 to summarize the law governing CIDs in a single book or even a single chapter, that soon became impossible. But it is instructive to consider particular aspects of CID legal development in one state. California is perhaps the best state to study, for several reasons. It has an estimated twenty-five thousand of the nation's one hundred fifty thousand homeowner associations—second only to Florida, which has forty thousand associations—and has had sufficient time to develop a significant body of law on the subject.[9] California and Florida are the only states where CAI has established a permanent legislative action committee. Through intense legal and political activity CAI has been able to wield substantial influence in the courts and legislature, and it has played a major role in two legislative task forces considering comprehensive CID law reform. California is also home to nearly one-eighth of the nation's population, and it has experienced enormous growth in population and housing units since World War II. For decades California in general and Los Angeles in particular have been at the cutting edge of American trends in use of zoning, restrictive covenants, suburbanization, and common-interest housing.[10]

Moreover, California has a standard court structure, with trial courts of general jurisdiction, intermediate appellate courts sitting in panels, and a seven-person Supreme Court sitting *en banc*.[11] The California court system for years has been considered a leader among appellate courts, and there has been considerable diffusion of California legal principles to other states.

California has also been required, in appellate court cases and legislation, to decide whether homeowner associations should be viewed by the law as governments, and also whether they should be seen as some sort of private business or nonprofit enterprise. The national and state constitutions limit the actions of government, particularly those that impinge on protected individual liberties. CIDs currently engage in many activities that would be prohibited if they were viewed by the courts as the equivalent of local governments. This definitional issue is often implicated when questions are raised concerning the power of the association to impose restrictions on individual members. On the other hand, businesses are subject to civil liability and are often required to pay damages to those they injure, negligently or intentionally. Associations have been sued by residents and others under various theories of tort liability. Either avenue—recognizing constitutional limitations as governments or civil liability as businesses—would provide a check on the actions of CID boards.

California courts have addressed both the government and business dimensions of CIDs. In different cases and under different circumstances, courts have called CID boards both "mini-governments" and "business establishments" and have sought to establish boundaries for their behavior along both lines. But when they have ruled contrary to the perceived interests of CID advocates, CAI and other groups have been aggressive

about obtaining relief from the state legislature. Their efforts were enhanced by their numbers and power and simplified by the absence of
consistent, organized opposition.

So far, California CID forces have been successful both in resisting
judicial and legislative action that would treat homeowner associations
as governments and in reducing the potential liability of board members
in lawsuits filed by homeowners, developers, and others. The result of
combined judicial activity and legislative intervention is that CIDs have
neither the limitations of a government nor the full potential for civil
liability of a business. In their competition with public governments,
these mini-governments are the beneficiaries of a double standard.

Tracing the history of legislative and judicial action on this issue in
California offers insights into the relationship between courts, the state
legislature and CID advocates in general, in a state where the outcome
matters a great deal.


## PRIVATE GOVERNMENT AND THE FOURTEENTH AMENDMENT

California's court decisions concerning whether CIDs boards should have
the legal status and responsibilities of private governments took place in
the context of a debate presented in a number of detailed law review
articles and elsewhere.[12] Most states had never addressed the problem in
published opinions, and others had it presented to them directly or
indirectly.[13] There was, however, precedent from the U.S. Supreme Court
that the California courts, and those of other states, could adopt if they
chose.

The precedent most often cited by those who wished to classify CID
activity as governmental is the U.S. Supreme Court decision in *Marsh v.
Alabama* (326 U.S. 501 [1945]). Grace Marsh was a Jehovah's Witness
who attempted to distribute religious literature in Chickasaw, Alabama,
a suburb of Mobile wholly owned by Gulf Shipbuilding Corporation. The
corporate town prohibited distribution of literature without a permit,
and Marsh was refused a permit. When she persisted in distributing the
literature, claiming it was her constitutional right, she was arrested for
trespassing.

The logic of Justice Hugo Black's opinion is simple. Chickasaw had
all the attributes of any other town except that it was private property
owned by a corporation. If any other town had arrested Marsh for dis-

tributing religious literature, it would have been unconstitutional. So, Black wrote, "our question then narrows down to this: Can those people who live in or come to Chickasaw be denied freedom of press and religion simply because a single company has legal title to all the town? For it is the State's contention that the mere fact that all the property interests in the town are held by a single company is enough to give that company power, enforceable by a state statute, to abridge these freedoms" (326 U.S. 501, 505).

The majority opinion stops short of calling the corporation a private government (though Justice Felix Frankfurter's concurring opinion is blunter: "A company town is a town as well as a congeries of property relations" [326 U.S. 501, 511]), but it finds ample state involvement (the arrest and the presence of a public highway) to justify application of the First Amendment rights of freedom of press and religion through the Fourteenth Amendment. "In our view the circumstance that the property rights to the premises where the deprivation of liberty, here involved, took place, were held by others than the public, is not sufficient to justify *the State's permitting a corporation to govern a community of citizens so as to restrict their fundamental liberties* and the enforcement of such restraint by the application of a state statute" (326 U.S. 501, 509; emphasis added).

The italicized language could include many kinds of organizations that political scientists call private governments, and it could be read to imply that fundamental constitutional guarantees apply to their activities. Indeed, Adolph Berle noted in his classic work *The Twentieth Century Capitalist Revolution* that in *Marsh v. Alabama* the court had "come within a biscuit-toss" of "applying constitutional limitations to corporations as such," and he opined that "when the case is squarely presented, the courts will cross the line, when it is made to appear that the corporation in fact has power, and in fact has used that power, without due process, in such manner as in fact to deprive an American of liberty of property or other constitutional rights."[14]

To date, that prophecy has not come to pass. But a second well-known U.S. Supreme Court precedent often cited by people challenging CID decisions is *Shelley v. Kraemer* (334 U.S. 1 [1948]), in which the court held that state enforcement of racially discriminatory restrictive covenants in land sales violates the Fourteenth Amendment's equal protection clause, which prohibits racial discrimination by the states. It is impossible for CIDs to function unless courts enforce their restrictive covenants. If this enforcement power is conditioned on the absence of constitutional violation, effectively the CID could be subject to constitutional regulation.

The emerging question was, Under what circumstances might the private conduct of CIDs and analogous private organizations be considered state action?[15] In 1968, in *Food Employees Local 590 v. Logan Valley Plaza, Inc.* (391 U.S. 1 308), the Warren court ruled that there is a First Amendment right to free speech in private shopping malls. The decisions seemed to recognize that private entities were now performing what had historically been government functions. Malls had become, in essence, the private equivalent of the *agora*, the public marketplace or Main Street where political activity had historically taken place. Consequently, these new privatized public spaces had to permit political activity to occur. This seemed consistent with the rationale of the *Marsh* opinion.

In subsequent decisions, however, the court backed away from the implications of these rulings. Eight years later, the Burger court overruled the *Logan Valley* decision in the 1976 case of *Hudgens v. NLRB* (424 U.S. 507), saying that there is no federal constitutional right to speak, picket, or petition government in a private shopping mall.

But in 1979 the California Supreme Court found that such a right did exist in the California state constitution *(Robins v. Pruneyard Shopping Center,* 23 Cal. 3d 899), over the objection of mall owners who claimed their property rights were being infringed upon. In the view of the mall owners, the state was taking their property without compensation—in violation of the Fifth Amendment "takings" clause—when it forced them to permit on their premises speech that they wished to prevent. The mall owners appealed to the U.S. Supreme Court, but the Court affirmed the California decision in 1980 *(Pruneyard Shopping Center v. Robins,* 100 S. Ct. 2035).

The upshot of the U.S. Supreme Court's rulings on the subject was something of a standoff: the would-be speakers had no federal First Amendment right to speak on private property, but the private property owner had no right under the Fifth Amendment to claim that his property had been taken for public use without just compensation, even if state law required him to permit free speech on his property. Consequently, variations from state to state were possible and legally permissible.[16]

## CALIFORNIA COURTS AND CID PRIVATE GOVERNMENT

Beginning in the early 1980s California appellate courts began to establish limits on the conduct of CID boards of directors. In doing so the courts considered the extent to which the boards were subject to governmental limitations and the degree to which they should be subject to ordinary tort liability as businesses. The court decisions that emerged from this case-by-case, common-law approach to CID conduct did not resolve the issues clearly.

In 1982 the California Court of Appeal for the Fourth District decided *Laguna Publishing Company v. Golden Rain Foundation of Laguna Hills* (182 Cal. App. 3d 816 [1982]). This hotly contested case led to an extremely long and convoluted opinion. The case was notable for the way it grappled, albeit inconclusively, with the issue of whether CID actions are governmental in nature.

The association governing the twenty thousand residents of the seniors' community Leisure World banned unsolicited delivery of all newspapers except for its house organ, the *Leisure World News*. The ban was enforced by private security guards. A competing newspaper publisher challenged the ban in court on a variety of constitutional grounds. At stake, in addition to constitutional principles, were millions of dollars in advertising revenue, because Leisure World is "a captive audience of 20,000 affluent people whom advertisers are trying to reach" (131 Cal. App. 3d 834).

The court held that *Marsh v. Alabama* was inapplicable because "there are no retail businesses or commercial service establishments in Leisure World" but then said that the community had attributes that "bring it conceptually close to characterization as a company town, and such attributes do weigh in our decision" (131 Cal. App. 3d 836). Later in the opinion the court called Leisure World a "hybrid in this sense" (131 Cal. App. 3d 843).

Next the court addressed the so-called shopping center cases dealing with citizens' rights under the California Constitution to free speech at a privately owned shopping center *(Robins v. Pruneyard Shopping Center,* 23 Cal. 3d 899; *Pruneyard Shopping Center v. Robins,* 447 U.S. 74). The court then tried to place CID conduct in the *Pruneyard* context: "To this we add that the gated and walled community is a new phenomenon on the social scene, and, in the spirit of the foregoing pronouncement, the ingenuity of the law will not be deterred in redressing grievances which arise, as here, from a needless and exaggerated insistence upon private property rights incident to such communities where such insistence is irrelevant in preventing any meaningful encroachment upon private property rights and results in a pointless discrimination which causes serious financial detriment to another" (131 Cal. App. 3d 839).

Then, putting the case in terms of discrimination, the court went on to analogize the situation to *Mulkey v. Reitman* (64 Cal. 2d 529, [1966]), the case in which the California Supreme Court struck down a statewide ballot measure, passed overwhelmingly by the voters, that would have guaranteed to people the "right" to discriminate against minorities in selling houses. The *Mulkey* decision was based on *Shelley v. Kraemer* and extended the concept of state action to "the significant aid of any state agency, even where the actor is a private citizen motivated by purely personal interests" (64 Cal. 2d 538). Leisure World's discriminatory conduct was its refusal to allow distribution of any papers but the house organ.

After adding all these constitutional bits and pieces together, the court said the question was

> whether its town-like characteristics compel Golden Rain's yielding to certain constitutional guarantees as a consequence of its adding discrimination to the picture. When that element is added, the balance tips to the side of the scale which imports the presence of state action per *Mulkey* and the lunch counter cases. In other words, Golden Rain [the CID corporation with power to enforce the restriction], in the proper exercise of its private property rights, may certainly choose to exclude *all* give-away, unsolicited newspapers from Leisure World, but once it chooses to admit one, where that decision is not made in concert with the residents, then the discriminatory exclusion of another such newspaper represents an abridgement of the free speech, free press rights of the excluded newspaper secured under our state Constitution. (131 Cal. App. 3d 843; emphasis in original)

The state action was "the implicit sanction of the state's police power" (131 Cal. App. 3d 844). As if to emphasize the narrowness of its holding and to make it clear that Leisure World's regime based on private restrictive covenants was still intact, the court added,"The rule we announce as the basis for resolution of this phase of the case will not result in requiring unrestricted admittance to Leisure World of religious evangelists, political campaigners, assorted salespeople, signature solicitors, or any other uninvited persons of the like. . . . [T]he owners of this private property still remain in *complete* control of who shall enter Leisure World." (131 Cal. App. 3d 845; emphasis in original).

One year later the same court, in an opinion by the same justice, decided the case of *Cohen v. Kite Hill* (142 Cal. App. 3d 642 [1983]), which dealt with the zoning-like activities of CID boards. The board had permitted the Cohens' neighbor to construct a fence that did not conform to the CC&Rs, and the Cohens sued the board for approving the nonconforming fence.

The court overruled a demurrer to the suit, holding that the Cohens could sue the board for failing to properly enforce the covenants. In doing so, the court quoted at length from a well-known law review article cowritten by Wayne Hyatt.[17] That article described the homeowner association as a "quasi-governmental entity paralleling in almost every case the powers, duties, and responsibilities of a municipal government," and called it a "mini-government" (142 Cal. App. 3d 651).

The court then compared the handling of variances by CIDs with the administration of zoning regulations: "The Kite Hill Community Association's approval of a fence not in conformity with the Declaration is analogous to the administrative award of a zoning variance. . . . Hence, what the California Supreme Court has stated with regard to judicial review of grants of variances applies equally well to the Association's actions herein. . . . [We] conclude that the courts must be available to protect neighboring property interests from arbitrary actions by homeowner associations" (142 Cal. App. 3d 652).

During oral argument, the Kite Hill Community Association contended that a decision could be considered arbitrary by an individual owner and yet reasonable in light of the overriding interest of the whole. The court dismissed this contention abruptly, and again returned to the government analogy. "Nonsense. Like any community, Kite Hill consists of individual members who form in the aggregate an organic whole. Thus, *like any government,* the Association must balance individual interests against the general welfare" (142 Cal. App. 3d 652–53; emphasis added).

For failing to perform this governmental responsibility, the association could be subject to lawsuit for breach of fiduciary duty. But it was unclear whether CIDs actually were to be treated as mini-governments or whether they were merely like governments in some respects. For example, government officials are protected by certain kinds of immunities against such tort lawsuits.

When the California Supreme Court considered the nature of CID regimes in other cases, it viewed the mini-government concept as more of an analogy than a reality and instead began treating CIDs as a form of business. In 1983 the court held that nonprofit homeowner associations are "business establishments" within the meaning of the Unruh Civil Rights Act (California Civil Code, sec. 51). Under that statute they were prohibited from enforcing age restrictions on residency *(O'Connor v. Village Green Owners Association,* 33 Cal. 3d 790 [1983]). The provision at issue banned residency by anyone under age eighteen. The court said,

> The Village Green Owners Association has sufficient business-like attributes to fall within the scope of the act's reference to "business establishments of every kind whatsoever." . . . In brief, the association performs all the customary business functions which in the traditional landlord-tenant relationship rest on the landlord's shoulders. A theme running throughout the description of the association's powers and duties is that its overall function is to protect and enhance the project's economic value. Consistent with the Legislature's intent to use the term "business establishments" in the broadest sense reasonably possible . . . we conclude that the Village Green Owners Association is a business establishment within the meaning of the act. (33 Cal. 3d 796)

This case was a serious blow to developers who wished to target-market child-free CID housing to affluent seniors. A campaign was mounted to have the state legislature rewrite the Unruh Act so as to overrule the Supreme Court's decision. In 1984 the legislature amended the Unruh Act to exempt seniors' housing from its terms, permitting them to engage in age discrimination.[18]

Three years later the California Supreme Court once again tried to decide what legal definition to apply to CID private governments, in a case arising from the same development. In *Frances T. v. Village Green Owners Association* (42 Cal. 3d 490 [1986]), the issue was whether an owners' association and the individual board members could be held civilly liable for the rape and robbery of a unit owner. The board knew the development was in a high-crime area and nonetheless refused the unit owner's request for permission to install exterior lighting at her unit. She sued for negligence, breach of contract, and breach of fiduciary duty.

Again the court viewed the CID as a sort of business enterprise, holding the board members to the standards expected of a landlord in protecting tenants against the acts of criminals. The court stated that "the Association is, for all practical purposes, the Project's 'landlord.'" The court briefly mentioned *Pruneyard v. Robbins, Shelley v. Kraemer,* and *Marsh v. Alabama* in a footnote and in passing: "Constitutional and common law protections do not lose their potency merely because familiar functions are organized into more complex or privatized arrangements" (42 Cal. 3d 490, n.6). There is no indication, however, that these cases played any substantial role in the decision.[19]

The *Frances T.* case was another major judicial setback for the CID movement because it allowed suits against not only the homeowner association itself as a corporation but against the individual directors themselves. So the job of volunteer director became less desirable than ever. Directors were expected to do this responsible and often controversial work without compensation, and they were putting their personal assets at risk every time they made a decision. There was general concern within the industry that few CID residents would be willing to serve as directors under such terms, a situation that would undermine the entire concept of homeowners volunteering to enforce the developer's restrictions and maintain the common areas.

Once again CID advocates petitioned the state legislature for relief, asking in two separate legislative sessions that the *Frances T.* decision be overruled by an amendment to the law. The legislature responded by establishing tort immunity for association directors in 1988 and then expanding it in 1992, giving board members protections not unlike those of municipal officials. The law provided immunity for volunteer CID directors for acts performed in the course of their duties, in good faith and without gross negligence, as long as the association itself had adequate liability insurance.[20]

Although the individual directors were immune from suit, the association itself could still be sued.[21] This approach ensured that the injured party had a "deep pocket" from which to seek recovery. But in making the job of volunteer director less hazardous, this immunity reduced the incentive for board members to be consistently cognizant of the consequences their actions might have, for residents and others.

## THE COMMON INTEREST DEVELOPMENT ACT

Through the early 1980s pressure was building for comprehensive legis-lation regarding the place of CIDs in California law. Court decisions, with their case-by-case, piecemeal approach, were leaving many questions unanswered and, sometimes, from the perspective of the CID movement, creating more problems than they solved. This pressure led to the cre-ation of a legislative task force that ultimately produced the Davis-Stirling Common Interest Development Act (CIDA), enacted in 1985.

The CIDA was the product of the Assembly Select Committee on Com-mon Interest Subdivisions, which was formed "to identify problems with the law of condominiums, planned developments and cooperatives and to suggest changes to correct the problems."[22] The committee, chaired by Assemblyman Larry Stirling, a Republican from San Diego, held hear-ings and conducted meetings with professionals who dealt with CIDs.[23] The committee also established a task force of representatives from "affected industries" who were primarily responsible for drafting the act. The senior consultant to the committee was Katharine Rosenberry, a law professor at California Western University in San Diego and a national officer (and later national president) of the Community Associations Institute. Rosenberry's activities were central to the shape and content of this legislation, giving CAI what amounted to direct participation in the writing of the act.

Other members of the task force whom Rosenberry identified as the principal drafters of the act, and the entities they represented, included David Van Atta, California State Bar; Doris Agee, Executive Council of Homeowners (ECHO); Peter Saputo, Building Industry Association; Mar-tin Dingman, California Department of Real Estate; Ron Kingston, advo-cate for the California Association of Realtors; Curtis Sproul, homeowner association attorney; Collyer Church, California Land Title Association; Mike Packard, national president of the Community Associations Insti-tute; Gary Aguirre, attorney and CAI member specializing in represent-ing CIDs in construction defect litigation; and Wayne Hanson, property manager (and graduate of the Professional Community Association Manager Program sponsored by CAI).[24]

It is apparent from Rosenberry's description that the CID movement, and CAI in particular, had more influence over the legislation than any other interest group. Of the eleven task force members, including Rosen-berry, six are identified with CAI or ECHO or are legal advocates for CIDs.

No other interest group, such as developers or lenders, had comparable influence on the legislation, and all the principal drafters represented private interests.

The powerful influence of the CID movement is also apparent from the issues it chose to address, which together form a sort of wish list for CID boards of directors and the industries organized to serve them. Rosenberry, in a 1985 article, identified thirty-seven problems the task force decided to address.[25] Many of them are technical matters of concern only to associations and their lawyers, such as the definition of a planned development.

Some issues were matters of convenience, such as the problem that the law governing CIDs was difficult to locate because it was spread through a variety of codes, including Civil, Business and Professions, and Corporations. The task force successfully sought to consolidate provisions affecting CIDs in the Civil Code.

In truth, a number of the issues Rosenberry identified as problems are more properly characterized as requests for more power for CID boards. For example, she points out that "Civil Code Section 1725, which places restrictions on the penalties the association may impose for failure to pay delinquent assessments, is unclear. It is unclear whether associations may charge interest on the delinquent assessments and whether attorney's fees may be recovered in the absence of filing a lawsuit. (The latter issue may be clearer than association attorneys would like to think.)"[26]

Here Rosenberry's goal is to secure for associations the power to charge interest and attorney's fees associated with collecting delinquent assessments without filing a lawsuit against the homeowner. No such power existed, and there was nothing unclear about it, as her parenthetical joke indicated. The problem was not lack of clarity but lack of legal authority.

The task force also identified some of the broad issues related to CIDs, including the explosive contention often voiced by CID advocates that CID residents pay a double tax. Rosenberry listed it as a problem about which the task force was concerned. "Owners in common-interest subdivisions are subjected to a potentially unfair tax burden. Since the passage of Proposition 13, local governments have attempted to save money by requiring developers to build 'public improvements' such as parks and pass the cost of maintenance of the improvements to the owners in the common interest project. Thus, while these individuals are paying for maintenance of public parks in standard subdivisions, through their taxes, the owners in standard subdivisions are not paying to keep up the parks in the common interest projects."[27]

Advocates of CIDs have long contended that the assessments residents pay to their associations are the equivalent of property taxes because the assessments go toward the maintenance of services and facilities ordinarily provided by local government. They contend that if they are paying for their own trash removal, for maintenance of their own streets, and for upkeep on their own park, they should not have to pay property tax assessments for such services as public trash removal and street and park maintenance. Paying both the full measure of property tax and common areas assessments is unfair, they feel. The solution, from their perspective, would be to permit CID residents to deduct some or all of their assessments from their property tax bills. In areas with large numbers of CIDs, this could amount to a serious loss of local government revenues.

The double taxation argument does not emphasize the fact that CID residents have access to the public streets and other facilities supported by their taxes and those of nonresidents of CIDs, though nonresidents do not have access to the private facilities supported by CID assessments. One logical but impossible implication of the double taxation argument would be that CID residents, once relieved of their tax burden, would be banished from public streets, parks, and other facilities supported by property taxes.

Regardless of the degree to which CID residents use public facilities, they benefit from the existence of such facilities, which are essential to the overall environment in which their developments exist. For example, their food supply arrives through public streets maintained by local property tax, and the public parks serve an important, even indispensable, social function of providing a place for people to gather and play. A metropolitan area lacking such facilities would have a very different character from those to which most people, including CID residents, are accustomed.

In fact, the private facilities enjoyed exclusively by CID owners are luxuries that they purchased and for which they are consequently expected to pay. Public facilities are open to everybody, and for that reason everybody pays taxes to support them. Many people do not use public parks because they belong to health clubs or use public libraries because they are college professors who have access to superior research facilities. They pay for these assets in one way or another, but they are not permitted to avoid property tax liability as a consequence. Public services are not provided on a pay-as-you-go basis.

Whatever its problems, the double taxation argument has persisted, and it was discussed by the task force. It represents a wedge that, some say, could forge unity among CID owners and make them into a force in electoral politics. This issue ultimately was not acted upon by the legislature in the CIDA, and double taxation remains a rallying cry for CID advocates. In 1991 a prominent lobbyist wrote that "no issue is likely to have more political fallout at the state and local level, to galvanize a constituency where once there was no constituency, than that of the taxation/double taxation of community associations. And yet this issue is being all but ignored by policy-makers."[28]

Rosenberry and the task force also addressed another issue that the legislature did not act upon: the degree to which CIDs should be restricted by constitutional standards or other strictures meant for governmental entities—i.e., the issue of whether CIDs are private governments. Rosenberry writes:

It is unclear whether the United States and California Constitutions apply to common interest projects. The court in *Laguna Publishing Co. v. Golden Rain* held that the U.S. Constitution did not apply to the planned development in question, but that the state constitution did. If courts decide that either constitution applies to common interest projects, numerous questions are raised. Does developer-weighted voting and one-unit-one-vote, violate the principle of "one-person-one-vote"? Could an association that unconstitutionally interferes with a unit owner's due process rights, by passing a restriction against leasing, be liable for damages on a theory of inverse condemnation? Are the board members who enforced age restrictions prior to the *O'Connor* decision liable for punitive damages if age restrictions are found to be unconstitutional? Do security projects violate one's right to privacy? The questions go on and on![29]

Rosenberry views the issue in terms of its negative implications, inclining in the direction that imposing constitutional limitations is a bad idea. She goes on to question the *Cohen v. Kite Hill* decision, saying that, even if the state and federal constitutions did not apply to CIDs, "it is unclear whether the boards will be held to the same standard as municipalities." If so, she wondered, would they have to have findings of fact to support their decisions, as would a city? If they restricted commercial uses in a development, would they be in violation of antitrust laws? And, "If the association is a mini-government, are the board members protected by any type of governmental immunity?"[30]

Absent from the issues discussed in Rosenberry's article, some would say, is the fact that CIDs exercise governmental authority over residents without any of the restrictions normally associated with that authority—at least in the United States. The Common Interest Development Act failed to establish procedures for limiting board power over members or curbing abuses of discretion. One member of the task force said that the group considered whether to recommend to the legislature adoption of the CAI-devised Community Association Members' and Residents' Bill of Rights but decided against it. Ultimately, it would have made little difference, because the Bill of Rights emphatically stated that CIDs were neither governments nor businesses and should not be subject to "the full panoply of governmental limitations." The document is less a statement of liberties than an information sheet advising CID residents of the limitations on their rights.[31]

After the Common Interest Development Act became law in 1985, debate continued in legal and legislative circles about the many unresolved issues. Assemblyman Dan Hauser, chair of the Housing Committee, headed a new Select Committee on Common Interest Subdivisions convened in 1990. The California Legislative Action Committee of CAI immediately met with Hauser and his consultants and announced to its members that "CLAC will be expected to provide the select committee with its ideas and concerns about issues affecting community associations and to comment on specific bills that come before the committee. Through the select committee's work, CLAC can have an important influence over the nature of legislation that addresses issues of concern to our members."[32]

The committee considered dozens of proposals for new legislation and could have made sweeping changes in the law governing CIDs. But a new state ballot measure slashed the budget of the legislature, and the select committee was dissolved.[33] Ultimately it produced only fourteen "spot" bills—interim measures designed to occupy legislative space until they can be revised.[34] In 1991, however, Hauser's regular Housing and

Community Development Committee took up a number of these proposals, as well as other measures dealing with CID housing.

By the end of the 1992 sessions the CID movement was able to claim yet another set of successes in the legislature, though the governor was not as reflexively friendly to CID interests. Robyn Boyer Stewart, a lobbyist for CID (and a former consultant to Hauser's select committee) identified forty-one bills related to CIDs. Of these, she noted seven bills that passed both houses and were sent to the governor for signature and that were, in her view, "critical to the common interest constituency." They included the following:

· A.B. 730, sponsored by Hauser, which authorized CID boards to impose fines on members for rule violation, regardless of whether the CC&Rs gave them that power. The bill was vetoed.

· A.B. 790, sponsored by Hauser and proposed by ECHO (Stewart's client), and A.B. 2049, also proposed by ECHO, which together repealed the California Residential Earthquake Recovery Fund program and, between passage of the repeal and the date it went into effect, eliminated CID board obligations under the fund, an insurance program that required all California homeowners to pay up to sixty dollars per year for fifteen thousand dollars in mandatory earthquake coverage.

· A.B. 867, sponsored by Hauser, which created mandatory, nonbinding arbitration for disputes between CID boards and their members. The bill was vetoed.

· A.B. 1384, sponsored by Hauser, which authorized CID boards to amend the CC&Rs to eliminate provisions dealing only with the developer's completion and marketing of a project.

· A.B. 2693, proposed by ECHO, which expanded the tort immunity created for CID board members by Civil Code Section 1365.7.

· A.B. 3554, which gave CID boards the authority to regulate members' installation of solar energy equipment in the same manner as other architectural modifications.

· A.B. 3708, which immunized CID associations and their boards against cross-complaints by developers and other parties sued by the association in negligence actions.[35]

The CID industry rolled up a number of significant victories and suffered no major legislative setbacks.[36] Stewart concluded on her "report card" that the legislature "as a body, receives an A! On the important measures rolling through the Legislature in 1992, the overwhelming majority of the Members of both houses supported our issues." She reported that 79 percent of the legislature voted in favor of all seven bills and that an additional 21 percent of each house voted in favor of six of the seven. Not a single member of the Assembly or Senate voted against more than one of the bills.[37]

## THE RULE OF REASON

In the absence of a clear decision by the courts or the legislature regarding the legal classification of CID boards as either governments or businesses, and in the absence of meaningful public regulation, their enforcement actions have come to be judged by a nebulous judicial standard of "reasonableness." This is a venerable principle of the common law of "equitable servitudes" that was codified in Civil Code section 1354. The section states that "the covenants and restrictions in the declaration shall be enforceable equitable servitudes, unless unreasonable."[38] The statute provides no other standard for evaluating a restriction, which leads to litigation as residents challenge the reasonableness of the private laws that govern their lives. The question then becomes one of determining what constitutes a reasonable restriction. CID boards and their advocates would prefer that the law presume the restrictions reasonable, requiring the accused resident to prove it unreasonable. The accused homeowner would rather have the association be forced to prove the reasonableness of its actions under all the circumstances in each case.

This ambiguity led to a court decision in 1992 that CID advocates considered a disaster. Natore Nahrstedt, a resident of the Lakeside Village Condominiums in the Los Angeles suburb of Culver City, felt that it was reasonable for her to keep three cats in her condominium unit. But the condominium association considered its deed restriction reasonable. The restriction read: "No animals (which shall mean dogs and cats), livestock, reptiles or poultry shall be kept in any unit." After the board assessed fines against her that amounted eventually to five hundred dollars per month, she filed suit. A Superior Court judge dismissed her case in the face of what appeared a clear violation of the deed restriction.

Nahrstedt appealed, however, and two of three appellate court judges reversed the trial court and reinstated her complaint. In a ruling that could pose a serious threat to CID board authority over residents, the court held that

> the question of whether the pet restriction at issue in the case before us is an enforceable equitable servitude under Civil Code section 1354 is a mixed issue of law and fact which can only be resolved in the context of the particular circumstances of this case.... Restrictions in CC&Rs are enforceable under Civil Code section 1354 when they prohibit conduct which, while otherwise lawful, in fact interferes with, or has a reasonable likelihood of interfering with, the rights of other condominium owners to the peaceful and quiet enjoyment of their property.
>
> Defendants argue that the blanket pet restriction they seek to enforce against plaintiff is reasonable and enforceable because it avoids a situation where they must always take a "wait and see" position on pets and then litigate over pets that are causing problems in the condominium project. We reject this contention. First, it runs contrary to the philosophy of *Portola Hills* and *Bernardo Villas* [two cases that invalidated as unreasonable the enforcement of restrictions], which is to judge situations on their own specific facts. Plaintiff's condominium home is her castle and her enjoyment of it should be by the least restrictive means possible, conducive with a harmonious communal living arrangement. Second, if carried to its logical conclusion, defendants' argument could be used to support all-inclusive bans on such diverse things as stereo equipment, social gatherings and visitors between the ages of two and eighteen. We cannot envision the courts finding that blanket restrictions against such things are reasonable; yet it is certainly conceivable that allowing Fluffin, Muffin and Ruffin to live inside plaintiff's condominium will pose less of a threat to the peace and quiet of the parties' communal living arrangement than would stereo equipment, parties or young visitors.[39]

Under the law as this court understood it, no restriction was enforceable as a blanket provision, apart from the particular facts of the alleged violation. The association would not be allowed to enforce a restriction as a mere technical violation of the letter of the provision. Instead, restrictions would only be enforceable if, under all the particular circumstances, enforcement was "reasonable," meaning that the violation interfered with other residents' lives. As the court explained it, "If the pet restriction at issue here is found to be unreasonable as applied to plaintiff because plaintiff's conduct in keeping her cats has not interfered with and does not have a reasonable likelihood of interfering with the rights of other owners to the peaceful and quiet enjoyment of their property, then by the very terms of section 1354, it is not enforceable against plaintiff, even though she bought her unit with at least constructive knowledge that keeping cats in the project was forbidden."[40]

Under this rule, residents could knowingly violate a developer's restrictions, then require the association to prove that the violation interfered with the lives of other residents. The court decision was a serious threat to the legitimacy of CC&Rs as systems of private law whose validity had heretofore not been questioned any more than the law against homicide or petty theft.

One justice dissented, arguing that the case was not a "mixed issue of law and fact," as the majority concluded, but a question of law alone.

The courts should leave the enforcement of covenants and restrictions to the homeowners' associations unless there are constitutional principles at stake, enforcement is arbitrary, or the association fails to follow its own procedures. . . . Not only from the standpoint of an already overburdened court system, but from the standpoint of property owners who rely on the enforcement of CC&Rs when they contracted to buy and as they continue to own and live in their property, it is vital to resolve any litigation stemming from such enforcement as early as possible. . . . The majority's new rule will place a tremendous burden on both the condominium owners and the courts by requiring a trial in virtually every lawsuit over the validity of such restrictions.[41]

The dissenting justice went on to argue that old principles of real property law, such as the rule of reasonableness, might have become obsolete, and that CID residents would simply have to adjust to a life of reduced personal freedom dictated by the nature of their housing:

> Legal rules borrowed from real property principles developed during feudal times may prove inappropriate tools as this court, in the late twentieth century, tries to accommodate competing interests involved in the use of a condominium. . . . What is true of the law is even more true of metaphor. An Englishman's home may be a castle. Increasingly, however, a Californian's home is a condominium, and I must question the majority opinion's attempt to recast the respondent's incidents of ownership by calling a condominium a "castle." I have never seen a condominium that even remotely resembled a castle. . . . [C]ondominium living involves increased density, shared and intensified use of common areas and facilities, and a heightened proximity to neighbors. Therefore it necessarily involves the principle that to promote the health, happiness, and peace of mind of the majority of the unit owners, individual unit owners must relinquish a degree of freedom of choice that they might otherwise enjoy in separate, privately owned property. It therefore becomes essential to successful condominium living and the maintenance of the value of these increasingly significant property interests that the owners as a group have the authority to regulate reasonably the use and alienation of the condominiums.[42]

The opinions in the *Nahrstedt* case set the stage for a major legal conflict between the rights of homeowners and the powers of CID boards. At stake was the enforceability of deed restrictions, and consequently the power of every CID board, in the state of California. The majority view sought to limit overly technical and petty rule enforcement and to make sure that CC&R violations would only be prosecuted if they involved some provable harm or inconvenience to other owners. This approach would tend to preserve the sense of privacy, freedom, and control implied in traditional home ownership. The dissent favored the CID industry's freedom-of-contract view and emphasized the need for placing the force of law behind private covenants and sacrificing privacy and individual rights in order for common interest housing to work.

The California Supreme Court decided on November 19, 1992, to review the case, and the CID industry prepared once again to appeal to the legislature for a bill reversing the decision if the Supreme Court failed to do so. Robyn Boyer Stewart described the case as follows in her newsletter:

Word from several quarters—legal, managerial and legislative— that the August 28, 1992, decision by the Second District Appeals Court in the *Nahrstedt v. Lakeside Village Condominium Association* case is nothing less than a CC&R bombshell! . . . The court held that blanket restrictions in CC&Rs are *unreasonable* and, therefore, unenforceable unless the association can show that the conduct essentially infringes on other owners' rights to the peaceful and quite enjoyment of their property. The burden of proof shifts from the offending homeowner to the association which must prove that its blanket restrictions are reasonable in each specific case. Sounds like a dream-come-true for the litigators; watch for legislative action next year on this one.[43] (Emphasis in original)

Her prediction came true on February 19, 1993, when Assemblyman Dan Hauser introduced a bill that would, if passed, "supersede the holding in *Nahrstedt v. Lakeside Village Condominium Association.*"[44]

Although the *Nahrstedt* case and the controversy it created were important in the CID industry, there was still no immediate prospect for clarifying how homeowner associations were to be regarded by the law. Although scholars in several disciplines had no trouble categorizing them as private governments, California lawmakers and judges would go no farther than admitting that CIDs are "like" governments. They were governments only by analogy and were not subject to the limitations on their power normally associated with cities. At the same time, while CIDs were classified as "businesses" for some purposes, the legislature carved out special protections for associations and boards against lawsuits by members and outsiders, including tort immunity similar to that received by municipal officials. As a result of this quasi-government, quasi-business status, CID board activity remained relatively freer from public regulation than it would have if lawmakers had placed them exclusively in one category or the other. Consequently, there was no pressure from CAI or any other industry group for a clear decision. The ambiguous identity of CID private governments was an asset rather than a liability from the standpoint of CID advocates, and, because of the lack of any substantial organized opposition, no change appeared likely.

The regular legislative success of CID lobbyists and interest groups in California was only one indication of the degree to which those involved in common-interest housing were becoming an important factor in politics and society. Yet in California and elsewhere, the full implications of the rise of CID housing remained unexamined.

# 8

## Conclusion: Reflections on Privatopia and the City

I am trying to envision what happens when 10 or 20
per cent of the population has enough income to bypass
the social institutions it doesn't like in ways that only the
top fraction of 1 per cent used to be able to do.
—Charles Murray

The continuing debate over whether the wealthy
are paying their fair share of taxes obscures a larger
issue, with more profound implications for America:
the fortunate fifth is quietly seceding from
the rest of the nation.
—Robert Reich

Samuel Johnson ends his novel *Rasselas* with a conclusion in which, he
tells the reader, "nothing is concluded." This final chapter is less an
attempt to conclude than to discuss some of the broad themes raised thus
far and particularly to consider some of the social and political consequences being wrought in urban America by the spread of CID housing.
   At the end of the nineteenth century, Ebenezer Howard envisioned a

175

new kind of city that would, he believed, gradually transform society if enough of them could be built. His vision combined both physical planning and social engineering ideas. When the garden city idea was transplanted to the United States it was put into practice by real estate developers who wished merely to maximize profits and did not share Howard's utopian social beliefs. Consequently, they emphasized the physical at the expense of the social, paying far more attention to the layout of streets, the location of swimming pools and parks, and the colors of houses than to the nature of the communities they were creating. American CIDs thus took on a bifurcated nature: their physical planning became ever more sophisticated, benefiting from constant study and innovation, but their "constitutions" remained antiquated and inadequate. Residents were expected to run each other's lives through private governments empowered by a stack of boilerplate deed restrictions, endlessly replicated and unchanged since before the Great Depression.

Despite the developers' general lack of interest in transforming society, Howard was right in believing that making many copies of a new kind of city, as American community builders have done, could lead to wider social change. Howard anticipated that the superiority of the garden city and the life it afforded its residents would become so apparent that people would leave the old cities, property values would collapse, and urban neighborhoods would become slums. This, he felt, was a good thing, because it would lead to the city itself being reconstructed on the garden city model: "London must die. . . . Elsewhere new cities are being built: London then must be transformed." A "new city," he believed, would "rise on the ashes of the old."[1]

Ninety-one years after Howard anticipated the death of the city and its replacement by a new form of planned community, Robert H. Nelson, an economist in the U.S. Department of the Interior, wrote that homeowner associations could gradually replace existing municipal governments. Nelson, like Howard, envisioned that CID housing and its particular form of private government would not be confined to new construction in outlying areas but that the model would prove superior to public local government and could gradually replace it. "The provisions of RCAS [residential community associations] could be extended to the private governance of existing neighborhoods that consist now of individually owned properties. Using the RCA model, the concept would be to establish the private neighborhood as a building block for metropolitan political and economic organization."[2]

Nelson anticipated that the gradual replacement of cities by CID private governments would have "the potential for making some changes of fundamental importance for the political and economic organization of metropolitan areas." "If RCAs were to become the prevailing mode of social organization for the local community, this development could be as important as the adoption in the United States of the private corporate form of business ownership. We would have two basic collective forms of private property ownership—the condominium (or RCA) form for residential property and the corporate form for business property."[3]

It is too early to say whether Howard and Nelson are right about the demise of the city, but they were right in recognizing that the existence of an alternative form of political and social organization could bring about broad social and political change. CIDs present the city with a set of profound challenges arising from the idea of the garden city as a new form of social and political life.

Although it has not taken the benign direction Howard anticipated, CID housing may represent the realization of at least part of Howard's social vision: it has the potential to threaten and undermine the city. In its present form, however, it does so without providing the utopia he offered. In place of Howard's utopia is privatopia, in which the dominant ideology is privatism; where contract law is the supreme authority; where property rights and property values are the focus of community life; and where homogeneity, exclusiveness, and exclusion are the foundation of social organization. There is no reason to believe that CID housing, as currently produced, offers a superior form of social organization to the municipality.

Nonetheless, in the context of American urban politics it is clear that CIDs are not only the present but the future of American housing. The construction of residences is a private undertaking that is increasingly dominated by large corporate developers who have adopted CID housing as the norm for mass production. A century ago such developments were simply a way to offer exclusive use of recreational facilities to affluent buyers. Later, modern community builders used the same vehicle to build large quantities of middle-class housing in an environment of rising land costs and resulting high density. To offer green open spaces and other facilities while keeping density high, developers created common ownership arrangements. These arrangements required ongoing management and maintenance. Cities and counties expressed no desire to undertake that responsibility, and developers had no interest in subjecting themselves to a greater degree of involvement with government regulation, so residential private governments evolved as the standard approach. All these factors make CID housing popular with developers.

Because the development industry will continue to build CID housing unless prevented from doing so, and because so much CID housing has already been constructed, governments now have no choice but to address the social and political consequences of the spread of this form of housing. The best and most logical way to do this is to view the spread of CID housing as a de facto privatization decision and evaluate it in that context.

## CID HOUSING AS PRIVATIZATION

The Advisory Commission on Intergovernmental Relations called the rise of CID housing "the most significant privatization of local government responsibilities in recent times." As ACIR notes, "very little is actually known about the extent to which RCAs substitute private for public expenditures." But it is clear that privately providing what would otherwise be municipal and county services to some thirty million people must result in substantial, albeit undetermined, savings to local governments.[4]

It is no accident that the use of this particular form of privatization began to increase greatly in the mid-1970s, when local governments found themselves facing demands for more services despite their shriveling revenues. Local tax revolts and reduced federal aid to cities coincided with a deliberate shifting of responsibility for many social and regulatory matters from the national level to state and local government. The result, for many cities, was the specter of budget deficits and potential insolvency.[5] At the same time, the administrations of Presidents Carter, Reagan, and Bush promoted, subtly or explicitly, an existing popular dislike for government and a general confidence in private enterprise. Together, the twin demands of budget deficits and renewed belief in the private sector legitimized a search for new ways to perform government functions. As John D. Donahue notes in *The Privatization Decision*, "The confluence of these two trends has led to great hopes and claims for 'privatization,' the practice of delegating *public* duties to *private* organizations."[6]

The rapid spread of CID housing was clearly a part of the overall privatization movement and was spurred by the trends Donahue discusses. The sudden acceleration in CID construction began in the mid-

1970s, when deficits began to loom as demands increased. Cities and counties had a greater incentive to permit, and even encourage, developers to build subdivisions complete with what amounted to a private infrastructure because it allowed for increasing property tax revenues by adding more residences, but at reduced public cost.

To view CID housing as a kind of privatization requires consideration of the meaning of the word. Donahue observes that the term is imprecise, in part because the idea was imported to the United States from Europe, notably Great Britain, where it meant something different:

In other countries, privatization has been mostly a matter of selling off parts of an abundant stock of public assets. Through the mid-1980s the Thatcher government sold British Gas, British Telecom, Jaguar, British Airways, the Sealink ferry service, all or part of its stakes in British Sugar, British Aerospace, British Petroleum, and British Steel, as well as nearly one million public housing units and various public utilities. . . . But America never could equal other countries in selling off government enterprises and assets for one simple reason: America has never *had* all that many government enterprises and assets. . . . Accordingly, as other countries were pondering or pursuing their version of privatization—severing the government connection with segments of the commercial economy—in the United States, privatization had a quite different meaning. Aside from a strictly limited number of asset sales, it meant (and continues to mean) enlisting private energies to improve the performance of tasks that would remain in some sense public. (Emphasis added)[7]

The uniquely American meaning of privatization highlights the complexity of the issues involved in any such decision. Donahue seeks to provide guidelines for determining when private performance of public tasks is a good idea. He argues for getting beyond the "tidy labels" of public and private and concentrating instead on two factors: efficiency and accountability.[8] Whether the issue is privatized prisons, trash collection, or job training, he argues, these remain the two critical dimensions.

Donahue's approach to privatization illuminates the degree to which the spread of CIDs was, and is, different in important ways from other efforts to privatize. It also suggests that serious questions need to be asked regarding this particular application of private energies to a public task.

# DE FACTO PRIVATIZATION

The title of Donahue's book—*The Privatization Decision*—makes what most people would consider a safe assumption: that privatization involves a conscious public decision to shift a public function to some form of private payment or delivery. This would imply that public officials would consider various approaches and specific plans, evaluate the costs and benefits, consult experts, hold public hearings, and *decide* to privatize. In the case of CID housing, this decision was never made. Instead, the move toward privatization was a matter of inaction. It was de facto privatization; it was done over decades, without a public discussion of whether it should take place; it happened not by government action, but by inaction, as private developers gradually transferred local government functions to private corporations. The risks and benefits of various approaches were never calculated and presented to the public for a decision. Although millions of Americans have purchased units of CID housing, they have done so without realizing that they were to become part of a collective decision to privatize local government, and without knowing the implications of that decision.

Although governments may have abdicated certain responsibilities in permitting a form of de facto privatization to occur, it is unlikely that the process will continue unexamined. CIDs have created a number of problems for local and state governments that must now be addressed. By the early 1990s only willful blindness could keep governments from recognizing that CID housing involves privatization of important public functions, with significant public consequences. Governments will soon be considering some of the fundamental questions that would have been asked at the outset had a conscious decision been made.

Beginning the evaluative process now, however, severely limits the options available to government. A non-CID nation is no longer possible, and policies must take into account a substantial CID housing sector. Governments are limited to asking such questions as whether there should be sixty million, or one hundred million, CID residents, and what kinds of intergovernmental relationships should exist between cities and their private counterparts. Moreover, the nature of CID private governments is already determined by their regimes of deed restrictions, and such private property arrangements are not easily changed by government action.

## PRIVATIZATION OF THE LAND PLANNING PROCESS

Donahue's conception of privatization contemplates the use of private energies to perform "public tasks," or "tasks that would remain in some sense public." CID housing differs from other forms of privatization because it involves the private takeover not only of such government functions as trash collection, street maintenance and zoning. At a deeper level, CID housing is a method for the conversion of large amounts of undeveloped land to residential real estate, something many believe to be a matter of public concern. But the policy process involved in real estate development has itself become privatized, and CID housing is an important part of that privatization.

Decades ago it was argued that urban land is a community resource, valuable to all and finite. Those who hold this view point out that the way in which urban land is developed affects the entire community. Consequently, to hold that important development decisions could be made by the landowner alone is, they feel, tantamount to arguing that factory owners should be permitted to pollute everybody's air at will because, after all, the factory is their private property. It has been suggested that government land planners should be viewed as "trustees" of the land as a public resource and accountable for its misuse, just as private trustees would be if they mishandled trust property.[9]

Common-interest developments pose special problems to the trustee theory. The nature of CID housing encourages an especially low level of public involvement in the process of real estate development, from the initial concept through day-to-day administration. Indeed, the self-sufficiency of CIDs—they allow a city or county to add taxpayers without having to pay for a full range of new infrastructure in return—is viewed as a major selling point in persuading local government officials to grant building permits. CIDs are sold as turnkey "packages" with substantial private infrastructures that will not place additional burdens on the existing community. Consequently, public officials can in some way justify being less concerned about the details of a CID than they would about a subdivision that would require substantial public expenditures. This is not to deny the substantial role local officials play in granting building permits; but CID construction tends to shift public scrutiny to the impact of the development on the surrounding community rather than to the internal nature of the new community. In this sense CID housing makes it easier for whatever public interest there is in the use of America's urban land to be submerged beneath the private values calculus of the corporate developers.

There is a larger sense in which CID housing reflects a movement toward privatization of the entire real estate development process. Such housing is a vital part of what Marc Weiss calls "the rise of the community builder," who "designs, engineers, finances, develops and sells an urban environment."[10] As Weiss demonstrates, "Subdividers who engaged in full-scale community development also performed the function of being private planners for American cities and towns."[11] At every turn in the history of CID housing, the ideas and initiatives have come from private developers who, as Weiss puts it, have seen their innovations "fully incorporated as public values to be standardized and emulated."[12]

In short, CID housing represents more than the privatization of certain local government services. It constitutes and facilitates privatization of the land planning function itself and of the process by which it is decided where and how people will live in American urban areas. CID housing is the product of privatized policy making in which most of the key decisions were made by NAREB, NAHB, ULI, CAI, and other private organizations and individuals. Such government agencies as FHA have for the most part ratified and legitimized those decisions. This is privatization at a deeper level than normal usage of the term would contemplate.

## ACCOUNTABILITY AND THE PRIVATIZATION OF LOCAL GOVERNMENT

Donahue argues persuasively that any decision to privatize must involve provisions for accountability to the public.

A special burden of accountability accompanies grants of public authority. This is so for three potent reasons. First, some of the most crucial functions of any society must be carried out collectively. Because weighty choices are at stake, we worry about accountability in public tasks. Second, the public at large—precisely because it is so large and diverse a category—is particularly exposed to failures by authorities to take into account its interests. Third, the individual is inherently vulnerable before the powers of government in ways that history richly illustrates, which the Constitution (and America's other defining documents) seek ingeniously to remedy. While accountability is a fundamental aspect of social existence, it is most often seen as a *problem* in the area of government. (Emphasis in original)[13]

Judged by any or all of these criteria, the privatization represented by CID housing, if it is to occur, should be accompanied by provisions for accountability. The functions involved, including the specific local services and land planning itself, are costly and of great importance, and they clearly expose the public to the consequences of "failures by government to take into account its interests." Moreover, the individual CID resident is exposed to treatment that would be unconstitutional had these government functions not been privatized.

Yet the delegation of governmental powers to private entities was done without adequate provisions for accountability. Nowhere is this more apparent than in the reliance CID housing has on untrained, unregulated, volunteer directors, who are elected from among the residents to run private local governments.

At the outset, it is apparent that CID "volunteers" are different than those who volunteer for charitable purposes in other nonprofit institutions. Jon Van Til, one of the leading figures in the study of voluntarism, discusses the important functions performed in the "third sector," which exists apart from business and government. He defines the term *volunteering* as "a helping action of an individual that is valued by him or her, and yet is not aimed directly at material gain or mandated or coerced by others. Thus, in the broadest sense, *volunteering* is any uncoerced helping activity that is engaged in not primarily for financial gain and not by coercion or mandate. It is thereby different from work, slavery, or conscription."[14]

Using Van Til's definition, residents in CIDs are not volunteers, because membership in the homeowner association is mandated. Residents are, in essence, "conscripted" into the association automatically, and that conscription undermines the legitimacy of a regime supposedly based on voluntary consent.

But the situation is more complex for those residents who, once drafted into the association, choose to serve as directors. For them, altruistic and materialistic motives are intertwined because of the nature of common property ownership. They are volunteers because they are not paid and because they are not coerced into serving on the board.

Yet if their motivation to serve comes from a desire to to protect and enhance their own property values, then materialistic considerations are involved. Some people undoubtedly serve because they feel that they are among the few residents qualified, by education and experience, to handle the responsibilities involved in protecting the development's market value. Others may serve because they enjoy wielding power over their neighbors.

Whatever their motivations, CID directors are essential to the operation of residential private governments, and in that sense they are not like other participants in the third sector. In fact, they are functioning in the governmental sector, and the way they perform their role is perhaps the most critical variable in the success or failure of CID housing, no matter how those terms are defined. Consequently, CID housing is a unique form of privatization, placing the fate of the experiment in the hands of untrained, uncompensated amateurs; establishing no qualifications for their participation; creating no public institutional support structure for on-the-job training; and leaving the directors essentially free of public regulation, increasingly with immunity from private regulation through lawsuit.

If a city government interested in privatization proposed to have the community's garbage collected or its policing done or its fires extinguished by volunteers, it would ensure that the volunteers were held accountable in some fashion, offering compensation or training, requiring minimal qualifications, imposing regulations, or establishing some other kind of oversight.[15] Steps would be taken to ensure that the public task being delegated to this private agent was being done properly. A government would be considered irresponsible if it did otherwise. Yet no accountability mechanisms were established for what the Advisory Commission on Intergovernmental Relations calls "the most significant privatization of local government responsibilities in recent times." In that sense as well, the decisions behind CID housing differ from other privatization decisions.

Byron Hanke and others understood as early as 1964 the critical importance of CID board members and the need to establish institutional support for them. It was this awareness that led to the creation in 1973 of the Community Associations Institute, whose purposes include the standardizing and professionalizing of CID governance through the training of board members, managers, lawyers, accountants, and others. This effort has been a significant step toward filling the "accountability gap," but it is insufficient and raises another question of privatization. There is no provision for ensuring that the idea of governance held by CAI is acceptable to the larger community or that CAI is pursuing its objectives efficiently and effectively.

In fact, CAI has evolved into a trade association controlled largely by lawyers, property managers, and others who have an economic interest in seeing that CID private governments remain heavily dependent on professionals like themselves. These individuals, and the standards of their respective professions, can be seen as a way of ensuring a kind of limited accountability for CID boards. But this arrangement leaves the definition of proper CID governance in the hands of professionals who are not under any public mandate to treat CID boards differently from any other corporate client—a situation that can ensure only the kind of board accountability corporate directors have to their shareholders. These professionals can be counted on only to encourage CID directors to use good business judgment, follow accepted management practices, honor their fiduciary duty to the membership, and strictly enforce the developer's rules. This accountability mechanism includes no provisions for responsibility to the larger community. Indeed, lawyers or property managers who advised a CID board to place a high value on the interests of nonresidents might be violating their professional duty to the client.

It is questionable whether strict adherence to the corporate managerial model is advisable. Board members and residents have to live together as more than shareholders and more than neighbors; they constitute an involuntary political community.

The managerial model of governance and what has been called the neighborly community model are the two roles within which CID residents and boards typically understand the board's activities. That is, the boards are urged by professionals to act as managers, but residents often expect them to just act like good neighbors. In fact, as sociologists Greg Barton and Carol Silverman argue, neither of these models is adequate because both are inherently private; neither takes note of the public and political character of this form of home ownership. It is not enough for board members to simply follow good management practices; neither is it enough to just act like good neighbors might in a development without common property ownership.[16]

The CID boards are neither businesses nor voluntary third sector neighborhood organizations. They are private governments that have been charged with what would otherwise be public responsibilities—a fact that would seem to require a means for ensuring that the volunteers who operate them will act as though they were running governments. Yet no mechanism exists to ensure accountability of CID boards as governments. There is no method in place to move CIDs away from one extreme of excessive reliance on managers and lawyers or the other extreme of excessive informality, and toward becoming functioning, evolving, self-governing communities.

## AMERICA: A HOUSE DIVIDED?

The privatization of local government brought about by the rise of CID housing is unusual in one other sense: the privatized services are provided only for some and not for others, and the same services must continue to be provided for the rest of society. Consequently, those paying for and receiving the private services can be expected to resent paying for duplicate public services they do not need. For this and other reasons, this "privatization for the few" has the potential for creating and amplifying social division and conflict between CID residents and local governments. Some feel this division is reaching the point at which many CID residents may develop an attenuated sense of loyalty and commitment to the public communities in which their CIDs are located, even to the point of virtual or actual secession.

CIDs give city residents the opportunity to leave the urban setting. The departure could be literal, as in a move to a new suburban private community. It could also be functional, as in the privatization of an existing neighborhood or in a move to a fortified condominium in a redeveloped downtown. In either case, given sufficient numbers of a sufficiently desirable alternative, the result could be a gradual secession from the city that would leave it stripped of much of its population and resources. Ultimately, at least in theory, the city could become financially untenable for the many and socially unnecessary for the few. Certainly this steady secession would make the lives of those who remained in the city increasingly difficult.

Robert Reich connects the privatization inherent in CID housing with a trend he calls "the secession of the successful": "In many cities and towns, the wealthy have in effect withdrawn their dollars from the support of public spaces and institutions shared by all and dedicated the savings to their own private services. . . . Condominiums and the omnipresent residential communities dun their members to undertake work that financially strapped local governments can no longer afford to do well—maintaining roads, mending sidewalks, pruning trees, repairing street lights, cleaning swimming pools, paying for lifeguards and, notably, hiring security guards to protect life and property."[17]

From the other end of the political spectrum comes a similar observation by Charles Murray, who sees the growth of CIDs as a symbol of America's becoming a "caste society." He anticipates that privatized local government services will facilitate the emergence of a new caste as a powerful political force. "I am trying to envision what happens when 10 or 20 per cent of the population has enough income to bypass the social institutions it doesn't like in ways that only the top fraction of 1 per cent used to be able to do. . . . The Left has been complaining for years that the rich have too much power. They ain't seen nothing yet."[18]

Once able to "bypass" the city by virtue of privatized services and political power, this new caste would, Murray thinks, come to view urban centers in much the same way mainstream America views Indian reservations today. Cities would be seen as places of squalor for which the new caste would acknowledge no responsibility.

The schism Reich and Murray anticipate is likely to become most apparent in the context of electoral politics at the state and local level. The specific issues involved in these impending political conflicts will most probably stem directly from the privatization of government services for some and not others. The cleavage produced by this differential privatization is intertwined with, and reinforced by, other divisions. These include homeowners versus renters, suburbs against the cities, and the differences in race, class, and age that are associated with home ownership and residence.

## Suburb versus City

The division between CID residents and others is reinforced by the existing cleavage between suburbanites and the city. Most CID residents are suburbanites, and suburbanites, it appears, are developing a distinct and significant political profile on issues related to taxation and the city.[19]

In an article entitled "The Suburban Century Begins," William Schneider pointed out that the 1992 presidential election would be the first in which a majority of the voters were suburbanites.[20] After decades of suburbanization, America had become a "suburban nation with an urban fringe and a rural fringe." This, he argued, would have enormous impact on electoral politics, in large part because of the privatization of public life in the suburbs. This privatization includes transportation by private auto instead of public conveyance; entertainment in the home by television and videotape instead of in public places; and shopping in malls instead of in city streets. Schneider quotes architects Andres Duany and Elizabeth Plater-Zyberk, who said, "The suburb is the last word in privatization, perhaps even its lethal consummation, and it spells the end of authentic civic life." Schneider amplifies on this idea: "To move to the suburbs is to express a preference for the private over the public. . . . Suburbanites' preference for the private applies to government as well. Suburban voters 'buy' private government—good schools and safe streets for the people who live there. They control their local government, including taxes, spending, schools, and police. . . . A major reason people move out to the suburbs is simply to be able to buy their own government. These people resent it when politicians take their money and use it to solve other people's problems, especially when they don't believe that government can actually solve those problems."[21]

The privatized atmosphere of suburban life produces a gap between city and suburb where certain issues are concerned, particularly those dealing with property ownership and taxes. As Schneider observes, "Can suburban voters, then, be said to have a defining characteristic? Yes: suburban voters are predominantly property owners. And that makes them highly tax-sensitive."[22]

When political issues related to the social and economic problems of the city emerge, these factors converge. Suburbanites live in a privatized environment in which their own needs are satisfied largely through private funds and by private means. Moreover, they bear the burden of property tax, the principal source of revenue for local government services. Schneider summarizes the result in a hypothetical question and response: "But isn't it 'in the national interest' to bail out the cities? The suburbs have given their answer: walled communities."[23]

## Homogeneous Communities?

The prospects for concerted political action, particularly at the state and local level, could be enhanced by the degree to which CID residents

were homogeneous, or similar in ways that might contribute to shared
political values, interests, and attitudes. Critics of CID housing, and of
suburbia in general, often point to what they consider an unhealthy
homogeneity of population. They point to the concentrations of white
middle-class homeowners in the suburbs and of less affluent, minority
renters in the cities.

A number of sociologists and urban theorists have debated the existence and desirability of age, race, and class homogeneity in American
suburbs and in CIDs. Some argue that heterogeneous communities, such
as those Howard anticipated for his garden city, enrich community life,
promote tolerance and reduce social conflict, provide children with a
broadened education about the diversity of humankind, and expose people to alternative ways of living. Homogeneous communities, they contend, do the reverse: they deprive people of social resources and thus
stultify their lives; promote isolation and conflict between residents of
the community and the rest of society; stunt children's ability to relate to
people unlike themselves; and leave residents frozen in their present
way of life.[24]

Others, including Herbert Gans, argue in favor of "selective homogeneity at the block level and heterogeneity at the community level."
Gans maintains that "whereas a mixture of population types, and especially of rich and poor, is desirable in the community as a whole, heterogeneity on the block will not produce the intended tolerance, but will lead
to conflict that is undesirable because it is essentially insoluble and thus
becomes chronic. Selective homogeneity on the block will improve the
tenor of neighbor relations, and will thus make it easier—although not
easy—to realize heterogeneity at the community level."[25]

Gans acknowledges that the suburbanites he studied "want some
homogeneity for themselves." But he emphasizes the heterogeneity of
interests, activities, and backgrounds that can be found within an apparently homogeneous neighborhood. This, he believes, left the residents
"pleased with the diversity they found among their neighbors."[26]

Both the critics of suburbia and its defenders agree that separation
of America's rich and poor into separate communities is highly undesirable and would produce political conflict. Gans observes that

communities should be heterogeneous because they must reflect
the pluralism of American society. Moreover, as long as local
taxation is the main source of funds for community services,

community homogeneity encourages undesirable inequalities. The high-income community can build modern schools and other high-quality facilities; the low-income community, which needs these facilities more urgently, lacks the tax base to support them. As a result, poor communities elect local governments which neglect public services and restrict the democratic process in the need to keep taxes minimal. Both financial inequity and its political consequences are eliminated more effectively by federal and state subsidy than by community heterogeneity, but so long as municipal services are financed locally, communities must include all income groups.[27]

It is in this sensitive area of economics—not just social characteristics—that CIDs promote homogeneity. To the extent that CID housing is increasingly the norm in new construction, CID buyers as a whole may reflect about the same level of diversity in age, race, and income that exists among homeowners generally.[28] But the most important ways in which CID residents are homogeneous have to do with critical similarities of economic circumstances that are reinforced by social factors.

The primary common characteristic of CID purchasers is that they are homeowners, a group that is older, whiter, and wealthier than the general population. In 1990 the home ownership rate for people below age 24 was only 17.1 percent; it was 45.3 percent for those between 25 and 34. Yet those between 45 and 54 had a home ownership rate of 75.3 percent; those between 55 and 64, a rate of 79.7 percent; and those between 64 and 74, a rate of 78.8 percent.[29] In 1991, 67.3 percent of all white households were owner-occupied, as compared with only 42.4 percent of black households and 39.0 percent of Hispanic households; 55.7 percent of black households and 61.0 percent of Hispanic households were renter-occupied, versus just 30.8 percent of white households.[30]

The class division between owners and renters in America is hardening. Since the mid-1970s it has become increasingly difficult for people of low to moderate income to make the jump from renting to owning. Consequently, as Apgar and Brown note, "America is increasingly becoming a nation of housing haves and have-nots." There is a large and widening income gap between owners and renters.[31]

The divisions between these two groups are politically significant. Each has a different relation to local government because of government's heavy reliance on property tax, which only owners pay, to fund services that benefit renters as well. To many suburbanites, it seems that "we" pay property taxes to support "them." Owners and renters are also affected very differently by the prospect of rising or falling property values in the community and neighborhood. To a homeowner whose only investment is a house, this issue can determine whether he or she will have a comfortable retirement and college-educated children. To a renter, a drop in community property values may not be entirely bad; although public services might decline, rents may drop, and the transition to home ownership may become easier.

Reinforcing this important cleavage between owners and renters is the fact that CID owners share a kind of property ownership that carries different burdens, responsibilities, and privileges. Whatever degree of sameness exists among homeowners generally is reinforced by the common economic interests among CID owners. Not only are they linked by a commitment to a privatized lifestyle—and are at least as homogeneous as other American homeowners or suburbanites—but they are identically affected by state and local government decisions regarding whether, and how, to build, maintain, and pay for public services and facilities that duplicate their private ones. Over time, these categories have been merging: the group known as homeowners is gradually becoming that of CID owners.

Adding to these similarities is the intentional homogeneity created by CID builders for marketing purposes. Within particular CIDs there is often a high degree of homogeneity because the developments were built with certain groups of buyers in mind. Pricing decisions for large neighborhoods of mass-produced housing promote class or income homogeneity. Marketing efforts have become more targeted, aiming at specific subgroups who may be most attracted to CID living, including "empty-nesters," "working couples," "singles," "retirees," "first-time buyers," and "investors."[32] It is often intended from the design stage that particular CIDs would be composed of people who wished to live in an enclave promoting a certain lifestyle.

This marketing effort contributes to homogeneity on a larger scale as well. Because some parts of the country and sections of metropolitan areas appeal to certain population groups, concentrations of specialty CIDs can occur. For example, the network of retirement communities in parts of Florida, California, Arizona, and elsewhere in the sunbelt can create substantial concentrated populations of people with similar social characteristics and political concerns. Indeed, the prospect of finding such homogeneous communities is a magnet for many buyers.

If home ownership rates continue to differ widely between young and old, white and nonwhite, and along income or class lines, the potential exists for several cleavages to reinforce each other, heightening the probability of political conflict. If, as Reich, Murray, and others believe, the additional variable of CID housing further promotes the creation of private communities of the affluent and public communities of the poor, the "undesirable inequalities" and resulting "political consequences" anticipated by Gans loom larger.

## MASS POLITICS FOR PRIVATOPIA?

There is ample evidence that sufficient commonalities exist among those who live in and serve CIDs to generate demands on the political system. In a number of states with much CID housing, CAI and other groups have already become a significant factor in interest group politics at the state level. People close to the heart of the industry recently have begun to speak openly of a new dimension in CID politics: actively organizing CID residents for mass political action.

The Advisory Commission on Intergovernmental Relations anticipated this possibility in 1989 after conducting a nationwide survey of CID boards: "As a significant proportion of the population in a given area—or in a state, for that matter—gets membership in RCAs, they gain potential political power. Because of the differences between their service and financial relationships to local governments, as compared to the non-RCA citizen, RCA residents may be inclined to vote differently on tax and service issues, and on bond referendums that will not directly benefit them. In addition they may organize to push for greater tax equity, or for public services to their areas, or for some other RCA-related interest. In Massachusetts, a Greater Boston Association of RCA Presidents has been formed for such purposes."[33]

The task of mobilizing such concerted action is simplified because CID residents are already organized. The board of directors can notify every resident regarding a candidate, a meeting, or an issue by posting notices in common areas and dropping notes in mailboxes, just as would be done to announce the annual meeting time or an assessment increase.

Moreover, CIDs generally have a large, common meeting place, such as a recreation room or lounge. Consequently, those who wish to mobilize a CID vote are tantalized by how ripe the prospect seems. But without an issue of sufficient visibility and seriousness, these voters do not see themselves as a group with a common political interest. The issue that is raised most often as the key to mobilizing a CID vote arises directly from the unique nature of this form of privatization: the contention that CID residents are victims of double taxation because they allegedly pay twice for the same services—once through property tax and again through homeowner association assessments. As one local politician put it, "I predicted ten years ago, when we first started approving these projects, that the day would come when people would refuse to pay taxes because they are already paying for these services through their homeowners' associations."[34]

CID owners, among others, can also be motivated to oppose something that might hurt property values, such as the building of new developments near their own. Los Angeles has seen the emergence of a substantial "no-growth" movement centered in neighborhood homeowner associations.[35] Either or both of these issues—taxes and growth—could become the focus for a mass politics involving CID owners.

*Common Ground,* published by CAI, recently described common-interest developments as a "force in the ring" of electoral politics. The article recounts numerous instances of organized CID residents "landing blows in the political arena" over double taxation and in opposition to growth. In Naugatuck, Connecticut, an organized CID contingent made double taxation an issue in a local election and claimed to have "turned the town around from being completely Democratic controlled to Republican controlled. . . . We were a force to be reckoned with. We turned this town on its ears."[36] Similar organizing efforts are recounted in Florida, California, North Carolina, Texas, New Jersey, Illinois, Maryland, and Virginia.

Steve Harvill, CAI president in 1993 and a Dallas property manager, emphasized that this force is more than interest-group politics: it is an effort to influence politicians by proving that the movement can deliver an organized base of voters. "That's what the politicians care about," said Harvill, "They care about their votes." *Common Ground* provides detailed advice on influencing the political system from four "experts" with "lengthy experience in government or as lobbyists."[37]

One of these experts is an attorney who described how he organized a mass demonstration of CID residents to stop a plan to build shopping centers and a subdivision near Sunshine Ranches, a CID in Fort Lauderdale, Florida. The attorney, a CAI member who represented some 40 percent of the condominiums in the county, worked through a group of CID associations to gather three thousand signatures on petitions opposing the plan. He also arranged a "media event" in which the residents of Sunshine Ranches "circled the entire area with a four-mile wagon train, defending their homes like the early pioneers. The stunt worked."[38]

Efforts to turn CID residents into a voting bloc are not confined to CAI. In California, lobbyist Robyn Boyer Stewart, who represents the Executive Council of Home Owners (ECHO), works to organize and mobilize a CID mass constituency that, she believes, could dwarf such legislative powerhouses as the public employee unions and trial lawyer organizations. She makes what she describes as a constant, systematic series of "exhortations to political action" aimed at unifying CID owners not only on specific CID-related issues, but, she hopes, on "other, broader issues" as well. "I exhort people to make a commitment," she says.[39]

She believes legislators have begun to recognize the existence of this constituency, and she has done her best to tell them about it. In 1991, she wrote an article for *California Journal,* a publication widely read by California politicians, which began, "Heads up, politicians. There's a new political bloc making headway in California and, at latest count, it's over three million votes strong. Its components are organized by neighborhoods, operated variously like a corporation or a mini-government, and structured (most of the time) according to democratic principles. Sound like a new political party or labor union? A candidate's dream? Give up? They're California's latest version of The Good Life—common-interest developments (CIDs) and their attendant community associations."[40]

She identified ten mayors and city council officials who used service on CID boards as their political training ground and electoral springboard. She quoted Marian Bergeson, a state senator, as saying that "community associations are clearly a stepping stone to running for city council," and Gil Ferguson, a state assemblyman, who stated that "every U.S. president in the last four elections campaigned in Leisure World. . . . That goes for senators and governors, too. . . . They go to Leisure World rather than the cities."[41]

In a 1992 address, Stewart recounted the CID lobby's major legislative successes of the year. "I'd like to say that the successes we have achieved are because of my abilities as a lobbyist, but that would not be entirely truthful. The fact is, I am only a messenger, and the message has got to be that the common interest constituency, that rag-tag of 3.5 million California homeowners, is organizing, watching how their legislators vote on CID issues, and acting based on what they see."[42]

Stewart makes the political equation clear: in California, voting power has shifted to the suburbs, and, "in California, the suburban voter is the common interest community voter."[43]

Like most CID advocates, Stewart is convinced that the issue of double taxation is the key to persuading CID owners to see themselves as a group with common political interests. "No issue is likely to have more political fallout at the state and local level, to galvanize a constituency where once there was no constituency, than that of the taxation/double taxation of community associations. And yet this issue is being all but ignored by policy-makers. . . . It is only a matter of time before the tax-and-equity bomb blows. . . . As yet there is no clearly identified champion for the people who live in CIDs. . . . The politician who manages to capture this constituency, speak to its needs and offer it a voice, will be amply rewarded with gratitude and votes. Those time bombs are ticking, but is anyone listening?"[44]

It would appear that legislators in New Jersey and elsewhere are listening to this new constituency, because they have responded to the double taxation charge by providing for special tax rebates to CID owners. Early in 1993 a law was approved in New Jersey requiring all cities to reimburse CIDs for the cost of providing for their own snow removal, street lighting, and leaf, recycling, and trash collection, or to provide CIDs those services "in the same fashion as the municipality provides these services on public roads and streets."[45] Property tax rebate measures have also been put in place in Houston, Kansas City, and Montgomery County, Maryland.[46]

The probability for mobilizing a CID constituency is greatest at the state and local level, where political decisions often directly affect property values and where the conflict between funding of public and private services occurs. But there is at least one national issue that could galvanize a nationwide CID voting bloc. As Robert Jay Dilger explains, "Another tax equity issue involves the national government. It allows taxpayers to deduct their property taxes from their taxable income when determining national tax liability. RCA [residential community association] members are not allowed to deduct their association fees from their taxable income even though a portion of their fees is used to provide services similar to those provided by property tax dollars. To promote tax equity, RCA members want the national government to allow them to deduct from their taxable income the portion of their assessment fees used to pay for services that are provided by their local government to other residents in their community."[47]

Whether the issue is local property tax or federal income tax, the central concept is the same: to CID advocates, "tax equity" means that people who are paying for exclusive services in their own neighborhood should not have to contribute to the cost of providing similar services for the rest of the community. Yet CID residents could use and benefit from the public services for which they would not have to pay, while outsiders could not use or benefit from the private services for which CID residents nonetheless would claim a tax deduction. Advocates of CIDs are trying equate the payment of assessments to a contribution to the public welfare. The analogy to property taxes is inapposite, however. These private payments do not benefit the public in the same sense as property taxes. Property taxes represent an individual taxpayer's contribution toward supporting clean streets not only in his or her own neighborhood but throughout the city. CID assessments are targeted for small pieces of private property from which the public can be, and often is, excluded.

It is emblematic of the CID movement that this distinction is lost. In effect, advocates identify the CID interest with the community interest because, from their perspective, the CID is the community. Having attended to the property they own, CID residents would be deemed to have satisfied their duties to the community at large, and would be free to take advantage of its benefits without further obligation. This is an extension of the unique idea of citizenship promoted in CIDs, in which one's duties consist of satisfying one's obligations to private property. The double taxation argument would extend that concept: one's duty to the entire surrounding community would be satisfied by paying the CID assessment. The CID definition of citizenship would be extended to the community at large. This entire line of argument, and the fact that it is stated so confidently, as though the unfairness of double taxation should be obvious to anyone, are evidence of the "quiet secession" Robert Reich noted.

Should a mass politics coalesce around this ideology of privatism, it could harness enormous energies and resources in the service of dismantling local government. Yet government is itself a variable in this equation. It is not clear whether the emergent relationship between public and private governments will be cooperative or conflictual. The Advisory

Commission on Intergovernmental Relations has made recommendations that seem to contemplate both dimensions. On the one hand, ACIR recommends that state and local governments "recognize the potential problems" of CIDs, and "give careful attention to the intergovernmental issues raised by their existence and activities." On the other, ACIR ultimately recommends as well that government should "cooperate with the private sector and local homeowners to facilitate appropriate development and successful operation of residential community associations."[48]

These two objectives may not be compatible. It is not clear that governments will be as inclined as before to encourage further proliferation of CIDs in their present form before coming to grips with the issues that would present. The privatization represented by CID housing is largely the product of unregulated private policy making. As awareness increases of the attendant social and political consequences, public scrutiny and regulation beyond simple consumer protection may result. Regulatory efforts could be aimed at making CID governance more democratic and less managerial, reducing the burden of CID disputes on local courts, countering secessionist tendencies, resisting the construction of new CIDs, or other issues.

But such regulatory efforts have the potential to provoke a political response from the industries that build and support CIDs and may themselves mobilize CID residents to organize for mass political action. Ultimately, electoral politics may become the arena in which it will be determined whether, as Ebenezer Howard predicted, the city as we know it will die and a new kind of city "rise on the ashes of the old."

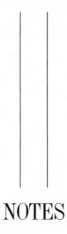

# NOTES

## Chapter 1

1. Dugald MacFadyen, *Sir Ebenezer Howard and the Town Planning Movement* (Manchester, Eng.: Manchester University Press, 1933), 20.

2. Edward Bellamy, *Looking Backward: 2000–1887* (Ticknor and Company, 1887; reprint, New York: Random House, 1917).

3. Ibid., 276.

4. MacFadyen, *Sir Ebenezer Howard,* 20.

5. Ibid., 21.

6. Ebenezer Howard, *Garden Cities of Tomorrow* (Cambridge, Mass.: MIT Press, 1965).

7. Ibid., 127–46.

8. Lewis Mumford, "The Garden City Idea and Modern Planning," in Howard, *Garden Cities of Tomorrow,* 29; and Jane Jacobs, *The Death and Life of Great American Cities* (New York: Vintage, 1961), 19.

9. Howard writes, "Shortly stated, my scheme is a combination of three distinct projects which have, I think, never been united before. These are: (1) the proposals for an organized migratory movement of population of Edward Gibbon Wakefield and of Professor Alfred Marshall; (2) the system of land tenure first proposed by Thos. Spence and afterwards (though with an important modification) by Mr. Herbert Spencer; and (3) the model city of James Silk Buckingham." Yet he notes that he had not seen the proposals of Marshall or Wakefield "till I had got far on with my project . . . nor had I seen the work of Buckingham" *(Garden Cities of Tomorrow,* 119).

10. Mumford, "The Garden City Idea," 33.

11. Howard, *Garden Cities of Tomorrow,* 76.

12. Howard actually deemphasized the details of his plan, noting repeatedly that the actual plan could not be drawn until a site had been selected. See ibid., 52–53, diagrams 1 and 2.

13. See ibid., 140. Howard states that building on farmland would be "disastrous" because "the beauty and healthfulness of the town would be quickly destroyed . . . by the process of growth."

14. Ibid., 69. See Howard's elaborate calculations for the rents, 58–69.

15. Ibid., 58.

16. Ibid., 87–88.

17. Ibid., 92–94. Together, the Central Council and the departments would be called the Board of Management. But because the Central Council comprises nothing more than the chairmen and vice-chairmen of the departments, it is not clear what governmental functions, if any, the Board of Management would perform.

18. Ibid., 92.

19. Ibid., 95.

20. Ibid., 92–93.

21. Ibid., 96–103.

22. Ibid., 138–50.

23. See Timothy Barnekov et al., *Privatism and Urban Policy in Britain and the United States* (Oxford: Oxford University Press, 1989), 8–9.

24. For a thorough, if uncritical, recounting of the English experience with new town construction, see Frederic J. Osborn and Arnold Whittick, *The New Towns: The Answer to Megalopolis* (New York: McGraw-Hill, 1963). As Barnekov et al. point out, there is a tradition of privatism in British urban planning as well, to which the postwar experience with new town construction was an exception.

25. Sam Bass Warner, *The Private City: Philadelphia in Three Periods of Its Growth* (Philadelphia: University of Pennsylvania Press, 1968), x. See also the discussion of this subject in Barnekov et al., *Privatism and Urban Policy.*

26. Dennis Judd, *The Politics of American Cities: Private Power and Public Policy,* 2nd ed. (Boston: Little, Brown, 1984), 412–13.

27. Beginning in the 1880s, business and government leaders saw home ownership as an antidote to social, political, and labor conflicts in America's rapidly growing cities. It was felt that workers who had invested their savings in a house would have an economic and emotional stake in the nearby company for which they worked and would be less likely to resign or strike. See Delores Hayden, *Redesigning the American Dream* (New York: W. W. Norton, 1984), 32–34. As Kenneth Jackson observed, "Business and political leaders were particularly anxious for citizens to own homes, based on the hope, as Friedrich Engels had feared, that mortgages would have the effect of 'chaining the workers by this property to the factory in which they work'" (Kenneth Jackson, *Crabgrass Frontier: The Suburbanization of the United States* [New York: Oxford University Press, 1985], 51).

There were other reasons for profit-seeking developers to offer privately owned homes and for industrialists and government to promote home ownership, apart from the domesticating effects on the American worker. Manufacturers and union leaders saw private home ownership as a way to expand domestic markets for consumer goods (Hayden, *Redesigning the American Dream,* 33). Moreover, Jackson points out that Americans preferred private home ownership "as a counterweight to the rootlessness of an urbanizing population," as a way to express individual tastes, and because European immigrants saw land ownership "as a mark of status, as well as a kind of sublime insurance against ill fortune" (Jackson, *Crabgrass Frontier,* 50–53). Considerations of economic security, status, and tax deductibility of mortgage interest still militate in favor of home ownership.

28. See Marc A. Weiss, *The Rise of the Community Builders: The American Real Estate Industry and Urban Land Planning* (New York: Columbia University Press, 1987).

29. MacFadyen, *Sir Ebenezer Howard and the Town Planning Movement,* 10–11.

30. W. A. Eden, "Ebenezer Howard and the Garden City Movement," *Town Planning Review* 19 (Summer 1947): 133.

31. Mumford, "The Garden City Idea," 30–31.

32. Marc A. Weiss and John W. Watts, "Community Builders and Community Associations: The Role of Real Estate Developers in Private Residential Governance," in Advisory Commission on Intergovernmental Relations, *Residential Community Associations: Private Governments in the Intergovernmental System?* (Washington, D.C.: Advisory Commission on Intergovernmental Relations, May 1989), 98.

33. Ronald J. Oakerson, "Private Street Associations in St. Louis County: Subdivisions as Service Providers," in Advisory Commission on Intergovernmental Relations, *Residential Community Associations,* 55–61.

34. Daniel Schaffer, *Garden Cities for America: The Radburn Experience* (Philadelphia: Temple University Press, 1982).

35. Clarence S. Stein, *Toward New Towns for America* (Cambridge: MIT Press, 1966). Stein was a member and leader of RPAA.

36. Charles S. Ascher, "The Extra-Municipal Administration of Radburn: An Experiment in Government by Contract," *National Municipal Review* 18 (June 1929): 442–46.

37. J. C. Nichols, *Mistakes We Have Made in Community Development,* Technical Bulletin no. 1 (Washington, D.C.: Urban Land Institute, 1945).

38. Urban Land Institute/Federal Housing Administration, *The Homes Association Handbook,* Technical Bulletin no. 50 (Washington, D.C.: Urban Land Institute, 1964), vi. The study classified associations in several ways and found that "470

subdivisions were reported to contain common property maintained by some type of home-owners association."

39. Weiss, *Rise of the Community Builders.*

40. James A. Clapp, *New Towns and Urban Policy* (New York: Dunellen, 1971); Theodore Roszak, "Life in the Instant Cities," *The Nation,* March 13, 1967, 336–40; and Uriel Reichman, "Residential Private Governments: An Introductory Survey," 43 *University of Chicago Law Review* 253 (1976).

41. Community Associations Institute, *Community Associations Factbook, 1988* (Alexandria, Va.: Community Associations Institute, 1988), and *Community Associations Factbook, 1993* (Alexandria, Va.: Community Associations Institute, 1993), 13. Although CAI statistics are almost universally relied on, it is important to keep in mind that there is no similar government tally. The Bureau of the Census counts only condominiums and cooperatives, not planned-unit developments (Advisory Commission on Intergovernmental Relations, *Residential Community Associations,* 3).

42. Advisory Commission on Intergovernmental Relations, *Residential Community Associations,* 4.

43. Ibid., 3.

44. Ibid., 3–4.

45. Rancho Bernardo Community Planning Board, *Rancho Bernardo Community Plan* (San Diego, Calif.: City of San Diego, 1989), 15.

46. Richard Louv, *America II* (New York: Penguin, 1983), 92. Louv's perceptive treatment of such "capitalist communes" as Rancho Bernardo and their role in what he calls the "shelter revolution" is one of the most accessible and influential to date.

47. Rancho Bernardo Community Planning Board, *Rancho Bernardo Community Plan,* 7–8. The plan was developed by Summers and, after extensive negotiation with the city of San Diego, was adopted by the City Council in 1962. It was revised in 1966, 1971, 1978, 1981, 1982, 1986, 1987, and 1988.

48. Louv, *America II,* 93–94.

49. Ibid., 93.

50. Ibid., 94.

51. *Bernardo Villas Management Corp. v. Black,* 190 Cal. App. 3d 153; 235 Cal. Rptr. 509 (1987).

52. Louv, *America II,* 94–95. I spent several evenings attending meetings of the Bernardo Home Owners Corporation, a body that does not enforce architectural restrictions but supports the other associations in a variety of ways. The group spent a good deal of time discussing how to help a neighborhood association appeal a case it lost against a homeowner. The association had cited a Trails homeowner for violating the rule against television antennas by installing a satellite dish, which he had concealed from view inside a structure. The point, members of the BHOC argued, was that a satellite dish is an antenna. The fact that in this case it neither looked like an antenna (in fact, it was not visible to anyone) nor sat atop the roof was deemed irrelevant by the board.

53. This was discussed at a BHOC meeting on March 21, 1989, that was observed by the author.

54. Harold Keen, "A New Town that Works," *San Diego Magazine,* March 1981, 113.

55. This reference to bus transportation and other political structure is contained in a mailer sent to residents by the BHOC as part of its 1989 membership drive.

56. "Don't Tread on Rancho Bernardo," *San Diego Magazine,* March 1979, 77–79.

57. Keen, "New Town that Works," 193.

58. A 1988 survey of associations belonging to the Community Associations Institute, conducted jointly by ACIR and CAI, found the average CID to have 537 units. The figure may overstate the national average, however, because CAI believes larger associations are more likely than smaller ones to join CAI. See *Residential Community Associations,* 4. Another study of 579 California associations yielded a median size of forty-three units; see Stephen E. Barton and Carol J. Silverman, *Common Interest Homeowners' Association Management Study* (Sacramento: California Department of Real Estate, 1987). Both studies were based on responses to mailed questionnaires, however, so neither reflects a representative sample. These conflicting estimates underscore the difficulty of studying CIDs, which are not subject even to the kind of centralized state government listings and record-keeping required of such simple consumer services as auto repair shops.

59. On display of the flag see Louv, *America II,* 128. On newspaper distribution see *Laguna Publishing Company v. Golden Rain Foundation of Laguna Hills,* 131 Cal. App. 3d 816 (1982). And on political gatherings see Ralph C. Meyer, "The Dictator Syndrome" (Paper presented at the Fourteenth Annual Conference of the Community Associations Institute, 1977); see also Ralph Meyer, "Democracy or Dictatorship: Are Association Leaders Listening?" *Common Ground,* May–June 1988, 18.

60. William K. Stevens, "Condominium Associations: New Form of Local Government," *Los Angeles Daily Journal,* September 8, 1988, p. 22.

61. United Press International, "Court Finds Wife Too Young for Retirement Condo," *San Diego Daily Transcript,* December 11, 1987.

62. Stevens, "Condominium Associations."

63. "Traffic," *San Diego Tribune,* July 5, 1988, p. B-1.

64. Mary Shepardson, "Homeowners Join Forces, Find Strength in Numbers," *San Diego Business Journal,* March 26–April 2, 1990, 17.

65. "Members Can Be at Mercy of Owners Group," *San Diego Union,* March 11, 1990, p. F-3.

66. United Press International, "Couple Sues to Lift Ban on Condo Door," *Los Angeles Times,* October 8, 1989, part 8, p. 21.

67. John Singh, "Fat Dog Isn't Welcome in the Land of Fat Cats," *Orlando Sentinel Tribune,* March 12, 1992, p. B-4; and John Singh, "Scales of Justice Tip in Favor of Pudgy Dog in Subdivision," *Orlando Sentinel Tribune,* March 17, 1992, p. B-3.

68. Steve Goldstein, "Don't Even Think About Pink Flamingos," *Philadelphia Inquirer,* October 27, 1991, p. 1.

69. Kathy Boccella, "Homeowners Group Coming Up Empty-Handed in a Dues Dispute," *Philadelphia Inquirer,* January 24, 1992, p. B-3.

70. Marie McCullough, "It's a Swing Set! There Goes the Neighborhood," *Philadelphia Inquirer,* October 9, 1991, p. 1.

71. See "Kissing and Doing Bad Things: Grandmother Feels Lash of Intrusive Condominium Association" and "Kissing Incident Apology Falls Short," *Los Angeles Times,* June 21, 1991, pt. B, pp. 6, 8; and "Condo Apologizes for 'Kiss' Accusation," *USA Today,* June 20, 1991, p. 3A. The association's attorney suggested that the security

guard who reported the incident had seen not the fifty-one-year-old grandmother but a seventeen-year-old girl.

72. Barton and Silverman, *Management Study,* 13. For a discussion of rule enforcement—which for many associations leads to conflict between board and residents, as well as to expensive litigation—see Stephen E. Barton and Carol J. Silverman, "The Political Life of Mandatory Homeowners' Associations," in Advisory Commission on Intergovernmental Relations, *Residential Community Associations,* 31–37.

73. Housing cooperatives are typically included with PUDs and condominiums as varieties of common-interest housing. The cooperative movement has a distinct history, however, and in many cases a very different ideology from the privatism that characterizes other CIDs. According to Clifford J. Treese in his unpublished draft of the 1993 *Community Associations Factbook,* co-ops were intended to "respond to housing shortages, especially after each world war, and the need for quality low-moderate income housing by deemphasizing the profit motive for the builder and the unit owner and stressing housing as a social investment which would simultaneously improve people's lives" (p. 23). Co-op developments are a small fraction of total CID housing and are "localized in New York and practiced elsewhere by community development corporations engaged in low-moderate income housing and neighborhood revitalization" (p. 29.) Although I stress the role of the Community Associations Institute as the leading trade association for CIDs, many co-op residents and directors would consider their primary organizational representative to be the National Association of Housing Cooperatives. The story of cooperative housing is separate in many ways from that of the growth of CID housing, and it is not told here.

74. The case generally cited as the earliest judicial approval of a restrictive covenant is *Packenham's Case* (Y.B. Hil. 42 Edw. 3, pl. 14 [1368]), in which it was held that a prior who had promised always to sing at religious services in the manor's chapel could be forced to sing by the lord's successors. The right to enforce the promise was not personal to the lord but "ran with the land."

75. Jesse Dukeminier and James E. Krier, *Property* (Boston: Little, Brown, 1981), 1042–44.

76. Advisory Commission on Intergovernmental Relations, *Residential Community Associations,* 18.

77. Federal Housing Administration, *Planned-Unit Development with a Homes Association,* Land Planning Bulletin no. 6 (Washington, D.C.: Urban Land Institute, 1964).

78. Urban Land Institute/Federal Housing Administration, *Homes Association Handbook,* 12.

79. Stanley Scott, "The Homes Association: Will 'Private Government' Serve the Public Interest?" *Public Affairs Report* 8, no. 1 (February 1967).

80. Urban Land Institute, *Open Space Communities in the Marketplace,* Technical Bulletin no. 57 (Washington, D.C.: Urban Land Institute, December 1966).

81. Scott, "Homes Association."

82. Robert Reich, "Secession of the Successful," *New York Times Magazine,* January 20, 1991, 42.

83. Charles Murray suggests that this new upper caste will become a powerful political force: "I am trying to envision what happens when 10 or 20 per cent of the population has enough income to bypass the social institutions it doesn't like in ways that only the top fraction of 1 per cent used to be able to do. . . . The Left has been

complaining for years that the rich have too much power. They ain't seen nothing yet" (Irwin M. Stelzer, "The Shape of Things to Come," *National Review,* July 8, 1991, 29–30).

84. Frank E. Manuel and Fritzie P. Manuel, *Utopian Thought in the Western World* (Cambridge, Mass.: Harvard University Press, 1979), 27.

85. Urban Land Institute, *Homes Association Handbook,* 4.

86. The literature of the Urban Land Institute and Community Associations Institute is replete with similar statements about finding community through common property ownership. I have chosen to evaluate those statements as serious assertions rather than regard them as marketing ploys intended to capitalize on widespread feelings of social alienation. I recognize that either interpretation is possible.

87. Rosabeth Moss Kanter, *Commitment and Community: Communes and Utopias in Sociological Perspective* (Cambridge, Mass.: Harvard University Press, 1972), 8.

88. Ibid.

89. See Robert Fishman, *Bourgeois Utopias: The Rise and Fall of Suburbia* (New York: Basic Books, 1987), an invaluable contribution to understanding the historical evolution of suburbia as a cultural and physical expression of middle-class utopian aspirations.

90. For contemporaneous accounts of the nineteenth-century utopian commune movement in the United States see John Humphrey Noyes, *History of American Socialisms* (New York: Dover, 1966); William Alfred Hinds, *American Communities* (Secaucus, N.J.: Citadel, 1973); and Charles Nordhoff, *The Communistic Societies of the United States* (1875; reprint, New York: Hillary House, 1961).

91. Kanter, *Commitment and Community,* 2.

92. Carol J. Silverman and Stephen E. Barton, "Common Interest Communities and the American Dream," Working Paper no. 463 (Berkeley, Calif.: Institute of Urban and Regional Development, September 1987), 16–17.

## Chapter 2

1. Charles S. Ascher, "How Can a Section of a Town Get What It Is Prepared To Pay For?" *The American City,* June 1929, 98–99; and Charles S. Ascher, "The Extra-Municipal Administration of Radburn: An Experiment in Government by Contract," *National Municipal Review* 18 (June 1929): 442–46.

2. Ascher, "Extra-Municipal Administration," 446.

3. This history is drawn from Jesse Dukeminier and James E. Krier, *Property* (Boston: Little, Brown, 1981), 959–61.

4. Ibid., 962–63.

5. *Packenham's Case,* Y.B. Hil. 42 Edw. 3, pl. 14 (1368). These principles were put together in *Spencer's Case* (5 Co. 16a, 77 Eng. Rep. 72 [1583]), though Dukeminier and Krier note that "attempts were made to read *Spencer's Case* as permitting covenants between neighboring owners to run to successors, but these attempts ultimately failed" *(Property,* 1026). But the case does set out principles that eventually became central to the English, and, especially, American law of covenants.

6. *Tulk v. Moxhay,* 2 Phillips 774, 41 Eng. Rep. 1143. Chancery was a court of equity to which parties could take cases based on general principles of fairness—cases that would be thrown out of courts of law, which followed stricter rules of pleading. The

facts leading to the court decision are taken from the opinion itself and from the detailed account in Charles S. Ascher, "Private Covenants in Urban Redevelopment," in Coleman Woodbury, ed., *Urban Redevelopment: Problems and Practices* (Chicago: University of Chicago Press, 1953), 228.

7. See Robert Fishman, *Bourgeois Utopias: The Rise and Fall of Suburbia* (New York: Basic Books, 1987).

8. Cleveland Rogers and Rebecca Rankin, *New York: The World's Capital City* (New York: Harper and Brothers, 1948), 253.

9. Urban Land Institute/Federal Housing Administration, *The Homes Association Handbook,* Technical Bulletin no. 50 (Washington, D.C.: Urban Land Institute, 1964), 39.

10. Marc A. Weiss and John W. Watts, "Community Builders and Community Associations: The Role of Real Estate Developers in Private Residential Governance," in Advisory Commission on Intergovernmental Relations, *Residential Community Associations: Private Governments in the Intergovernmental System?* (Washington: Advisory Commission on Intergovernmental Relations, May 1989), 98.

11. Ascher, "Private Covenants," 230.

12. Ronald J. Oakerson, "Private Street Associations in St. Louis County: Subdivisions as Service Providers," in Advisory Commission on Intergovernmental Relations, *Residential Community Associations.*

13. Kenneth Jackson, *Crabgrass Frontier: The Suburbanization of the United States,* (New York: Oxford University Press, 1985), 76.

14. Ibid., 77–78.

15. Marc A. Weiss, *The Rise of the Community Builders: The American Real Estate Industry and Urban Land Planning* (New York: Columbia University Press, 1987), 3.

16. By 1928 the average duration of a restrictive covenant was 34.4 years, according to the study by Helen Monchow. See Helen Monchow, *The Use of Deed Restrictions in Subdivision Development* (Chicago: Institute for Research in Land Economics and Public Utilities, 1928), 56; and Weiss and Watts, "Community Builders and Community Associations," 98–99.

17. Weiss, *Rise of the Community Builders,* 45.

18. Ibid., 43–44.

19. Ibid., 4–6.

20. Ibid., 2–8, 13.

21. Ibid., 3–4.

22. Ibid., 3.

23. Jackson, *Crabgrass Frontier,* 177–78, 258–59.

24. Weiss, *Rise of the Community Builders,* 4.

25. William S. Worley, *J. C. Nichols and the Shaping of Kansas City: Innovation in Planned Residential Communities* (Columbia: University of Missouri Press, 1990), 164–65.

26. Ibid., 168–69.

27. Ibid., 166–67.

28. Ibid., 166. Worley suggests that developers like Nichols may have been

inspired to create homeowner associations by observing the activities of Civil War–era "village improvement societies," which were organized voluntarily in New England and elsewhere. Composed of prominent citizens, they lobbied city officials to build parks, plant trees, repair roads, and create uniform property restrictions regarding setbacks, fences, and even the colors of houses (pp. 159–60). For a discussion of these associations see David P. Handlin, *The American Home: Architecture and Society* (Boston: Little, Brown, 1979), 91–116.

29. Worley, *J. C. Nichols,* 167–68.

30. J. C. Nichols, "A Developer's View of Deed Restrictions," *Journal of Land and Public Utility Economics* 5, no. 2 (May 1929): 140. See also J. C. Nichols, *Mistakes We Have Made in Community Development,* Technical Bulletin no. 1 (Washington, D.C.: Urban Land Institute, March 1945).

31. Nichols, "A Developer's View," 140 n. 2.

32. J. C. Nichols, "Housing and the Real Estate Problem," *Annals of the American Academy of Political and Social Science* 51 (January 1914): 132–33.

33. Monchow, "Deed Restrictions," 47, 50.

34. Ibid., 27.

35. Ibid., iii.

36. Ibid., 28–31.

37. Ibid., 39–42.

38. Ibid., 46–50.

39. Ibid., 50.

40. Ibid., 61–64.

41. Weiss and Watts, "Community Builders and Community Associations," 99.

42. Monchow, "Deed Restrictions," 66–70.

43. Ibid., 71.

44. This biographical sketch is drawn from Ascher's obituary, *New York Times,* February 5, 1980, p. D17; and from *Who Was Who in America,* vol. 7, 1977–81 (Chicago: Marquis, 1981), 18.

45. City Housing Corporation built two influential projects—Sunnyside Gardens in Queens, and Radburn, New Jersey—and then fell victim to the depression. After the demise of City Housing Corporation, which went into bankruptcy in 1934, Ascher went on to a distinguished career in public administration and political science. He was a founder and the first executive secretary of the Public Administration Clearing House in Chicago from 1932 to 1936. During and after World War II he served as regional director in New York of the National Housing Agency. In 1947 he went to Paris as an executive officer for urban planning at the United Nations Educational, Scientific, and Cultural Organization, beginning an involvement in international consulting on housing affairs with the United Nations and other organizations that lasted through the 1970s.

In 1948 he joined the political science department at Brooklyn College, a department he chaired from 1949 until he retired in 1966, and where he continued in an adjunct and emeritus capacity until his death. His academic career included a term as president of the American Society for Public Administration, and he was one of the founders of the Maxwell School of Public Administration at Syracuse University.

46. The RPAA was led by Clarence Stein and included Bing, Frederick L. Ackerman, Robert D. Kohn, Lewis Mumford, and Henry Wright (also a central figure at

CHC); Appalachian Trail designer Benton MacKaye; Charles H. Whitaker (editor of the *Journal of the American Institute of Architects,* which became a forum for RPAA ideas), Frederick Bigger, John Bright, Stuart Chase, Tracy Augur, Edith Elmer Wood, and Catherine Bauer (Clarence S. Stein, *Toward New Towns for America* [Cambridge, Mass.: MIT Press, 1966]). In his introduction to Stein's book Mumford recalls that the core members of RPAA met actively from 1923 to 1933, generally two or three times a week for lunch or dinner, and had occasional weekend meetings, which were more formal, at Hudson Guild Farm in Netcong, New Jersey. Stein went to England after World War I and saw Welwyn while it was under construction. He "returned to America a disciple of Ebenezer Howard and Raymond Unwin" and approached Bing with the idea of building a garden city in America (Stein, *Toward New Towns,* 19). See also Carl Sussman, *Planning the Fourth Migration: The Neglected Vision of the RPAA* (Cambridge, Mass.: MIT Press, 1976).

47. Daniel Schaffer, *Garden Cities for America: The Radburn Experience* (Philadelphia: Temple University Press, 1982), 38–41, 108.

48. Alexander M. Bing, "Can We Have Garden Cities in America?" *The Survey* 54, no. 3 (May 1, 1925): 172. See also Schaffer, *Garden Cities,* 45, 113. A 1925 advertisement for CHC enticed potential investors with the promise of modest but sure profits and a contribution to a better society. "You can help build the future garden cities of America," the ad read. It asserted that limited-dividend financing was "the only effective means for providing good housing for families of moderate income standards." The appeal was directed to "thoughtful men and women who have been glad to invest in a safe business enterprise and to accept a return limited to six per cent so as to participate in the most notable housing movement in twenty-five years" *(The Survey* 50, no. 3 [May 1, 1925]: 125). The CHC board of directors included Eleanor Roosevelt.

49. See Stein, *Toward New Towns,* chap. 2.

50. See Schaffer, *Garden Cities,* chap. 9. Schaffer describes the RPAA as "a think tank with a sponsor, a group of intellectuals with access to capital" (p. 219) whose efforts to strike a compromise between Howard's utopian socialism and American capitalism confronted them with "an uncomfortable, almost hopeless task" (p. 230). Ultimately, Schaffer argues, RPAA was unable to make this compromise work because the organization "often had difficulty calling the rules it wanted to follow because it feared losing its place at the table where the political game was played" (p. 231).

51. Mumford and MacKaye were comfortable with regional plans. See Lewis Mumford, "Regions—To Live In," *The Survey* 54, no. 3 (May 1, 1925): 151, and "The Theory and Practice of Regionalism," *Sociological Review* 19 (June 1928): 24. See also Benton MacKaye, "The New Exploration: Charting the Industrial Wilderness," *The Survey* 54, no. 3 (May 1, 1925): 153. Frederick L. Ackerman, though, felt that planning should be done at the national level. Of all RPAA members, he was probably the most fundamentally critical of capitalism. See Frederick L. Ackerman, "Nation Planning," *National Municipal Review* 8 (January 1919): 15–25.

52. Schaffer, *Garden Cities,* 192–94.

53. Ibid., 172–73.

54. The first project for CHC was a townhouse development in Queens known as Sunnyside Gardens, which also used restrictive covenants and had homeowner associations for each of its six courts. See Urban Land Institute/Federal Housing Administration, *Homes Association Handbook,* 87.

55. Bing, "Can We Have Garden Cities?" 190.

56. Schaffer, *Garden Cities,* 151.

57. Ascher, "Extra-Municipal Administration," 443. Ascher has stated in an

interview that he wrote the covenants (Schaffer, *Garden Cities,* 152). Clarence Stein, however, recalled in 1957 that the "plan for maintaining property and for a shared responsibility" was "based on the experience gained at Sunnyside" and was "developed under the able leadership of Louis Brownlow and Major John Walker" (Stein, *Toward New Towns,* 61). Ascher's account is more persuasive than Stein's. Ascher was an attorney, unlike Brownlow or Walker, and had the legal expertise needed to write the covenants. Monchow had submitted her detailed study of restrictive covenants to him for review in manuscript form. Moreover, Ascher's contemporaneous articles, as well as more recent writings, provide a detailed account of how he went about it.

58. Ascher, "Extra-Municipal Administration," 443.

59. Ibid.

60. *Report of the President's Committee on Administrative Management* (Washington, D.C.: Government Printing Office, 1937).

61. John P. Buenker and Edward R. Kantowicz, *Historical Dictionary of the Progressive Era, 1890–1920* (New York: Greenwood Press, 1988), 315–316. See also Bradley Robert Rice, *Progressive Cities: The Commission Government Movement in America, 1901–1920* (Austin: University of Texas Press, 1977), xii; and John P. East, *Council-Manager Government: The Political Thought of Its Founder, Richard S. Childs* (Chapel Hill: University of North Carolina Press, 1965).

62. Ascher, "Extra-Municipal Administration," 445.

63. Robert B. Hudson, *Radburn: A Plan of Living* (New York: American Association for Adult Education, 1934), 7; and Schaffer, *Garden Cities,* 178.

64. Ascher, "Extra-Municipal Administration," 444–46.

65. There are lessons to be learned about the internal politics of CIDs through examination of the economic and political forces arrayed behind the council-manager plan; see chap. 4.

66. *Wehr v. Roland Park Company,* 143 Md. 384 (1923).

67. *Sanborn v. McLean,* 233 Mich. 227 (1925).

68. *Neponsit Property Owners' Association, Inc. v. Emigrant Industrial Savings Bank,* 278 N.Y. 248 (1938). For a list of cases following *Neponsit* see Uriel Reichman, "Residential Private Governments: An Introductory Survey," 43 *University of Chicago Law Review* 253–306, n.15 (1976).

69. *Neponsit Property Owners' Association, Inc. v. Emigrant Industrial Savings Bank,* 278 N.Y. 248, 256.

70. Ibid.

71. The court cited *Tulk v. Moxhay* for the proposition that "enforcement of such covenants rests upon equitable principles," meaning that the decision is based on the court's evaluation of the overall fairness of the situation rather than on any specific legal principle.

72. *Neponsit Property Owners' Association, Inc. v. Emigrant Industrial Savings Bank,* 278 N.Y. 248, 262.

## Chapter 3

1. Bureau of the Census, *Historical Statistics of the United States, Colonial Times to 1970* (Washington, D.C.: Bureau of the Census, 1975), pt. 2, series N, 156–69.

2. Ibid.

3. Ibid.; and Bureau of the Census, *Statistical Abstract of the United States: 1992* (Washington, D.C.: Government Printing Office, 1992), table 1211, p. 710.

4. Ibid., 238–45.

5. William Schneider, "The Suburban Century Begins," *Atlantic Monthly,* July 1992, 34. See also Douglas S. Massey and Nancy A. Denton *American Apartheid: Segregation and the Making of the Underclass* (Cambridge, Mass.: Harvard University Press, 1993).

6. Michael N. Danielson, *The Politics of Exclusion* (New York: Columbia University Press, 1976), 1.

7. Richard Louv, *America II* (New York: Penguin, 1983), 114.

8. *Shelley v. Kraemer,* 334 U.S. 1 (1948).

9. Bureau of the Census, *Historical Statistics,* series C, 89–119.

10. Charles Abrams, *Forbidden Neighbors* (New York: Harper and Bros., 1955; reprint, Port Washington, N.Y.: Kennikat, 1971), 13.

11. See Richard Hofstadter, *The Age of Reform* (New York: Random House, 1955); and Dennis Judd, *The Politics of American Cities,* 2nd ed. (Boston: Little, Brown, 1984), 84–96.

12. Bureau of the Census, *Historical Statistics,* series C, 25–75.

13. Nicholas Lemann, *The Promised Land: The Great Black Migration and How it Changed America* (New York: Knopf, 1991), 6.

14. See Abrams, *Forbidden Neighbors,* 10–17, on reaction to the "white migration" from Eastern and Southern Europe; and 29–43, on hostility toward the "Far Eastern influx."

15. See Robert C. Weaver, *The Negro Ghetto* (1948; reprint, New York: Russell and Russell, 1967), 212–30; Charles S. Johnson, *Negro Housing* (1932; reprint, New York: Negro Universities Press, 1969), 35–51; and Abrams, *Forbidden Neighbors,* 81–136.

16. Pearl Janet Davies, *Real Estate in American History* (Washington, D.C.: Public Affairs Press, 1958), 58. NAREB was originally called the National Association of Real Estate Exchanges; it is now the National Association of Realtors.

17. Marc A. Weiss, *The Rise of the Community Builders: The American Real Estate Industry and Urban Land Planning* (New York: Columbia University Press, 1987), 15.

18. Davies, *Real Estate in American History,* 183.

19. Weiss, *Rise of the Community Builders,* 44–45.

20. Ibid.

21. Davies, *Real Estate in American History,* 83; and Weiss, *Rise of the Community Builders,* 18–28.

22. The Code of Ethics was published in Harry Grant Atkinson and L. E. Frailey, *Fundamentals of Real Estate Practice* (New York: Prentice-Hall, 1946), 428–29.

23. Abrams, *Forbidden Neighbors,* 154.

24. Atkinson and Frailey, *Fundamentals of Real Estate Practice,* v.

25. Ibid., 34.

26. Ibid., 131.

27. Ibid., 148.

28. Ibid., 295.

29. Abrams, *Forbidden Neighbors*, 157.

30. Miles L. Colean, *A Backward Glance—An Oral History: The Growth of Government Housing Policy in the United States, 1934–1975* (New York: Columbia University Oral History Research Office, 1975), 27.

31. Weiss, *Rise of the Community Builders*, 160. The quotation is attributed to Federal Housing Administration, "Confidential Report of the Planning Committee Meeting," Housing Advisory Council (Washington, D.C., January 18, 1935), 40–41.

32. Weiss, *Rise of the Community Builders*, 143–46.

33. Ibid., 160.

34. Ibid., 147. The quotation is attributed to Federal Housing Administration, "Operative Builders," Circular no. 4, December 15, 1934.

35. Ibid.

36. Ibid., 27–29; and Kenneth Jackson, *Crabgrass Frontier: The Suburbanization of the United States,* (New York: Oxford University Press, 1985), 203–4.

37. Jackson, *Crabgrass Frontier,* 203.

38. Ibid., 206.

39. Ibid., 207.

40. Federal Housing Administration, *Underwriting Manual* (Washington, D.C.: Government Printing Office, February 1938).

41. Federal Housing Administration, *Underwriting Manual* (Washington, D.C.: Government Printing Office, 1947).

42. Urban Land Institute, "Homes Associations, Their Establishment and Functions," *Urban Land* (June 1946).

43. Jackson, *Crabgrass Frontier,* 213.

44. Weaver, *Negro Ghetto,* 231.

45. For a detailed treatment of these ordinances see Johnson, *Negro Housing,* 35–40.

46. Ibid., 38.

47. Ibid., 39.

48. *Buchanan v. Warley,* 245 U.S. 60 (1917).

49. Johnson, *Negro Housing,* 36–37.

50. Weaver, *Negro Ghetto,* 231.

51. In her study of restrictive covenants, Helen Monchow noted that thirty-eight of the forty subdivisions she studied that had racial covenants had been built recently. "The device seems to be in rather general use in the vicinity of the larger eastern and northern cities which have experienced a large influx of colored people in recent years." Helen Monchow, *The Use of Deed Restrictions in Subdivision Development* (Chicago: Institute for Research in Land Economics and Public Utilities, 1928), 50.

52. Weaver, *Negro Ghetto,* 231. The quotation is attributed to Charles Abrams speaking to the Bar Association of the City of New York, February 19, 1947.

53. Johnson, *Negro Housing,* 40–41.

54. Weaver, *Negro Ghetto*, 214, 247.

55. John P. Dean, "Only Caucasian: A Study of Race Covenants," *Journal of Land and Public Utility Economics* (November 1947): 429.

56. Dean, "Only Caucasian," 432.

57. Abrams, *Forbidden Neighbors*, 171.

58. Dean, "Only Caucasian," 429.

59. Ibid., 431.

60. Jackson, *Crabgrass Frontier*, 234, 241.

61. Ibid., 241.

62. David Handlin, *The American Home: Architecture and Society, 1815–1915* (Boston: Little, Brown, 1979), 94–116.

63. William S. Worley, *J. C. Nichols and the Shaping of Kansas City: Innovation in Planned Residential Communities* (Columbia: University of Missouri Press, 1990), 159–61.

64. See the extensive discussion of this phenomenon in Abrams, *Forbidden Neighbors*, especially chap. 14. See also the detailed description of how real estate agents contributed to the creation of the Chicago ghetto in St. Clair Drake and Horace R. Cayton, *Black Metropolis: A Study of Negro Life in a Northern City* (New York: Harcourt, Brace, 1945), especially chap. 8.

65. See Abrams, *Forbidden Neighbors;* and Weaver, *Negro Ghetto*. See also Robert Schafer, *Racial Discrimination in the Boston Housing Market* (Cambridge, Mass.: Harvard University Department of City and Regional Planning, 1976); John Yinger, *Prejudice and Discrimination in the Urban Housing Market* (Cambridge, Mass.: Harvard University Department of City and Regional Planning, 1977); and Zorita Mikva, "The Neighborhood Improvement Association: A Counter-Force to the Expansion of Chicago's Negro Population" (Master's diss., University of Chicago, June 1951), 102.

66. Abrams, *Forbidden Neighbors*, 171. For a comprehensive evaluation of the pervasive role of real estate brokers in maintaining racial segregation see Davis McEntire, *Residence and Race* (Berkeley: University of California Press, 1960), chap. 14.

67. Weaver, *Negro Ghetto*, 233.

68. Mikva, "Improvement Association," 108.

69. Ibid., 99–100. A copy of the letter from the Los Angeles Realty Board is attached at 118–19. In it, the board says, "The threat of occupancy by Negroes of property in such areas depreciates the value of all home properties and constitutes a direct deterrent to investment in the construction or acquisition of homes of superior quality whenever and wherever Negroes have occupied homes in such areas. This has not only depreciated the values of the properties which they own but has depreciated the values of all surrounding properties. . . . The magnitude of the economic and social loss with which we are confronted is appalling. The widespread depreciation in value of homes, the instability of home ownership, and the discouragement of the construction and acquisition of homes are conditions that menace the family life of the nation as we have enjoyed it in the past. Additionally, the insistence of some Negroes upon moving into areas previously restricted exclusively to the occupancy of Caucasians will necessarily create racial tensions and antagonisms and do much harm to our national social structure."

70. Weaver, *Negro Ghetto*, 254.

71. McEntire, *Residence and Race*, 244–50.

72. Weaver, *Negro Ghetto*, 39–40.

73. For a vivid description of these methods see William H. Slavick, "Trouble Comes to Memphis," *Commonweal*, July 24, 1953, 392–94.

74. Johnson, *Negro Housing*, 46–47. See also Drake and Cayton, *Black Metropolis*, 178.

75. Chicago Commission on Race Relations, *The Negro in Chicago* (Chicago: University of Chicago Press, 1922), xv.

76. Ibid., 639.

77. The long-term effects of these institutional practices are discussed in Abrams, *Forbidden Neighbors*, 149; McEntire, *Race and Residence*, especially chaps. 4 and 5; and Chicago Commission on Race Relations, *The Negro in Chicago*, 639.

78. Catherine Bauer, "Good Neighborhoods," *Annals of the American Academy of Political and Social Science* 242 (November 1945): 105.

79. Weaver, *Negro Ghetto*, 229. Yet Weaver's 1944 proposal to replace race restrictive covenants with restrictions based on social class has to be seen as promoting homogeneous neighborhoods.

80. "Real Estate: Exclusive . . . Restricted," *U.S. News and World Report*, May 14, 1948, 22.

81. The option of enforcing racial covenants through different means was outlawed by the U.S. Supreme Court in *Barrows v. Jackson* (346 U.S. 249 [1953]).

82. Bureau of the Census, *American Housing Survey for the United States in 1987* (Washington, D.C., December 1989), table 1A-1.

83. Abrams, *Forbidden Neighbors*, 179–80.

84. Robert C. Weaver, "Race Restrictive Housing Covenants," *Journal of Land and Public Utility Economics* 20, no. 3 (August 1944): 191.

85. "Real Estate," *U.S. News and World Report*, 23.

86. "We've Been Asked: About Status of Racial Bans," *U.S. News and World Report*, May 14, 1948, 50.

87. Mikva, "Improvement Association," 16–20.

# Chapter 4

1. William H. Whyte, Jr., *The Organization Man* (New York: Doubleday, 1956), 6, 310.

2. Herbert J. Gans, *The Levittowners: Ways of Life and Politics in a New Suburban Community* (New York: Random House, 1967), xvi. Gans·summarizes the view of many literary and social critics but takes issue with their view of suburban social life, dubbing it the "myth of suburbia" (pp. xv–xvi). For his thoughtful but ambivalent views on homogeneous and heterogeneous neighborhoods, see chaps. 8 and 15. Gans says that another word for homogeneity might be "compatibility" (p. 154), argues that the optimum solution is "selective homogeneity at the block level and heterogeneity at the community level" (p. 172), and concludes by saying, "I should like to emphasize once more that whatever its imperfections, Levittown is a good place to live" (p. 432).

3. See Robert C. Wood, "Suburbia as an Ideological Retreat," in Jeffrey K. Hadden et al., *Metropolis in Crisis* (Itasca, Ill.: F. E. Peacock, 1967), 155–75.

4. Charles Abrams, *The City Is the Frontier* (New York: Harper and Row, 1965). See also John C. Bollens, *The Metropolis: Its People, Politics, and Economic Life* (New York: Harper and Row, 1965); and, for brief but colorful excerpts from some of the most intense criticisms, Edward P. Eichler and Marshall Kaplan, *The Community Builders* (Berkeley: University of California Press, 1970), 4–7.

5. Robert Fishman, *Bourgeois Utopias: The Rise and Fall of Suburbia* (New York: Basic Books, 1987). Fishman shows in chaps. 3 and 4 how builders in England and later in America discovered that "land far beyond the previous range of metropolitan expansion could be transformed immediately from relatively cheap agricultural land to highly profitable building plots" (p. 10). He traces the emergence of the modern suburb in late-eighteenth-century England as the middle class merchant elite began to move from London to villas in the countryside, "allowing the women and children to remain wholly separate from the contagions of London while the merchants themselves commuted daily from their villas to London by private carriage" (p. 39).

6. For an an interesting distinction between utopian and arcadian visions see Carol A. Christensen, *The American Garden City and the New Towns Movement* (Ann Arbor, Mich.: UMI Research Press, 1986). She argues that utopianism involves social and institutional change and that arcadianism views organized society and nature as antithetical and envisions escaping the supposed evils of the city and embracing imagined rural peace, simplicity, innocence, harmony with nature, and "artless equality." Although this is a worthwhile observation, there has always been more to suburbanization than merely moving to the countryside. Moreover, the CID, with its private government, adds an institutional dimension to suburban life that promises a particular kind of social order. So, though I think the term *arcadian* is useful, I do not distinguish between that word and *utopian*.

7. Fishman, *Bourgeois Utopias,* x.

8. See Urban Land Institute, *New Approaches to Residential Land Development: A Study of Concepts and Innovations* (Washington, D.C.: Urban Land Institute, 1961).

9. Most early 1960s publications on CIDs share a tone of breathless enthusiasm. See, e.g., Federal Housing Administration, *Planned-Unit Development with a Homes Association,* Land Planning Bulletin no. 6 (Washington, D.C.: Urban Land Institute, 1964), 4. The FHA proclaims, on the basis of ULI data, that "the incidence of resident satisfaction and favorable market effect is extremely high. Problems are relatively few; solutions are available."

10. See Community Associations Institute, *Community Associations Factbook* (Alexandria, Va.: Community Associations Institute, 1988), 9. The *Factbook* also refers to the increased cost of land as a percentage of the total home construction cost, a figure that rose from 11 percent in 1950 to 25 to 30 percent by 1988 (p. 6).

11. Martin Mayer, *The Builders: Houses, People, Neighborhoods, Governments, Money* (New York: W. W. Norton, 1978), 13.

12. For a discussion of the legal dimensions of the struggle over who should bear the burden of these costs see Donald G. Hagman and Julian Conrad Juergensmeyer, *Urban Planning and Land Development Control Law,* 2nd ed. (St. Paul, Minn.: West Publishing, 1986), 202–13.

13. Builders' awareness of the desire to preserve open space increased their leverage as they campaigned for laws that permitted smaller lots and allowed them to leave some land in its natural state—saving development costs as they built at least as many homes. The public agency's ultimate weapon was down-zoning, but builders said that eminent domain was the only constitutional approach. There was also a middle ground. In 1959 William H. Whyte, Jr., proposed a way to preserve natural open space without using zoning to prohibit construction on it or buying it through eminent

domain. He urged that the public pay a land owner for not building on his or her land by purchasing a "conservation easement." The owner would retain title to the land, but the public would have bought the owner's right to "develop it into a subdivision or splatter it with billboards" (William H. Whyte, Jr., *Securing Open Space for Urban America: Conservation Easements,* Technical Bulletin no. 36 [Washington, D.C.: Urban Land Institute, December 1959], 8).

14. David B. Wolfe, *Condominium and Homeowner Associations that Work* (Washington, D.C.: Urban Land Institute/Community Associations Institute, 1978), 7.

15. Jon Rosenthal, "Cluster Subdivisions," Planning Advisory Service Information Report no. 135 (Chicago: American Society of Planning Officials, June 1960), 5. The report also notes the "look-alike" pattern of postwar developments: "Architecture, street pattern, setback, and yard spacing are unvaried" (p. 1).

16. Urban Land Institute, *New Approaches to Residential Land Development,* Technical Bulletin no. 40 (Washington, D.C.: Urban Land Institute, 1961), Foreword.

17. Urban Land Institute, *Innovations vs. Traditions in Community Development* (Washington, D.C.: Urban Land Institute, 1963), 12.

18. Ibid., 32–33.

19. Federal Housing Administration, *Planned-Unit Development.*

20. Ibid., 24. For a full description of the measure see Federal Housing Administration, *Land-Use Intensity* (Washington, D.C.: Federal Housing Administration, 1963.)

21. Author interview with Byron R. Hanke, January 9, 1993.

22. Urban Land Institute, *The Homes Association Handbook,* Technical Bulletin no. 50 (Washington, D.C.: Urban Land Institute, 1964). Hanke was heavily involved in producing new standards for multifamily housing for the administration, as well as *Land-Use Intensity* and *Planned-Unit Development.* He was instrumental in founding the Community Associations Institute. The close connection was exemplified by Seward Mott, who went from being the first head of the land planning division to a position as executive director of ULI. See Marc A. Weiss, *The Rise of the Community Builders: The American Real Estate Industry and Urban Land Planning* (New York: Columbia University Press, 1987), 68.

23. Author interview with Byron Hanke, January 9, 1993.

24. They were Waldemar Weichbrodt, director of the Appraisal and Mortgage Risk Division; William J. O'Connor, deputy director of the Architectural Standards Division; and John R. Lynch, chief of the Valuation Section. See *Planned-Unit Development,* 1.

25. Stanley Scott, "The Homes Association: Will 'Private Government' Serve the Public Interest?" *Public Affairs Report* 8, no. 1 (February 1967): 4.

26. David Clurman and Edna L. Hebard, *Condominiums and Cooperatives* (New York: John Wiley and Sons, 1970), 2.

27. Robert G. Natelson, "Comments on the Historiography of Condominium: The Myth of Roman Origin," 12 *Oklahoma City University Law Review* 17 (1987), 20. Natelson suggests that what he calls the myth of Roman origin was conveyed to Congress by the resident commissioner of Puerto Rico and the legislative director of the Puerto Rican Home Builders Association, whose "strategy was (in part) to convince Congress that condominium was a venerable institution which had been thoroughly time-tested in Europe and in Latin America" (pp. 39–40). There is also an archaeological basis for the myth: in Rome there are remains of attached houses connected by party walls and blocks of flats several stories high. But Natelson maintains that the

buildings were not condominiums. The bottom level of a house would have been the home of a wealthy family or the quarters for a commercial establishment, he says; the upper floors were apartments for the poor. Whatever its origin, the myth was apparently spread by those connected with the building industry. Natelson notes that in 1960 a title officer for Chicago Title and Trust Company, Charles E. Ramsey, wrote a pamphlet entitled "Condominium: The New Look in Co-ops," which contained this statement, unsupported by legal or historical authority: "The concept of property ownership to which [the condominium] pertains is literally as old as the hills—the hills of ancient Rome, where it is said to have its beginning." Ramsey spoke on this new and interesting subject, published articles in law periodicals, and spread the "hills of ancient Rome" image widely. Natelson shows how the erroneous concept began to appear in legal publications with great regularity.

28. Rudolf Huebner, *A History of Germanic Private Law* (1918; reprint, New York: Augustus M. Kelley , 1968), 174.

29. Clurman and Hebard, *Condominiums and Cooperatives,* 3.

30. Mike Davis, *City of Quartz: Excavating the Future in Los Angeles* (London: Verso, 1990), 224.

31. Natelson, "Historiography," 30.

32. House Committee on Banking and Currency, *Hearings on General Housing Legislation Before the Subcommittee on Housing,* 86th Cong., 2nd sess., 1960; and Senate Committee on Banking and Currency, *Hearings on Various Bills to Amend the Federal Housing Laws Before a Subcommittee,* 86th Cong., 2nd sess., 1960.

33. See Clurman and Hebard, *Condominiums and Cooperatives,* 4–6.

34. Community Associations Institute, *Community Associations Factbook, 1988,* 7. See also Clurman and Hebard, *Condominiums and Cooperatives,* 6.

35. Bureau of the Census, *American Housing Survey for the United States in 1987* (Washington, D.C.: Department of Commerce, December 1989), table 1A-1.

36. James A. Clapp, *New Towns and Urban Policy* (New York: Dunellen, 1971), 291–98, 118–19. Summary data on fifty-three new towns that were planned or under construction in 1964 showed an average size of fourteen thousand acres and fifteen thousand housing units. See Eichler and Kaplan, *Community Builders,* 185–86.

37. For a description of the English new town program see Frederic J. Osborn and Arnold Whittick, *The New Towns: The Answer to Megalopolis* (New York: McGraw-Hill, 1963).

38. Eichler and Kaplan, *Community Builders,* 24.

39. For an optimistic assessment of the ways in which "new towns can serve as demonstration laboratories for new approaches to more democratic local government" see Twentieth Century Fund, *New Towns: Laboratories for Democracy* (New York: Twentieth Century Fund, 1971).

40. Eichler and Kaplan, *Community Builders,* 34–35, 104–19.

41. Ibid., 105. Additionally, they note, community builders assumed that in areas around new communities there would be limited demand for cheaper housing and that people who wanted less expensive housing "will not find the extra amenities a special attraction."

42. Ibid., 114, 116.

43. Ibid., 116.

44. Ibid., 117.

45. Ibid., 116.

46. Ibid., 119.

47. Mayer, *The Builders,* 94.

48. Clapp, *New Towns,* 119.

49. See Mayer, *The Builders,* 96.

50. See Uriel Reichman, "Residential Private Governments: An Introductory Survey," 43 *University of Chicago Law Review* 253 (1976); Theodore Roszak, "Life in the Instant Cities," *The Nation,* March 13, 1967, 336–40; and James Ridgeway, "New Towns are Big Business," *New Republic,* October, 1, 1966, 15.

51. Reichman, "Residential Private Governments," 258–59.

52. Joseph B. Mason, *History of Housing in the U.S., 1930–1980* (Houston, Texas: Gulf, 1982), 100–101.

53. Ibid., 102–6.

54. See ibid., 107–8, for a listing "complicated and often bizarre series of formulas" that the corporate giants brought to the housing business.

55. There were other significant federal initiatives involving large-scale private housing construction. The Government National Mortgage Association (GNMA, or "Ginnie Mae") was enabled by the Housing and Urban Development Act of 1968. GNMA helped large corporations tap the investment market. As Joseph B. Mason puts it, "The new guaranteed Mortgage-backed securities paved the way for vast new investments by pension funds, trusts, insurance companies, and private investors" (Mason, *History of Housing,* 108).

56. See Joseph L. Arnold, *The New Deal in the Suburbs: A History of the Greenbelt Program, 1935–1954* (Columbus: Ohio State University Press, 1971).

57. Ibid. 88–89.

58. Ibid., 124–33. The Bankhead-Black Act, passed by Congress in 1936, made the Greenbelt towns subject to state civil and criminal jurisdiction, made provision for civil rights for residents, and authorized the Resettlement Administration to pay "sums in lieu of taxes" to the local communities deprived of property tax revenues by the retention of ownership by the federal government.

59. Ibid., 138–39.

60. Ibid., 191.

61. Ibid., 243.

62. Clapp, *New Towns,* 8–9.

63. Department of Housing and Urban Development, *An Evaluation of the Federal New Communities Program* (Washington, D.C.: Department of Housing and Urban Development, December 1984), table 2.1 and preceding page.

64. Ibid., Introduction.

65. The report itemizes the program costs as follows: repayments of defaulted loans, $298 million; accrued and defaulted interest, $147 million; grants, $137 million; administrative costs, $75 million; this is a total program cost of $657 million, which was offset by $96 million in recovered fees and payments for a net cost of $561 million (Department of Housing and Urban Development, *Evaluation,* iii, v, appendix 1, table 1).

66. Ibid., vi–vii.

67. Mayer, *The Builders,* 89.

68. For reasons of space and focus, I have chosen not to dwell on the complex economic vicissitudes of the 1970s and 1980s and their effects on the housing industry. These events included recessions, stagflation, and the debt-driven boom of the 1980s that spawned CIDS in unprecedented numbers. That memorable decade also featured the pillaging of the savings and loan industry, an episode that enriched many developers and helped to finance numerous CIDS that never stood a chance of being economically viable and eventually were taken over by the federal government. For various accounts of the saving and loan meltdown see Robert Sherrill, "The Looting Decade: S&Ls, Big Banks, and Other Triumphs of Capitalism," *The Nation,* November 19, 1990, 589.

69. Marc A. Weiss and John W. Watts, "Community Builders and Community Associations: The Role of Real Estate Developers in Private Residential Governance," in Advisory Commission on Intergovernmental Relations, *Residential Community Associations: Private Governments in the Intergovernmental System?* (Washington: Advisory Commission on Intergovernmental Relations, May 1989), 101.

70. Christensen, *American Garden City,* 128.

## Chapter 5

1. Both ULI and NAHB maintain substantial libraries at their respective Washington, D.C., headquarters, as well as lists of their own publications that can be purchased on site or through the mail. ULI also prepares what it calls InfoPackets, which are collections of articles and reports on specific subjects. For example, Info-Packet no. 326 is titled "New Towns/Planned Communities" and contains fourteen articles from the ULI journal *Urban Land* and twenty other publications.

2. Community Associations Institute, *Community Associations Factbook, 1988,* (Arlington, Va.: Community Associations Institute, 1988), 9. Byron Hanke, the author of the *Homes Association Handbook,* which originated the 1962 figure, conducted a national survey that located 233 associations and estimated that "we missed about half of them," leading him to the widely reported conclusion that there were fewer than five hundred associations (author interview with Byron Hanke, January 9, 1993).

3. Bureau of the Census, *Statistical Abstract of the United States: 1989* (Washington, D.C.: Government Printing Office, 1989), table 1229, p. 700.

4. House Committee on Government Operations, Subcommittee Hearings on Federal Trade Commission Decisions and Policies, 91st Cong., 1st sess., April 30, 1975.

5. Department of Housing and Urban Development, *Condominium and Cooperative Study* (3 vols.) (Washington, D.C.: Department of Housing and Urban Development, July 1975).

6. Marc A. Weiss and John W. Watts, "Community Builders and Community Associations: The Role of Real Estate Developers in Private Residential Governance," in Advisory Commission on Intergovernmental Relations, *Residential Community Associations: Private Governments in the Intergovernmental System?* (Washington: Advisory Commission on Intergovernmental Relations, May 1989), 101.

7. Urban Land Institute, *Homes Association Handbook,* 253–56.

8. Ibid., 256.

9. Author interview with Byron Hanke, January 9, 1993; letter from Richard Canavan to Ford Foundation, August 20, 1966; and letter from Ford Foundation to Richard Canavan, August 29, 1966.

10. Author interview with Byron Hanke, January 9, 1993.

11. There is some ambiguity regarding who was actually a member of the design group and who was a consultant to the group. Rhame recalls that Wolfe was a consultant, but Hanke believes Wolfe was a member. The plan for CAI's first year, CAI Design '74, lists Wolfe as an "advisor on design." Additionally, from the outset the membership of CAI reflected considerable ambiguity over which interest group a particular individual represented. The CAI brochure "Meet the Board of Trustees," issued in 1975, identifies Stahl as a "colleague representative," and attorney Wayne Hyatt is listed as a "homeowner representative" (Byron Hanke files).

12. On the first CAI board were May Russell (managers); Rhame (developers); Canavan (public officials); Cummings (homeowners); and John Gunther (professionals).

13. The former executive vice-president of CAI, C. James Dowden, recalls testifying before Congress on an issue and explaining that his organization represented neither consumers nor developers but "the process of creating these things." He also explained the consensus provision. As a result, he says, CAI received thirty minutes to testify, and the National Association of Home Builders lobbyist was allotted only ten minutes (author interview with C. James Dowden, January 13, 1993).

14. Author interviews with Byron Hanke and Lincoln Cummings, January 20, 1993.

15. This statement appears on CAI publications. See, e.g., David B. Wolfe, *Condominium and Homeowner Associations that Work*, (Washington, D.C.: Urban Land Institute/Community Associations Institute, 1978), ii.

16. Hanke's recollection was that the target was $500,000. David Rhame recalled it as $600,000, with $200,000 from the building industry, $200,000 from government agencies, and $200,000 from foundations. Had major foundations taken greater interest in CID housing and the idea that private governments, run by amateurs, were necessary to its operation, CAI would not have had to depend so heavily on the development and property management industries and the professionals who serve CIDs. Such professionals became the major source of financial support for CAIS, contributing heavily and buying advertising in CAI publications. Had powerful business and trade interests not been so essential to the existence of CAI, it is likely that the organization would have better reflected considerations of the overall public interest and the interests of homeowners.

17. Rhame recalls the net from the conference as "about a hundred thousand dollars."

18. The HUD-sponsored CAI publications were *Creating a Community Association: The Developer's Role in Condominium and Homeowner Associations* and *Community Associations: A Guide for Public Officials*. See the account of CAI's founding in its booklet "Ten Years of Growth and Success—1973–1983." That booklet also lists the twenty-three founding developers who contributed at least three thousand dollars each to start CAI.

19. Author interview with Lincoln Cummings, January 16, 1993.

20. Community Associations Institute, 1992 Annual Report, *Common Ground* (November–December 1992): 24–31.

21. Advisory Commission on Intergovernmental Relations, *Residential Commu-*

*nity Associations: Private Governments in the Intergovernmental System?* (Washington, D.C.: Advisory Commission on Intergovernmental Relations, 1989).

22. The organizational structure of CAI, before the changes described below, was set forth in the November 1988 issue of *CAI News,* the national CAI newsletter. The California Legislative Action Committee publishes regular legislative updates advising members of the California chapters of the progress of all bills in which CAI has an interest.

23. See Community Associations Institute, 1992 Annual Report, 26.

24. Community Associations Institute, *Community Associations Factbook, 1993* (Arlington, Va.: Community Associations Institute, 1993).

25. Community Associations Institute, 1992 Annual Report, 31.

26. Author interview with David W. Gibbons, January 15, 1993.

27. Author interviews with Byron Hanke, January 9 and 16, 1993; and Lincoln Cummings, January 16, 1993.

28. Letter from Lincoln Cummings to David Gibbons, March 7, 1992.

29. Ibid.

30. CAI Statement of Core Purpose, 1992 Annual Report, 27. The rest of the statement describes CAI as "the catalyst in the dynamic development and presentation of educational experiences as a vehicle for the ongoing advancement of the community associations industry and competent performance of its participants; the leading promoter of research in the community association field; the premier resource center on current and future trends and practices; the developer of innovative concepts for the creation and operation of community associations; dedicated to the betterment of the greater community." Although the statement was drafted by the same Strategic Planning Committee that decided to place increased emphasis on legislative advocacy, nothing in the statement identifies the organization as a group with a political agenda.

31. Author interview with David Gibbons, January 15, 1993.

32. "Legislative Action Links CAI With Federal, State Governments," CAI 1992 Annual Report, *Common Ground* (November–December 1992): 26.

33. Author interviews with Byron Hanke and Lincoln Cummings, January 20, 1993.

34. Author interview with J. Stephen Cottrelle, president of MCHA, January 20, 1993; and MCHA literature, including its newsletter, *Communicator.*

## Chapter 6

1. Thomas Hobbes, *Leviathan* (New York: J. M. Dent and Sons, 1976), 117–18.

2. Arthur F. Bentley, *The Process of Government: A Study of Social Pressures* (Bloomington, Ind.: Principia Press, 1908), 268.

3. Charles E. Merriam, *Public and Private Government* (New Haven: Yale University Press, 1944), 2–19.

4. Richard Eells and Clarence Walton, *Conceptual Foundations of Business* (Homewood, Ill.: Richard D. Irwin, 1961), 134.

5. *Dartmouth College v. Woodward,* 4 Wheaton 518 (1819).

6. Eels and Walton, 134–35, 142.

7. Ibid., 305–8. See also Richard Eels, *The Meaning of Modern Business* (New York: Columbia University Press, 1960).

8. Adolph A. Berle, Jr., *The 20th Century Capitalist Revolution* (New York: Harcourt, Brace, 1954), 105–6.

9. Earl Latham, "The Body Politic of the Corporation," in Edward S. Mason, ed., *The Corporation in Modern Society* (Cambridge, Mass.: Harvard University Press, 1959), 218.

10. John McDermott, *Corporate Property: Class, Property, and Contemporary Capitalism* (Boulder, Colo.: Westview, 1991), 4–5.

11. Stephen E. Barton and Carol J. Silverman, *Common Interest Homeowners' Association Management Study* (Sacramento: California Department of Real Estate, 1987), 2.

12. See Department of Housing and Urban Development, *Condominium and Cooperative Study* (3 vols.) (Washington, D.C.: Department of Housing and Urban Development, July 1975); and Barton and Silverman, *Management Study*, 2.

13. See Federal Housing Administration/Urban Land Institute, *The Homes Association Handbook*, Technical Bulletin no. 50 (Washington, D.C.: Urban Land Institute, 1964), appendix F, art. N, sec. 1.

14. Author interview with Byron Hanke, January 20, 1993.

15. There are exceptions to this, one of the most notable being Columbia, Maryland. But the rule of "one-unit, one vote" still obtains in developments where renters are permitted to vote.

16. See, e.g., Albert A. Foer, Comment, "Democracy in the New Towns: The Limits of Private Government," 36 *University of Chicago Law Review* 379 (1969).

17. Barton and Silverman, *Management Study*.

18. Ibid., 13.

19. Ibid., 21. Physical deterioration of CID housing may become a serious issue in areas where a great deal of new construction was undertaken in the late 1970s through the 1990 recession. Many associations do not maintain adequate reserves for replacement of such building components as roofs, walls, and windows, which have a shorter useful life than many residents may realize. A defect in one component often causes damage to other components, hastening overall deterioration. This problem can be especially serious in condominiums and townhouses, where many residents live under one roof and share walls. For example, a leaking roof membrane that admits water into the interior of the structure can damage the plywood roof itself and cause dry rot of the drywall and even the beams and joists. Consequently, the ultimate cost of not maintaining a roof or replacing its outer surface on schedule can be monumental and exceed the residents' resources.

20. Ibid., 9.

21. See California Corporations Code, sec. 309.

22. Ibid.

23. "The Buck Stops with the Board" (interview with F. Scott Jackson), *Common Ground* (November–December 1992): 34.

24. See, e.g., *Raven's Cove Townhomes, Inc. v. Knuppe Development* 114 Cal. App. 3d 783, 799 (1981), which held that CID directors owe a fiduciary duty to their members.

25. Ralph Meyers has called this the dictator syndrome. See Ralph Meyers, "Democracy or Dictatorship," in the CAI pamphlet "The Successful Leader."

26. For discussion of the basic principles in these areas see Wayne Hyatt and Philip S. Downer, eds., *Condominium and Homeowner Association Litigation: Community Association Law* (New York: Wiley and Sons, 1987), chaps. 2 and 3.

27. Community Associations Institute, *Community Associations Factbook, 1993,* 25. In California, the ADR was reintroduced for the 1993–94 regular session on December 17, 1992 as Assembly Bill 55.

28. Latham, "Body Politic," 220.

29. Sanford A. Lakoff with Daniel Rich, *Private Governments: Introductory Readings* (Glenview, Ill.: Scott, Foresman, 1973), 1.

30. Ibid.

31. Grant McConnell, *Private Power and American Democracy* (New York: Knopf, 1966), chap. 5.

32. Barton and Silverman, *Management Study,* 13–14, 30.

33. See, e.g., Katharine Rosenberry, "The Application of the Federal and State Constitutions to Condominiums, Cooperatives and Planned Developments," 19 *Real Property, Probate and Trust Journal* 1 (1984).

34. See Community Associations Institute, 1992 Annual Report, *Common Ground* (November–December 1992): 27.

35. Hugh Mields, Jr., *Federally Assisted New Communities: New Dimensions in Urban Development* (Washington, D.C.: Urban Land Institute, 1973), 54.

36. Urban Land Institute/Community Associations Institute, *Managing a Successful Community Association* (Washington, D.C.: Urban Land Institute, 1974), 2.

37. Wayne S. Hyatt and James B. Rhoads, "Concepts of Liability in the Development and Administration of Condominium and Home Owners Associations, 12 *Wake Forest Law Review* 915 (1976).

38. Ibid., 3.

39. Theodore Roszak, "Life in the Instant Cities," *The Nation,* March 13, 1967, 339–40.

40. Lakoff with Rich, *Private Governments,* 228–42.

41. See Richard Louv, *America II* (New York: Penguin, 1983), 133–34. Louv derived some of these concepts from discussions with Ralph Meyer.

42. John Locke, *The Second Treatise of Government* (Indianapolis, Ind.: Library of Liberal Arts, 1952).

43. Robert Nozick, *Anarchy, State, and Utopia* (New York: Basic Books, 1974).

44. Louv, *America II,* 119.

45. Carol Snyder, *The Great Condominium Rebellion* (New York: Delacorte, 1981).

46. See, e.g., California Corporations Code, sec. 7140.

47. The author was involved as one of many attorneys in a lawsuit concerning a senior citizens' development consisting of 223 homes that was damaged because of an ancient landslide complex beneath the development. The homeowner association and the individual residents ultimately recovered about twenty million dollars in a series of lawsuits against the developer, insurance companies, and other defendants.

48. Adolph A. Berle, Jr., *The Twentieth Century Capitalist Revolution* (New York: Harcourt, Brace, 1954).

49. Barton and Silverman, *Management Study,* 13–14.

50. Ibid., 27–28.

51. Richard Louv, *Childhood's Future: Listening to the American Family* (Boston: Houghton Mifflin, 1990), 318.

52. Ibid., 317.

53. Mike Bowler and Evan McKenzie, "Invisible Kingdoms," 5 *California Lawyer* 55, 58 (December 1985).

54. Locke, *Second Treatise,* 9.

55. See, e.g., California Civil Code, sec. 1356.

56. One interestingly unsympathetic comment regarding this phenomenon appears in Curtis C. Sproul, "Is California's Mutual Benefit Corporation Law the Appropriate Domicile for Community Associations?" 18 *University of San Francisco Law Review* 695 (Summer 1984).

57. Robert Dahl, "The City in the Future of Democracy," *American Political Science Review* 61 (December 1967): 953.

## Chapter 7

1. The Florida Condominium Act is located at chap. 718 of the Florida Statutes.

2. Community Associations Institute, "Ten Years of Growth and Success—1973–1983" (Alexandria, Va.: Community Associations Institute, 1983), 5.

3. Ibid.

4. For a discussion of the history of these acts see Uniform Common Interest Ownership Act (Chicago: National Conference of Commissioners on Uniform State Laws, 1982), 6–8.

5. Ibid., 1–2.

6. Community Associations Institute, *Community Associations Factbook, 1993* (Alexandria, Va.: Community Associations Institute, 1993), 12.

7. See, e.g., Robert G. Natelson, *The Law of Property Owners' Associations* (Boston: Little, Brown, 1989); Robert C. Ellickson, "Cities and Homeowner Associations," 130 *University of Pennsylvania Law Review* 1519 (1982); Gregory S. Alexander, "Dilemmas of Group Autonomy: Residential Associations and Community," 75 *Cornell Law Review* 1 (November 1989); "Freedom, Coercion and the Law of Servitudes," 73 *Cornell Law Review* 883 (July 1988); Robert G. Natelson, "Consent, Coercion and 'Reasonableness' in Private Law: The Special Case of the Property Owners' Association," 51 *Ohio State Law Journal* 41 (Winter 1990); and James L. Winokur, "The Mixed Blessings of Promissory Servitudes: Toward Optimizing Freedom, Economic Utility, Individual Liberty and Personal Identity," 1989 *Wisconsin Law Review* 1 (January–February 1989), and Rejoinder, "Reforming Servitude Regimes: Toward Associational Federalism and Community," 1990 *Wisconsin Law Review* 537 (March–April 1990). See also Richard Epstein, "Notice and Freedom of Contract in the Law of Servitudes," 55 *Southern California Law Review* 1353 (1982).

8. Wayne S. Hyatt and Philip S. Downer, eds., *Condominium and Homeowner Association Litigation: Community Association Law* (New York: John Wiley and Sons, 1987).

9. See Stephen E. Barton and Carol J. Silverman, *Common Interest Homeowners'*

*Association Management Study* (Sacramento: California Department of Real Estate, 1987), 28. In California CIDS are not required to be incorporated. Those that have incorporated are "mutual benefit corporations," a category that includes many other kinds of organizations. Consequently, it is difficult to calculate their numbers or population. See Community Associations Institute, *Community Association Factbook, 1993.*

10. For the critical role played by Los Angeles in the creation of modern zoning ordinances see Marc A. Weiss, *The Rise of the Community Builders: The American Real Estate Industry and Urban Land Planning* (New York: Columbia University Press, 1987). On Los Angeles as the model for the auto-dependent suburbanized metropolis see Kenneth Jackson, *Crabgrass Frontier: The Suburbanization of the United States,* (New York: Oxford University Press, 1985). On Los Angeles as the new "technoburb" see Robert Fishman, *Bourgeois Utopias: The Rise and Fall of Suburbia* (New York: Basic Books, 1987). See also Mike Davis, *City of Quartz: Excavating the Future in Los Angeles* (London: Verso, 1990).

11. All data on the structure and attributes of the state courts was taken from *State Court Organization, 1987* (Williamsburg, Va.: National Center for State Courts, Conference of State Court Administrators, 1988).

12. See Mike Bowler and Evan McKenzie, "Invisible Kingdoms," 5 *California Lawyer* 55 (December 1986); Ellickson, "Cities and Homeowner Associations"; Albert A. Foer, Comment, "Democracy in the New Towns: The Limits of Private Government," 36 *University of Chicago Law Review* 379 (1969); Wayne Hyatt and James B. Rhoads, "Concepts of Liability in the Development and Administration of Condominium and Homeowner Associations," 12 *Wake Forest Law Review* 915 (1976); Uriel Reichman, "Residential Private Governments: An Introductory Survey," 43 *University of Chicago Law Review* 253 (1976); Katharine Rosenberry, "The Application of the Federal and State Constitutions to Condominiums, Cooperatives and Planned Developments," 19 *Real Property Probate and Trust Journal* (1984); Katharine Rosenberry, "Actions of Community Association Boards: When Are They Valid, and When Do They Create Liability?" 13 *Real Estate Law Journal* 315 (Spring 1985); Katharine Rosenberry, "The Legislature Addresses Problems in the Law of Condominiums, Planned Developments, and Other Common Interest Projects," 3 *California Real Property Journal* 24 (Winter 1985); Katharine Rosenberry, "Condominium and Homeowner Associations: Should They Be Treated Like Mini-Governments?" 8 *Zoning and Planning Law Report* 153 (October 1985); and Curtis C. Sproul, "Is California's Mutual Benefit Corporation Law the Appropriate Domicile for Community Associations?" 18 *University of San Francisco Law Review* 695 (Summer 1984).

13. See the Florida Fourth District Court of Appeal's decision that the actions of homeowner associations are not state action in *Brock v. Watergate Mobile Home Park Association, Inc.* (502 So. 2d 1380 [1987]).

14. Adolph A. Berle, Jr., *The Twentieth Century Capitalist Revolution* (New York: Harcourt, Brace, 1954), 105.

15. Two main tests were developed to decide whether apparently private action constituted state action. The public function test considered whether the actions of the private person or organization were essentially public in nature, as in *Marsh*. The state involvement test considered the nexus between the state and the challenged activity. If the connection was close enough, the private action could be considered state action.

16. In *Brock v. Watergate Mobile Home Park Association, Inc.* (502 So. 2d 1380 [1987]), the Florida Fourth District Court of Appeal held that a homeowner association's conduct did not constitute state action because the association "lacks the municipal character of a company town," being based on ownership alone; because the

association's services "are merely a supplement to, rather than a replacement for, those provided by local government," so that the association does not act "in a sufficiently public manner"; and because "the association's maintenance, assessment, and collection activities are not sufficiently connected to the State to warrant a finding of state action." Accordingly, the court said, "We conclude that the association in this case does not stand in the position of a government" (1382).

17. Hyatt and Rhoades, "Concepts of Liability."

18. The provision allows age discrimination in developments with "accommodations designed to meet the physical and social needs of senior citizens," which can mean people as young as fifty-five. See California Civil Code, secs. 51.2 and 51.3, which define senior housing in more detail.

19. *Frances T. v. Village Green Owners Association,* 229 Cal. Rptr. 456 (1986). The court allowed the unit owner to proceed against the association and the directors in negligence, but not under theories of breach of contract or breach of fiduciary duty.

20. The law allows tort immunity for associations that maintain at least $500,000 in insurance for developments of fewer than one hundred units and at least $1 million for larger developments. See California Civil Code, sec. 1365.7.

21. Advocates of CIDs also secured reversal of a case that limited the ability of CID boards to file lawsuits against developers regarding construction defects. This was *Friendly Village Community Association, Inc., v. Silva & Hill Construction* (31 Cal. App. 3d 220 [1973]), which held that owners' associations could not file such suits because the owners were the real parties in interest. Under pressure from CAI advocates and the Executive Council of Homeowners, the legislature reversed the decision by passing California Code of Civil Procedure, sec. 374, giving these associations standing to sue as the real party in interest. See Evan McKenzie, "Private Covenants and Public Law: A Perspective on the Rise of Residential Private Governments in Common Interest Housing" (Ph.D. diss., University of Southern California, 1989), chap. 7. Section 374 led to a flood of multimillion-dollar construction cases against developers in California, most of which would never have been filed if the individual owners in a development had been required to agree. As of this writing the board can file the suit on its own authority on behalf of the corporation, without joining or even informing the members.

22. California Senator Larry Stirling, "Form Letter for Background on A.B. 314, 315, 316, 438 and 439," February 22, 1985.

23. Stirling, who subsequently became a state senator and then a Superior Court judge, was described as "an active advocate for community associations in the California Legislature" ("Legislative Affairs Report of the California Legislative Action Committee" [Summer 1987]). At the 1987 National CAI Conference in San Diego, Stirling opposed a package of ethics bills considered by the legislature. The bills would have prohibited lawmakers and their staff members from lobbying the legislature for one year after leaving office. Stirling said the measures would curtail contact between lawmakers and the public. He said he believed it was a good thing that special interests influence the legislature, and he defined these special interests as being every California citizen or group with a common interest.

Still, Stirling referred to the consumer lobby group California Common Cause as "communist" and to its leader, Walter Zelman, as a "man of extreme liberal views who believes in statism, who believes in state power, who believes in redistribution of wealth, believes that he should be in charge, and that's why he's running for public office." Zelman was at the time considering a run for the newly created office of state insurance commissioner. *(Los Angeles Times,* San Diego edition, September 15, 1989, p. B-1.)

24. Rosenberry drafted and signed the Stirling "Form Letter for Background," from which this information was obtained.

25. Katharine N. Rosenberry, "The Legislature Addresses Problems in the Law of Condominiums, Planned Development and Other Common Interest Projects," 3 *California Real Property Journal* 24–27 (Winter 1985).

26. Ibid., 25.

27. Ibid., 27.

28. Robyn Boyer Stewart, "Homeowner Associations Sally Forth into the Political Wars," *California Journal* (April 1991): 269–72. Stewart anticipates that the double taxation issue will be "the next Proposition 13" and will one day be the subject of a statewide ballot issue. When property tax reform came to California in 1978, it happened through an initiative because the state government failed to agree on a plan. By the time the governor and legislature arrived at a proposal, the popular momentum behind the more drastic measure, Proposition 13, was too great to be diverted. It is conceivable, as Stewart suggests, that this pattern may repeat itself. Stewart also served as a legislative consultant in 1991–92 to the Assembly Select Committee on Common Interest Subdivisions, which considered and recommended amendments to the Common Interest Development Act in 1991. (Author interview with Robyn Boyer Stewart, January 19, 1993.)

29. Rosenberry, "Legislature Addresses Problems," 28.

30. Ibid.

31. Author interview with Gary Aguirre. On March 31, 1985, CAI adopted an "approved draft" dated March 29, 1985. That draft, described as an "official policy statement" of the CAI Board of Trustees, contains references to the legal authorities, including cites to *Cohen* and *O'Connor*. The document has a section entitled "Background" that gives some indication of CAI's limited view of member rights. "Community associations are subsocieties with power to affect the quality of members' and residents' lives. As entities that are neither governments nor businesses, community associations should provide basic rights of a constitutional nature to all members and residents, *but not impose the full panoply of governmental limitations on the process.* All members and residents of community associations should be treated fairly, reasonably, and without invidious discrimination. All *owners* should have a voice in, and an opportunity to shape the actions of their community association" (emphasis added). The CAI position, if adopted by the state, would not hold associations to the standards prescribed for either governments or businesses. *Laguna Publishing, O'Connor,* and *Cohen* all would be legislatively overruled. Note also the expressed intention not to extend "governmental limitations" to CID action, and the restriction of political participation rights to owners. The remainder of the document is a listing of procedural matters, largely parliamentary, that are the "rights" reserved for the owners—all of which are "subject to the community association's duty to fulfill its purposes, and subject to the need for timely response to emergencies." These "rights" are more properly characterized as the duties corporate managers typically owe their shareholders, including annual membership meetings, regular reports from the board, fair elections, and ethical management. The document does not really place any part of the individual's life beyond the reach of private government because the rights are surrounded by words such as "reasonable," "as appropriate," and "in light of needs and circumstances." For example, the right to privacy merely provides that the association shall "minimize intrusion into the privacy of individual units, individual affairs and personal records."

This "bill of rights" does not include any right to an independent judiciary, leaving the association board with the power to make the rules, charge people with violating them, and try the violators. The accused has merely the right to "notice and an opportunity to be heard," but the association board has the power to levy fines, including "imposition of special charges or fees for misconduct," which seems to suggest almost a quasi-criminal jurisdiction.

32. "CLAC to Have Important Role in Hauser's Select Committee," *CAI-CLAC Legislative Bulletin,* February 1990.

33. Proposition 140, passed in 1990, reduced the legislative budget by 40 percent, leading to mass layoffs of professional staff. The measure also established term limits of six years for members of the assembly and eight years for state senators.

34. Author interview with Stephen Holloway, January 12, 1993. Holloway is a consultant to Hauser's committee, the Assembly Committee on Housing and Community Development.

35. A.B. 3780 was initiated by the San Diego law firm of Aguirre & Eckmann, which represents homeowner associations in multimillion-dollar lawsuits against developers regarding construction defects. Developers had been using these cross-complaints to force the plaintiff association to contact its liability insurance carrier, which would then hire an additional attorney to defend the association against the cross-complaint. This tactic would create the specter that somehow the association would be required to indemnify the developer for the damages it owed the association—a somewhat bizarre concept—and would introduce the potential for conflict between the new attorney and the firm representing the association. The new law left in place the developer's ability to defend and offset his damages by asserting that the association had been responsible for causing or worsening its own damages—for example, by failing to properly maintain a roof (see, e.g., *Jaffe v. Huxley Architecture,* 100 Cal. App. 3d 1188 [1988]).

36. The most significant regulatory legislation regarding CID boards to emerge from the select committee's work was a set of measures establishing requirements dealing with the maintenance and disclosure of reserves (A.B. 623 and 871, passed in 1991).

37. The bills are described *Common Interest,* September–October 1992. The "report card" appears in "Legislators' Honor Roll Announced—1992 a Good Year for Condos," *Common Interest,* November–December 1992.

38. California Civil Code, sec. 1354.

39. *Nahrstedt v. Lakeside Village Condominium Association,* 9 Cal. App. 4th 1, 18 (1992); review granted by California Supreme Court, November 19, 1992, SO29132.

40. *Nahrstedt v. Lakeside Village Condominium Association,* 9 Cal. App. 4th, 18–19.

41. Ibid., 25.

42. Ibid., 28–29.

43. *Common Interest,* September–October 1992, 4.

44. California Assembly Bill 530, 1993–94, regular sess.

## Chapter 8

1. Ebenezer Howard, *Garden Cities of Tomorrow* (Cambridge, Mass.: MIT Press, 1965), 156–57.

2. Robert H. Nelson, "The Privatization of Local Government: From Zoning to RCAs," in Advisory Commission on Intergovernmental Relations, *Residential Com-*

*munity Associations: Private Governments in the Intergovernmental System?* (Washington, D.C.: Advisory Commission on Intergovernmental Relations, May 1989), publication A-112, 45–46.

3. Ibid., 51.

4. Advisory Commission on Intergovernmental Relations, *Residential Community Associations,* 18. The lack of data on the degree to which CID expenditures substitute for public spending makes it difficult to answer one of the most basic questions regarding a decision to privatize: Is it more efficient to deliver the services privately than publicly?

5. For discussion of the evolving doctrine of federalism see Richard Nathan, "The Role of the States in American Federalism," in C. Van Horn, ed., *The State of the States* (Washington, D.C.: Congressional Quarterly Press, 1989), 15–32; for case studies of the consequences, see H. V. Savitch and John Clayton Thomas, *Big City Politics in Transition* (Newbury Park, Calif.: Sage, 1991); for a description of the ways in which this process has strengthened the hand of private corporate interests, see Scott Cummings, "Private Enterprise and Public Policy: Business Hegemony in the Metropolis," in Scott Cummings, ed., *Business Elites and Urban Development* (Albany: State University of New York Press, 1988), 3–21.

6. See John D. Donahue, *The Privatization Decision: Public Ends, Private Means* (New York: Basic Books, 1989), esp. chap. 7.

7. Ibid., 6–7.

8. Ibid., 10.

9. See Stanley Scott, "Urban Growth Challenges New Towns," *Public Management,* September 1966, 253–260; Jesse Dukeminier, "The Coming Search for Quality," 12 *U.C.L.A. Law Review* 707 (1965).

10. Marc A. Weiss, *The Rise of the Community Builders: The American Real Estate Industry and Urban Land Planning* (New York: Columbia University Press, 1987), 1.

11. Ibid., 3.

12. Ibid.

13. Donahue, *Privatization Decision,* 11.

14. Jon Van Til, *Mapping the Third Sector: Voluntarism in a Changing Social Economy* (New York: Foundation Center, 1988), 6.

15. See Donahue, *The Privatization Decision,* chap. 3.

16. See Stephen E. Barton and Carol J. Silverman, *Common Interest Homeowners' Associations Management Study* (Sacramento: California Department of Real Estate, 1987). See also "Management and Governance in Common Interest Community Associations" (Working Paper no. 461, October 1987); "Homeownership in the Common-Interest Development" (Working Paper no. 469, October 1987); and "Public Life in Private Governments" (Working Paper no. 471, November 1987), in which the neighborly community model and the property management business model are discussed (all published at Berkeley, Institute of Urban and Regional Development, University of California). Barton and Silverman persuasively argue that the dominance of these private models weakens the public life of CIDs.

17. Robert Reich, "Secession of the Successful," *New York Times Magazine,* January 20, 1991, 42.

18. Murray' is quoted in Irwin M. Stelzer, "The Shape of Things to Come," *National Review,* July 8, 1991, 29–30.

19. CAI, using HUD data and its own, estimates that of some 11.6 million CID housing units in the nation, almost six million are planned communities, which are overwhelmingly in the suburbs. Many of the more than 4.8 million units of condominium housing in the nation also are located in the suburbs. Only the 824,000 cooperative housing units are primarily urban. CAI, *Community Associations Factbook, 1993*, 13.

20. William Schneider, "The Suburban Century Begins," *The Atlantic*, July 1992, 33.

21. Ibid., 37.

22. Ibid.

23. Ibid., 35.

24. For a vehement criticism of suburban life see Lewis Mumford, *The City in History: Its Origins, Its Transformations, and Its Prospects* (New York: Harcourt, Brace, Jovanovich, 1961), 482–513. He writes, "Those who accept this existence might as well be encased in a rocket hurtling through space, so narrow are their choices, so limited and deficient their permitted responses. Here indeed we find 'The Lonely Crowd.' . . . Suburbia offers poor facilities for meeting, conversation, collective debate, and common action—it favors silent conformity, not rebellion or counter-attack. Suburbia has become the favored home of a new kind of absolutism: invisible but all-powerful" (512–13).

25. Herbert Gans, *The Levittowners: Ways of Life and Politics in a New Suburban Community* (New York: Random House, 1967), 172. Gans emphasizes, however, that "the criteria on which the advocacy of block homogeneity and community heterogeneity is based cannot justify racial homogeneity at either level" (p. 173). See also Herbert Gans, "The Balanced Community: Homogeneity or Heterogeneity in Residential Areas," *Housing Urban America*, Jon Pynoos et al., eds. (New York: Aldine, 1980), 141.

26. Gans, *The Levittowners*, 166–67.

27. Ibid., 173.

28. See Barton and Silverman, *Management Study*, 6. The authors found California CID residents to be "quite diverse" in the aggregate. But they acknowledge that less than half of the CIDs they studied had a minority ethnic group population of 5 percent or greater—a figure that represents only a fraction of the minority population of California. The authors also attach considerable significance to the presence of renters as a sign of diversity, but these individuals generally have no say in CID decisions.

29. Bureau of the Census, *Statistical Abstract of the United States, 1992* (Washington, D.C.: Bureau of the Census, 1992), table 1226.

30. Bureau of the Census, *Statistical Abstract of the United States, 1992* (Washington, D.C., 1992), tables 41, 44.

31. William C. Apgar, Jr., and H. James Brown, *The State of the Nation's Housing—1988* (Cambridge, Mass.: Joint Center for Housing Studies of Harvard University, 1988), 1, 8.

32. See, e.g., Community Associations Institute, *Community Associations Factbook, 1993*, 18. Planned communities as large as Levittown and the city-sized new towns can, if their designers wish, offer the block homogeneity and community heterogeneity of which Gans speaks.

33. Advisory Commission on Intergovernmental Relations, *Residential Community Associations*, 6.

34. Illa Collin, supervisor of Sacramento County, quoted in Robyn Boyer Stewart, "Homeowner Associations Sally Forth into the Political Wars," *California Journal*, April 1991, 272.

35. See Mike Davis, *City of Quartz: Excavating the Future in Los Angeles* (London: Verso, 1990), chap. 3.

36. Kenneth Budd, "A Force in the Ring: How Condominium and Homeowner Associations are Landing Blows in the Political Arena," *Common Ground*, November–December 1992, 15.

37. Ibid., 16, 20. The headings for these "tips" explained by the CID lobbyists include "Inform the membership of the issues. . . . Get out the vote. . . . Establish a presence. . . . Do your homework. . . . Be honest and even tempered. . . . Create win-win situations. . . . Go through the proper channels. . . . Use the media."

38. Ibid.

39. Author interview with Robyn Boyer Stewart, January 19, 1993; letter from Stewart to the author dated January 19, 1993.

40. Robyn Boyer Stewart, "Homeowner Associations Sally Forth Into the Political Wars," *California Journal* (April 1991): 268–72.

41. Ibid., 270, 272.

42. Robyn Boyer Stewart, "Power to the People: The Growing Political Clout of Common Interest Development Associations" (Speech delivered at the California Society of Certified Public Accountants, Common Interest Realty Associations Conference, San Francisco, July 29, 1992).

43. Robyn Boyer Stewart, "Board Immunity Bill Now Law! EQ Insurance Program Repealed!" *Common Interest*, September–October 1992, 1.

44. Stewart, "Homeowner Associations Sally Forth," 271–72.

45. 1993 New Jersey Laws 6; C.40:67–23.2 as amended; 1992 Senate Bill no. 1154. Under the law reimbursement will gradually increase from 20 percent in 1993–94 to the "total cost of services" in 1997–98. Thereafter, "the municipality shall either provide the services . . . or enter into a written agreement to annually reimburse the qualified private community in full."

46. Robert Jay Dilger, *Neighborhood Politics: Residential Community Associations and American Governance* (New York: New York University Press, 1992), 28–29

47. Ibid., 29–30.

48. Advisory Commission on Intergovernmental Relations, *Residential Community Associations*, 7.

# INDEX

Abrams, Charles, 61, 70, 72, 76, 80, 211n
Ackerman, Frederick L., 46, 207n
Advisory Commission on Intergovern-
  mental Relations, 11, 22, 178, 192,
  196–97
Agee, Doris, 163
Aguirre, Gary, 163, 226n

Alabama, 59. *See also individual loca-
  tions*
Alaska, 86
Alternative dispute resolution, 132, 222n
*America II,* 13
*American Home, The,* 71
American Society of Planning Officials, 85

232

Index

Apgar, William C., Jr., 190
Architectural Forum, 71
Arkansas, 59
Arnold, Joseph, 101–2
Ascher, Charles S.: as author of Radburn restrictive covenants, 10, 208–9n; as designer of Radburn private government, 29–30, 31, 45–51; biography of, 46, 207n; mentioned, 88, 121
Ashland, Mass., 15
Augur, Tracy, 208n

Baltimore, Md., 74
Bauer, Catherine, 74–75, 208n
Belgium, 95
Bellamy, Edward, 1–2
Bentley, Arthur, 123
Bergeson, Marian, 194
Berle, Adolph, 125, 156
Beverly Hills Police Department, 15
Bigger, Frederick, 208n
Bing, Alexander M., 46, 48
Birmingham, Ala., 67
Black, Hugo, 155–56
Boca Raton, Fla., 16
Boston, 2, 44
Brazil, 86, 95
Bright, John, 208n
British East India Company, 124
Brock v. Watergate Mobile Home Park Association, Inc., 224–25n
Brookline, Mass., 35
Brown, H. James, 190
Brownlow, Louis, 49, 50, 209n
Buckingham, James Silk, 200n
Bucks County, Pa., 17
Business judgment rule, 130–31
Buttenheim, Harold S., 49

California, 10, 11, 19, 59, 114, 120, 130, 136, 193. See also individual locations
California Association of Community Managers, 120–21
California Journal, 194
California Real Estate Association, 76
Canada, 86
Canavan, Richard J., 91, 92, 110, 111
Chartwell, Pa., 17
Chase, Stuart, 208n
Chicago, 8, 69, 74, 93, 111
Chicago Commission on Race Relations, 74, 76
Chicago Real Estate Board, 73

Chicago Title and Trust Company, 73, 216n
Chickasaw, Ala., 155
Childs, Richard S., 49, 50
Christensen, Carol, 104, 214n
Christian Scientists, 8
Church, Collyer, 163
City Housing Corporation: as builder of Radburn, 46–48; bankruptcy of, 48; mentioned, 207n, 208n
City Is the Frontier, The, 80
Cleveland, Ohio, 74
Cohen v. Kite Hill Community Association, 160–61, 166–67
Colean, Miles, 63
Colt, John, 49
Columbia, Md., 100
Columbus, Ohio, 69
Committee on Negro Housing, 69
Common area: defined, 19
Common field system, 31–32, 84
Common Ground, 114, 193
Common-interest developments (CIDs): types of, 7, 126–27; location of, 11; quantities of, 11; population of, 12; micropolitics of, 18–21; conflict in, 19; legal characteristics of, 19; macropolitics of, 21; as utopian communities, 24–26; as force in electoral politics, 26, 192–97; models of governance of, 185; target-marketing of, 191–92. See also Private government; Restrictive covenants
Community Association Members' and Residents' Bill of Rights, 167, 226–27n
Community associations. See Common-interest developments
Community Associations Factbook, 114
Community Associations Institute: creation of, 27, 83, 110–13, 184–85; generally, 106–21; Legislative Action Committees, 114; role in national legislation, 152–53; mentioned, 136, 137, 138–39, 182, 203n, 204n, 205n, 225n
Community Associations Law Reporter, 114, 153
Community builders: and restrictive covenants, 36–43; and racial segregation, 58, 70–71; relations with Federal Housing Administration, 62–63; mentioned, 10, 31, 60, 82, 92, 96, 99
Condominiums: defined, 19; origins and history of, 94–96; Puerto Rican experience with, 215n; mentioned, 7, 126, 127

Construction defects, 108, 130, 142, 227n
Cooperatives, 7, 19, 127, 204n
Council of Condominium and Home-
 owner Associations, 120
Council of Housing Producers, 99–100
Council-manager form of city govern-
 ment, 10, 45, 50, 51
Country Club District, Kansas City, 39,
 91
Cuba, 86
Culver City, Calif., 169
Cummings, Lincoln C., 106, 111, 112,
 113, 116–17, 119

Dahl, Robert, 149
Daley, Richard J., 111
Dallas, Texas, 67, 116, 193
Danielson, Michael, 57
Davis, Alexander Jackson, 36
Davis, Mike, 95
Davis-Stirling Common Interest De-
 velopment Act, 114, 163–67
Dean, John P., 69–71
Deed restrictions. *See* Restrictive cove-
 nants
Delaware County, Pa., 16
Detroit, 69
Dickman, George, 2
Dilger, Robert Jay, 195
Dingman, Martin, 163
Dodd, Harold W., 49
Donahue, John D., 178–83
Donohoe, John P., 153
Double taxation, 164–66, 193, 195–96,
 226n, 230n
Dowden, C. James, 113, 219n
Duany, Andres, 188

Edison, Thomas, 36
Eels, Richard, 124–25
Eichler, Edward P., 79, 96, 97, 98
England, 20–21, 30, 31–32, 33, 214n
Environmental Protection Agency, 17
Executive Council of Homeowners
 (ECHO), 120, 163, 168, 194, 225n

Fairbanks Ranch, Calif., 15
Federal Housing Administration: guidelines for creating CIDs, 10; adoption of
 Urban Land Institute policies, 22, 27;
 advocacy of restrictive covenants, 27;
 promotion of racial segregation, 58, 60,
 64–67; creation of, 63; *Underwriting
 Manual, 1938,* 64–65; *Underwriting*

*Manual, 1947,* 65–66; promotion of
 CID housing, 88–93; decision to issue
 mortgage insurance for condomini-
 ums, 95; mentioned, 79, 82, 107, 121,
 127, 150–51, 182
Ferguson, Gil, 194
Fishman, Robert, 81, 214n
Florida, 11, 114, 193. *See also individual
 locations*
Florida Bureau of Condominiums, 152
Florida Condominium Act, 132
*Food Employees Local 590 v. Logan Val-
 ley Plaza, Inc.,* 157
Forest Hills, N.Y., 43, 48, 49, 91
Fort Lauderdale, Fla., 16, 194
Fort Wayne, Ind., 15
Foster City, Calif., 98, 139
France, 95
*Frances T. v. Village Green Owners Asso-
 ciation,* 150, 161–62
Frankfurter, Felix, 156
*Friendly Village Community Association,
 Inc., v. Silva & Hill Construction Co.,*
 225n
*Fundamentals of Real Estate Practice,*
 61–62

Gaithersburg, Md., 111
Gans, Herbert, 189–90, 213n, 229n
*Garden Cities of Tomorrow,* 2–6, 8
Garden city: physical plan, 3–4; political
 and economic organization, 4–6; men-
 tioned, 176
Georgia, 59
Germany, 94–95
Gibbons, David W., 115–16
Government National Mortgage Associa-
 tion, 217n
Gramercy Park, 9, 34
Great Britain, 7, 179
*Great Condominium Rebellion, The,* 142
Greater Boston Association of Residen-
 tial Community Association
 Presidents, 192
Greenbelt Towns program, 100–102,
 217n
Greenbelt, Md., 101
Greendale, Wis., 101
Greenhills, Ohio, 101
Gulf Shipbuilding Company, 155
Gulick, Luther H., 49

Hamner, Lee, 49
Handlin, Davis, 71

Hanke, Byron: involvement in FHA policy on CIDs, 91–93, 215n; role in founding of Community Associations Institute, 109, 110, 111–13, 184, 219n; views on restructuring of Community Associations Institute, 119; mentioned, 121
Hanson, Wayne, 163
Harvill, Steve, 193
Haskell, Llewellyn S., 35
Hauser, Dan, 167–68, 172
Hawaii, 11
Hayden, Delores, 201n
*History of Germanic Private Law, A,* 9, 94
Hobbes, Thomas, 123, 146
Home ownership: rates, 57, 190
*Homes Association Handbook, The,* 92–93, 109, 110, 127
Housing starts, 57, 107
Houston, Texas, 15, 113, 195
Howard County, Neb., 8
Howard, Ebenezer: influenced by Edward Bellamy, 1–2; influence of, 3, 46, 47; views on the city, 175–76, 177, 197; mentioned, 12, 82, 96, 104, 121, 189, 208n
*Hudgens v. National Labor Relations Board,* 157
Huebner, Rudolph, 94–95
Hyatt, Wayne, 138, 153, 160, 219n

Illinois, 59, 193
Immigration, 58–60
Indiana, 59. *See also* Fort Wayne, Ind.
*Innovations vs. Traditions in Community Development,* 88
Irvine, Calif., 100
Italy, 95

Jackson, F. Scott, 131
Jackson, Kenneth, 64, 67, 71, 200n
Jacobs, Jane, 3
Judd, Dennis, 7

Kansas City, Mo., 10, 39, 40, 42, 74, 195
Kanter, Rosabeth Moss, 24–25
Kaplan, Marshall, 79, 96, 97, 98
Kaufman and Broad, 92
Keen, Harold, 15
Kingston, Ron, 163
Knowles, Morris, 49
Kodak Company, 2
Kohn, Robert D., 46, 207n
Krasnowiecki, Jan, 91

*Laguna Publishing Company v. Golden Rain Foundation of Laguna Hills,* 158–60, 166
Lakeside Village Condominiums, 169
Lakoff, Sanford, 134–35, 139
Lambie, Morris, 49
Land costs: rise of, 83–84
Latham, Earl, 125, 133–34
*Leadership Update,* 114
Leisure World, 141, 158–60, 194
Letchworth, England, 3, 47
Levitt & Sons, 100
Levitt, Abraham, 71
Levitt, William, 71
Levittowns, 71, 229n
Linden Place, 35
Llewellyn Park, N.J., 36, 48
Local democracy: CIDs as examples of, 82, 216n
Locke, John, 140, 144, 145, 146
London, 2, 4, 33–34, 176
Long Island, N.Y., 71
*Looking Backward,* 1–2
Loring, William C., 91
Los Angeles, 38, 69, 154, 169
Los Angeles Realty Board, 73, 212n
*Los Angeles Times,* 18
Louisburg Square, 9, 34, 44, 91
Louisiana, 59
Louisville, Ky., 67, 74
Louv, Richard, 13–14, 57, 143–44

McConnell, Grant, 135
McDermott, John, 125–26
MacKaye, Benton, 208n
*Managing a Successful Community Association,* 137, 138
Manuel, Frank A. and Fritzie P., 23–24
*Marsh v. Alabama,* 155–56, 157, 158, 162
Marshall, Alfred, 200n
Marshall, John, 124
Martha's Vineyard, 35
Maryland, 11, 193. *See also individual locations*
Maryland Condominium and Homeowner Association, 120
Mayer, Martin, 83, 98
Memphis, Tenn., 74
Merriam, Charles E., 49, 123
Meyer, Ralph, 221n
Michels, Robert, 135
Michigan, 59
Mields, Hugh, 136

Migration, internal, 58–60
Mikva, Zorita, 77–78
Mission Hills, Mo., 40–41
Mississippi, 59
Mobile, Ala., 155
Monchow, Helen, 42, 43–45, 209n
Monroe, N.J., 15
Montgomery County, Md., 120, 132, 195
Montgomery Village, Md., 111
Mott, Seward, 215n
*Mulkey v. Reitman,* 159
Mumford, Lewis, 3, 8, 9, 207–8n, 229
Murray, Charles, 23, 175, 187, 192, 204–5n

*Nahrstedt v. Lakeside Village Condominium Association,* 169–73
Natelson, Robert G., 94, 223n, 215–16n
National Association of Home Builders: founding of, 60; cofounding of Community Associations Institute by, 83, 110, 111, 113; views on residential density, 86; mentioned, 91, 107, 120, 182, 219n
National Association of Housing Cooperatives, 204n
National Association of Real Estate Boards, 37, 60–62, 182, 210n
National Conference of Commissioners on Uniform State Laws, 119, 153
National Municipal League, 45, 49–50
Naugatuck, Conn., 193
*Negro Housing,* 69
Nelson, Robert H., 176–77
*Neponsit Property Owners' Association, Inc., v. Emigrant Industrial Savings Bank,* 53–55
New Communities Program, federal, 100–103
New Jersey, 11, 36, 59, 193. *See also* individual locations
New towns, 3, 10, 96–104
New York City, 34, 46, 69
New York Housing Commission, 46
New York state, 9, 11, 59, 70–71, 74, 204n
Nichols, Jesse Clyde, 38–43; role of in Urban Land Institute, 10, 60; views on expansion of home ownership, 55, 56; mentioned, 71, 89, 107
Norfolk, Va., 67
North Carolina, 193. *See also* Winston-Salem, N.C.
Nozick, Robert, 140–41

*O'Connor v. Village Green Owners Association,* 161
Ocean Grove, N.J., 35
Ohio, 59. *See also* individual locations
Orange County, Calif., 92
*Organization Man, The,* 80

Packard, Mike, 163
*Packenham's Case,* 33, 204n, 205n
Palos Verdes Estates, Calif., 43
Pennsylvania, 11, 59. *See also* individual locations
Perry, Clarence A., 49
Philadelphia, 7, 17, 69
Pittsburgh, Pa., 74
Planned-Unit Development with a Homes Association, 89–91, 93, 109
Plater-Zyberk, Elizabeth, 188
*Politics of Exclusion, The,* 57
*Private City, The,* 7
Private government: corporations, 29–30, 45–51; used by Jesse Clyde Nichols, 40–41; replacement of cities by, 176–77; volunteers in, 183–86
Private streets associations, 9, 35
Privatism, 7, 18–19, 196
*Privatization Decision, The,* 178, 180
Privatization, 22, 28, 26, 178–86
Privatopia, 12, 177
Project HOPE, 119
Property managers: influence of, 142–43
*Property Owners' Journal,* 74
*Pruneyard Shopping Center v. Robins,* 157, 158, 162
Puerto Rico, 95, 215n
Puritans, 145, 146

Quakers, 8

Racial zoning laws, 67–68
Radburn, N.J., 9, 10, 27, 30, 56, 88
Ramsey, Charles E., 216n
Rancho Bernardo, Calif., 12–15
Rancho Santa Fe, Calif., 16
*Rasselas,* 175
*Raven's Cove Townhouses, Inc., v. Knuppe Development Co.,* 221n
Regional Planning Association of America: Ebenezer Howard's influence on, 9; relation with City Housing Corporation, 46, 47; influence on Greenbelt Towns program, 100–101; membership of, 207–8n; mentioned, 74

Reich, Robert, 23, 175, 186–87, 192, 196
Reichman, Uriel, 99
Renters: disenfranchisement of, 128,
  221n; mentioned, 190–91
Reserve funds, 129–30, 221n
Residential community associations. *See*
  Common-interest developments
Reston, Va., 91, 100
Restrictive covenants: in luxury subdivi-
  sions, 9; at Rancho Bernardo, 13–14;
  enforcement of, 15–18, 32–33, 131–
  32; described, 20; racial, 21, 27, 35, 37,
  44, 68–74, 211n; as model for public
  zoning, 38; rule of reason as applied to,
  169–73. *See also* Monchow, Helen;
  Nichols, Jesse Clyde; Federal Housing
  Administration
Rhame, David, 110, 111, 219n
Richmond, Va., 67
*Robins v. Pruneyard Shopping Center,*
  157, 158, 162
Roland Park, Md., 43, 48, 49, 52
Roosevelt, Eleanor, 208n
Rosenberry, Katharine, 114, 136, 163,
  167
Roszak, Theodore, 11, 99, 139
Ruggles, Samuel, 34
Russell, May, 113

San Diego, Calif., 12, 13, 14, 16, 227n;
  police department, 15
*Sanborn v. McLean,* 52–53
Santa Ana, Calif., 17
Saputo, Peter, 163
Savings and loan institutions, 218n
Schaffer, Daniel, 48, 208n
Schneider, William, 57, 187–88
Scott, Stanley, 22, 93
*Shelley v. Kraemer,* 44, 75, 159
Silverman, Carol, 135, 142–43
Smith, Alfred E., 46
Social cities, 6
Social division: CIDs and, 186–92
Spain, 95
*Spencer's Case,* 205n
Spencer, Herbert, 200n
Sproul, Curtis, 163, 223n
St. Louis Real Estate Exchange, 73
St. Louis, Mo., 9, 35, 67, 73
Stahl, David, 111, 112, 113, 219n
Stein, Clarence, 46, 207n, 209n
Stewart, Robyn Boyer 168–69, 173, 194–
  95, 226n
Stirling, Larry, 163, 225n

Suburbs: English, 33–34, 214n; Radburn
  as, 48; homeowner associations in
  growth of, 56–78; critics of, 80; increasing land costs in, 80–84; as
  "bourgeois utopia," 81–82; new towns
  as, 104; in conflict with cities, 187–88;
  and privatism, 187–88; homogeneity
  in, 189; mentioned, 10, 19, 26, 28, 96,
  110, 139, 191
Summers, Harry L., 12
Sunnyside Gardens, 208n
Sunshine Ranches, Fla., 194
Super-majority voting requirements, 21,
  147
Sweden, 95

Texas, 11, 193. *See also individual loca-
  tions*
Third sector, 183–84
Tort immunity for CID directors, 162, 168
Townsquare Owners' Association, 17
Treese, Clifford J., 204n
Tugwell, Rexford, 100, 101
*Tulk v. Moxhay,* 33–34, 209n
*Twentieth Century Capitalist Revolution,
  The,* 156
Tyler Walk, Pa., 17

Uniform Common Interest Ownership
  Act, 153
Uniform Condominium Act, 153
Uniform Planned Community Act, 153
Uniform Unincorporated Nonprofit As-
  sociations Act, 119
U.S. Department of Housing and Urban
  Development, 119
U.S. Department of Justice, 119
Unwin, Raymond, 208n
Upson, Lent B., 49
Urban Growth and New Communities
  Act of *1970,* 102
Urban Land Institute: Community
  Builders' Council, 10; policy on open
  space, 22; as proponent of utopian
  thought, 24–25; and relations with
  Federal Housing Administration, 27,
  90–93, 127, 182; founding of, 39, 60;
  cofounding of Community Associations
  Institute by, 83, 110, 112; on increas-
  ing residential density, 86–89;
  mentioned, 107, 120, 121, 122, 136,
  137, 140, 205n, 218n. *See also* Hanke,
  Byron R.; Nichols, Jesse Clyde; Stahl,
  David

*U.S. News and World Report,* 75–76, 77
Utopian thought: of Edward Bellamy, 1–
  2; of Ebenezer Howard, 1–2, 7; nature
  of, 23–24; Urban Land Institute and,
  24–25; suburbs and, 81–82

Van Atta, David, 163
Van Til, Jan, 183
Village improvement societies, 207n
Virginia, 59, 193. *See also individual lo-
  cations*
Vista, Calif., 16
Volunteers: CID directors as, 183–84

Wakefield, Edward Gibbon, 200n
Walker, John, 209n
Walton, Clarence, 124–25
Warner, Sam Bass, 7
Washington, D.C., 69, 111

Washington, D.C., Real Estate Board, 73
Watts, John W., 104, 108
Weaver, Robert C., 56, 68–69, 72, 73, 75,
  76–77
*Wehr v. Roland Park Company,* 52
Weiss, Marc, 37, 63–64, 104, 108, 182
Welwyn, England, 3, 47
Whitaker, Charles H., 208n
White Plains, N.Y., 69, 74
Whyte, William H., 80, 214–15n
Williams, Wayne, 57
Winokur, James L., 223n
Winston-Salem, N.C., 67
Wolfe, David B., 84, 111, 219n
Wood, Edith Elmer, 208n
Woodlands, Texas, 103
Worley, William S., 71

Zelman, Walter, 225n